The

GREAT
SHAKESPEARE
FORGERY

BY BERNARD GREBANIER

The Truth about Shylock
The Heart of Hamlet
Thornton Wilder
Playwriting
The Other Love
Mirrors of the Fire
Fauns, Satyrs, and a Few Sages
Racine's *Phaedra,* an English acting version in verse
Molière's *The Misanthrope,* an English acting version
The Great Shakespeare Forgery

The
GREAT
SHAKESPEARE
FORGERY

Bernard Grebanier, 1903–

W · W · NORTON & COMPANY · INC ·
New York

LIBRARY OF CONGRESS CATALOG CARD NO. 65-18031

PRINTED IN THE UNITED STATES OF AMERICA

2 3 4 5 6 7 8 9 0

TO *S. N. Behrman,*
in affection and admiration,
and to the Lady of the Ramo Barziza,
with love and gratitude

Contents

✳ ✳ ✳ ✳ ✳ ✳ ✳ ✳ ✳ ✳ ✳ ✳ ✳ ✳ ✳ ✳

Illustrations

Foreword

It was a lucky concurrence of time and temperament (unlucky finally for all concerned) that made the astonishing career of William Henry Ireland possible. He lived in an age peculiarly auspicious for the rascality he practiced. The present account is, I believe, the first to place him in perspective.

Indeed, there has been to date only one honest study of him, that written by John Mair (1939), and long since out of print. William Henry's earlier biographers dutifully repeated all the misinformed slander and fabrications of his contemporaries; none of these distortions, though of a different order, were half as dramatic and absurd as the actual facts. Only recently an American theatrical magazine printed an article about him which contained a misstatement in nearly every sentence, and presented a picture of him as a "Teddy boy" of his times, a notion laughably at variance with William Henry's character. There exists also a tiny volume published by the Harvard University Press (1930) which hardly attempts to fathom this fascinating subject. It, too, is studded with inaccuracies. Even Mr. Mair's otherwise excellent book, I find, has several, understandable in a pioneering work.

But there are many facets of William Henry's hazardous activities that seem to have escaped Mr. Mair's attention. For years I found myself reverting to the question of what—aside from the meaningless obvious ones—the boy's real motives could have been. Many rereadings of William Henry's own confessions began to afford the clue between the lines. Then I came upon fresh material apparently unknown to Mr. Mair (of which but one example is the Farington Diary), which made clear that the nature of the mystery lay in the puzzling relationship that obtained among Ireland senior, his mistress Mrs. Freeman, and young Ireland; this revelation, in turn, strongly substantiated the hints I had already gleaned from William Henry's admissions; finally, this solution to the puzzle became almost unchallengeable when I considered passages in William Henry's later writings, which no one seems to have taken the trouble to read.

Ireland senior and junior thus stood in a new state of tension with each other, none the less dramatic for all the comedy involved. There was much more, in short, to be told about the story, especially about the persons of the drama, both principal and subsidiary. There were such matters as William Henry's strange relationship to Mrs. Freeman; his father's equally strange relationship to him and her; the facts of the murder which inspired the novel *Love and Madness*, a book that powerfully influenced William Henry; William Henry's courtship and marriage; the great day of the visit to Carlton House, the night at the Drury Lane Theatre which was the climax of William Henry's life; the immediate aftermath of that night and William Henry's subsequent behavior; the last days of Samuel Ireland; the disposition of his beloved possessions; the later life and career of William Henry; and the peculiar conduct of the minor characters of the story.

It was to supply these missing or incomplete passages and others like them—all of them fascinating, many of them at once amusing and pathetic—that the present work was undertaken. (While at it, I also have corrected a few of the errors in the printed record.) I have never enjoyed writing any book as much, for the exploits of my harebrained hero are diverting at every turn.

I wish to express my gratitude to Mr. Dan L. Levy of the Brooklyn College Library, who spared me a year of days in travel by procuring for me the loan of many rare, and in some cases unique, copies of material which greatly enriched my studies and added to their pleasure.

BERNARD GREBANIER
New York, 1965

The

GREAT
SHAKESPEARE
FORGERY

ONE

The Stage Set for William Henry

✳ ✳ ✳ ✳ ✳ ✳ ✳ ✳ ✳ ✳ ✳ ✳ ✳ ✳ ✳ ✳

FOR ANY MAN TODAY to state publicly his indifference to the beauties of Shakespeare would be as foolhardy as for him to declare his blindness to the beauties of the Alps. Such a man, unless protected by the immunity allotted actors, who are permitted any sort of impulsive pronouncement without contradiction (we don't expect *them* to like Shakespeare!), would instantly be read out of civilized society. The magnificence of Shakespeare and the Alps has long been axiomatic, beyond dispute. Yet the reputation of each was not always so secure.

When in the summer of 1793 the bumbling antiquarian Samuel Ireland brought his apparently backward and quiet-mannered son, William Henry, in reverence to Stratford-on-Avon, it had been only decades since the pre-eminence of Shakespeare and the Alps had begun to be appreciated. To be sure, those awesome Swiss peaks had had to wait longer and even a little later than Shakespeare for due recognition. From time immemorial they had been dreaded or disliked, but at last, in the days of Queen Anne, Addison was able to regard them as no worse for the traveler than a sometimes inescapable bore. It was indeed only three decades earlier than that visit to Stratford, so fateful to William Henry Ireland, that Rousseau had legislated his native mountains —or, to be more precise, their foothills—into sublimity. And even in 1793 people were not yet climbing them for the pleasure of risking their necks.

Though for most of its duration the eighteenth century was not fond of high places, Shakespeare, after almost a hundred years of neglect or outrage, had fared somewhat better.

But only gradually. For many years after Shakespeare's death, Stratford itself seemed unaware of the rare swan it had incubated. His son-in-law, Dr. John Hall, for instance, who until his own death lived at New Place, Shakespeare's final residence, has left us a book of memoranda on many of his patients and their maladies, but not a word on his wife's father. Two generations later, the vicar of Stratford, John Ward, though recording in his journal a story that Shakespeare had died after a drinking bout with Drayton and Jonson, made a note for himself that some day he must get around to reading Shakespeare's works. In London, meanwhile, the plays were either unproduced or else, usually, violated by abominable "improvements" to suit the taste of the time. Pepys was confiding to his diary (1661-62) that *A Midsummer Night's Dream* was "the most insipid, ridiculous play" he had ever seen and that *Romeo and Juliet* was of all dramas the world's worst.

At rare intervals a solitary admirer had made his way to Stratford to pay homage to its half-forgotten genius. Aubrey's *Brief Lives* (1681) gave an exceedingly scant account of Shakespeare, but encouraged the growth of an incipient mythology: "His father was a Butcher, and I have been told that when he was a boy he exercised his father's trade, but when he killed a calf he would do it in a high style and make a speech." Nevertheless, Aubrey added, Shakespeare had as a contemporary another butcher's son "not at all inferior to him for a natural wit, his acquaintance." The world, presumably, lost another master poet-dramatist by the premature death of this young butcher. After the turn of the new century Betterton, the celebrated actor, after a visit to Stratford, returned to London with a small stock of biographical data, much of it sheer fiction—like the myth that Shakespeare had to flee from Stratford because he stole some deer—or else misstatement of fact.

But by the time, one fine day in May, 1742, David Garrick and Charles Macklin were sitting in the garden of New Place, things were looking up for Shakespeare. His own texts, rather than those of his "improvers," were becoming available through the editorial efforts of Rowe, Hanmer, Pope, and Theobald, and Shakespeare was being read. While Garrick, only twenty-five, and Macklin, a generation older, sat in the garden of the last house in which Shakespeare had lived, they listened entranced as old Sir Hugh Clopton, the current owner of New Place, discoursed to them on various legends connected with the poet, and pointed out to them that the mulberry tree whose shade the three were enjoying had been planted by Shakespeare himself. Naturally both actors were enthralled; to a degree both of them were already sponsors of a new fame for Shakespeare on the stage.

Only the year before, Macklin had revolutionized stage tradition by daring to reject Granville's hideous distortion of Shylock into a ludicrous butt; he had awakened *The Merchant of Venice* from its century of slumber, and had presented the Jew as a powerful personality, a man of malign purpose speaking not Granville's lines but Shakespeare's. He had, moreover, enacted the role with an unheard-of "naturalism," which had overwhelmed the audience. The morning after George II had witnessed this performance of Shylock, Walpole had said, "I wish, your Majesty, it was possible to find a recipe for frightening the House of Commons," and the King, confessing he had not slept a wink that night, replied, "Vat you tink of sending dem to see dat Irishman play Shylock?"

And as for young Garrick, in the fall of the preceding year he had taken London by storm with his Richard III. His instantaneous success had decided the stage-struck young man at once to brave his family's wrath and settle upon acting as a career. Thereafter Garrick was to do more than any man of his century to reinstate Shakespeare in his rightful place on the stage. For that matter, it was to be Shakespeare who would do more than anyone else to raise Garrick to his unrivaled position as the leading actor of the age.

Garrick and the mulberry tree under which he sat as a young man were both destined to play a leading part in changing the climate of opinion on the subject of Shakespeare—and particularly in establishing and inflating a Shakespearean idolatry. Who knows? Perhaps the moving sight of the mulberry tree, the one certain link with Shakespeare the man (for the house itself at New Place had been remodeled in neoclassical style), was the inspiration for Garrick to make his particular mission the fostering of public enthusiasm for its original planter.

The tree had its own devious history. In 1753 New Place passed out of the hands of the Copton family into those of the Reverend Francis Gastrell, late of Cheshire. Gastrell unfortunately regarded his new possession as a home for himself instead of a national monument of which he was the privileged custodian. It is equally clear that he does not seem to have been a devotee of the Bard's. He "felt no sort of pride or pleasure in this charming retirement," says an early guidebook to Stratford, "no consciousness of his being possessed of the sacred ground which the Muses had consecrated to the memory of their favorite Poet."

Luckless Gastrell! Now the pilgrims were coming to Stratford in ever-increasing numbers, and the Mulberry Tree had become a shrine. His garden was overrun. When the berries were in season, urchins gleefully gathered them; in and out of season pious tourists carved their initials in the bark and broke off branches of the sacred tree as mementos of the Muses' darling. In our own century everyone would expect a Gastrell to regulate this enthusiasm and profit from it by charging a couple of shillings for admission to the garden. But whatever may be said of Gastrell, he was not minded to capitalize on his ownership of Shakespeare's property. For three years he put up with these harassments; then, in

6

1756, his exasperation prompted the deed which made his name infamous in the lexicon of Shakespearolatry. With the excuse that the Mulberry Tree was the cause of dampness in his house, "in an evil hour the sacrilegious priest ordered the tree, then remarkably large and at its full growth, to be cut down; which was no sooner done than it was cleft to pieces . . . to the great regret and vexation not only of the inhabitants, but of every admirer of our Bard."

By this time Shakespeare had admirers in Stratford, too, who professed outrage at the horrid deed. Shakespeare was beginning to be something of a supply of income to Stratford, and its citizens' emotions may well have exceeded mere astonishment. After the first shock "excited by the discovery of this profanation," says one chronicler, there succeeded "a general fury against the perpetrator, and the enraged populace surrounded the premises, and vowed vengeance against Gastrill [*sic*] and his family."

Understandably, Gastrell now preferred to spend much of his time away from the town, but whether from fear or disgust is not clear. In any case, New Place did not "long escape the destructive hand" of its owner. Deeply resenting the monthly assessments for maintenance of the poor, imposed upon his property despite his absence by a town he had no reason to love, he "in the heat of anger declared *that* house should never be assessed again: and to give his imprecation due effect, the demolition of New Place soon followed; for in 1759 he razed the building to the ground, disposed of the materials, and left Stratford amidst the rage and curses of its inhabitants."

The Mulberry Tree, though consigned to death, took on a postmortem life. Unlike Gastrell, the enterprising and well-named Thomas Sharp, carpenter of Stratford, was not indifferent to its commercial possibilities. That worthy had persuaded the irascible Gastrell to sell him most of the hacked-up Tree, and having a shrewd idea of its value to the world, began turning out a steady stream of souvenirs by converting every fragment he had bought into goblets, small boxes, tea chests, toothpick cases, tobacco stoppers, inkstands, and the like. The supply of wood from that same tree gave evidence of being truly inexhaustible as countless objects of turnery ware followed one another out of his shop. The skeptical began to think a grove of mulberries had been requisitioned.

It was only fitting that some portions of the Mulberry Tree should find their way into the keeping of Garrick, who had been so much exalted as a youth by viewing it where it grew, and who now, a generation later, with a host of Shakespearean triumphs behind him, was unrivaled as the Bard's chief interpreter. Every season he had presented no less than ten of Shakespeare's plays (though often these were but hideous adaptations), until the names of Garrick and Shakespeare were inextricably linked in the mind of the theatre-going public. Garrick was, moreover, always a cooperating victim of anyone with a Shakespearean relic to dispose of. He had already acquired a signet ring with the initials W. S., a bad piece of delft in the form of a saltcellar painted in blue and glaring yellow, a gray leather glove with metal embroidery at the cuff—all represented to him as having once been Shakespeare's. In 1762 he managed to buy for two guineas a half-dozen pieces of the true Mulberry Tree, and these he had made into a "Shakespeare chair." This revered object, weather permitting, was kept at his villa at Hampton in the Greek-porticoed octagonal building on the bank of the Thames, his Shakespeare Temple, which housed a statue of Shakespeare he had commissioned.

But the crucial acquisition was a gift sent to him by Stratford itself. The town had built a new Town Hall; in the north wall was a vacant niche waiting to be filled with a statue or a painting. It had been suggested that with the application of the unction of flattery, Garrick, known to be both rich and vain, might spare Stratford the expense of such an object of art by supplying a bust or painting of Shakespeare. In May, 1769, a committee delegated

8

by the mayor, aldermen, and burgesses of the town waited upon
Garrick in Southampton Street, London, and presented him with
a rarity made especially for him out of the one and only Mulberry
Tree: a box on which were carved "Fame Holding the Bust of
Shakespeare" (in case Garrick needed the hint), and "the Three
Graces Crowning Him with a Laurel"; on the sides were figures
representing Comedy and Tragedy; on the back was carved a
representation of "Mr. Garrick in the Character of King Lear in
the Storm Scene; and the top and corners were ornamented with
devices of Shakespeare's works, all curiously carved, and highly
finished."

Within this box Garrick found a document informing him that
the mayor, aldermen, and burgesses of Stratford had unani-
mously resolved that "being fully sensible of the extraordinary accomplishments and merits" of Garrick as a "judicious admirer and
representative" of their "incomparable poet," and being aware
how Garrick had "added (if possible) to that pleasing command
over the passions, which SHAKESPEARE in a most eminent degree,
and in numberless instances possessed," they had therefore
elected Garrick an honorary Burgess of Stratford, and herewith
presented him this copy of the freedom of the borough "in a small
neat chest constructed from a Mulberry-tree planted by SHAKE-
SPEARE himself."

By no means unprepared for these honors, Garrick responded
with a more than cordial letter thanking them for the freedom of
Stratford sent "in such an elegant and inestimable box." It would
be impossible for him, he concluded, ever to forget those who
had honored him by mentioning his own "unworthy name with
that of their immortal townsman."

This was the episode which was responsible for Garrick's decision to sponsor a Shakespeare Jubilee at Stratford. That imposing
event, while destined to be less than a success during the days it
was held, had the effect of gathering together the stray fragments
of reverence for Shakespeare and erecting out of them a formal

and official edifice of Shakespeare Worship, which was thereafter to render sacred every scrap that could be connected with the Bard.

It is always amusing to trace the mighty contests which rise from trivial things. Henry Angelo, son of the celebrated and wealthy fencing master, had often heard Garrick express to Angelo senior the desire to do something important for Garrick's "saint," Shakespeare. As the younger Angelo saw it, had the bad-tempered Gastrell not chopped down the Mulberry Tree, there would have been no wood from it to make into a box for Garrick, and hence there would have been no Shakespeare Jubilee. To put it less negatively, Gastrell's fury against the Bard's worshipers ended by vastly multiplying the number of idolaters. Gastrell cut down the Tree, Stratford had some of its wood made into a box for Garrick, Garrick sponsored the Jubilee, the Jubilee settled once and for all the sacredness of everything connected with Shakespeare. And, to carry this one step further: the Jubilee's settling the sacredness of everything connected with Shakespeare provided the incentive, at the end of the century, for the startling career of William Henry Ireland.

Stratford's overtures to Garrick had preceded by many months the ceremonious attendance upon him of the town's committee. He was well aware of that empty niche in the new Town Hall, and he lost no time in supplying for it both a painting and a sculpture. The figure was a copy of the statue by Scheemaker which graces the Poets' Corner at Westminister Abbey. The painting was Benjamin Wilson's *"Shakespeare in His Study,"* showing the poet sitting in a Jacobean chair near arched windows, pen in hand, and looking to the side where, beyond the limits of the canvas, Inspiration is apparently addressing him.

The town's Corporation, well pleased, informed Garrick that it would also be delighted to own a picture of *him*. For this Garrick needed no further encouragement, and he was soon urging Gainsborough to paint a canvas in which both Garrick and the

Bard would figure. When at length the painting was finished and hung in Stratford's new Town Hall, the Mulberry Tree (or, rather, *a* mulberry tree) was hymned on canvas. The picture showed Garrick, considerably taller than the facts warranted, leaning with negligent grace with his arm around a pillar surmounted by a bust of Shakespeare. Here the Bard looks vaguely as he does in the Westminster Abbey sculpture, though much more elegant. And over the inseparable pair hangs the luxuriant foliage of a mulberry tree.*

Shakespearean idolatry was still sufficiently in its infancy for no one to be troubled that the Jubilee took place five years after the bicentenary of Shakespeare's birth in 1564. No one in those days was yet much concerned about his dates. Some of the natives of Stratford, confounded by the preparations, were uncertain as to whether this was going to be a Jew Bill, a Jubilo, or a Juvilium, and were, moreover, quite in the dark as to just what all those mysterious terms signified. A fellow from Banbury, hired to bring a bass viol to the Festival, announced that it was to be employed for "the resurrection of Shakespeare."

Stratford was as busy as a hive during the spring and summer of 1769. Mr. Latimore came down from London to erect an octagonal wooden amphitheatre, seventy feet in diameter, on the very banks of the Avon. This proud building, in the style of the Rotunda at Ranelagh, was destined to accommodate a thousand spectators. Upon the banks of Avon thirty cannon were stationed; there too were made ready two wagonloads of fireworks and variegated lamps, sent from London by Angelo senior, in charge of illuminations. Multitudes of people flocked from adjacent counties to view the preparations. Some ten days before opening day, great numbers of the nobility and gentry arrived to be sure of lodgings, so that the town as well as villages in the neighborhood was completely filled. For the event Conventry manufactured the

---

* No one before now has identified the tree for what its leaves clearly indicate it to have been. This handsome painting, as well as Wilson's, was destroyed by fire.

Jubilee Ribbon, which "blended all the colors of the rainbow," inspired by a line from Johnson: "Each change of many-color'd life he drew." Mr. Westwood of Birmingham struck a medal for the Festival; on one face was a likeness of the Bard with this inscription from *Hamlet:* "We Shall not Look Upon His Like Again." The reverse read: "Jubilee at Stratford in Honor and to the Memory of SHAKESPEARE. Septr. 1769. D. G. Steward." These, in copper, silver, or gold, were quickly bought up.

The midsummer opening date had originally been set seasonably for August 6, 1769. But preparations had encountered too many obstacles. Despite the fury expended on Gastrell, many Stratfordians had never heard of Shakespeare; to most of them the name of Garrick meant nothing. Traditionally a Puritan town, Stratford looked upon the London workmen and their complicated equipment with suspicion; the glimpses caught of the rehearsals for the Festival seemed more than pagan to sober eyes. Some citizens were heard to express the conviction that these people would be raising Satan himself next. Others anticipated every kind of violence from robbery to riot from the incursion of out-of-towners.

Against such a background it is not surprising that operations lagged. By August the amphitheatre was still uncompleted, for local carpenters had stubbornly refused to lend the workmen their tools. Moreover, there were weeks of rain, and the swelling waters of the Avon were looking less than gentle. Lamps for the illumination of the Rotunda, sent by Garrick from the Drury Lane, arrived in smithereens; a friend of his, at Stratford for a preview, was warned as he walked the bank of the river not to cut his shoes on the pieces.

Nevertheless, every spare bed in the town, whether in attic, cellar, or shed, every rentable bit of floor-space was snapped up by the visiting aristocracy and gentry at exorbitant rates. Among their distinguished numbers were the dukes of Dorset and Manchester; the earls of Hertford, Plymouth, Northampton, Carlisle,

Shrewsbury, and Denbigh; the lords Beauchamp, Grosvenor, Pigot, Windsor, Catherlough, Archer, Spencer, Craven; many of their duchesses, countesses, and ladies; and a vast assortment of baronets and members of parliament. The theatrical and literary world was there too: Boswell, Macklin, Colman, Murphy, Kendrick, Hugh Kelly, Samuel Foote, among others.

Before setting out for Stratford, Boswell went to an embroiderer in Bow Street, London, and left a paper pattern for "a Corsican Cap, and ordered VIVA LA LIBERTA to be embroidered on the front of it, in letters of gold." Two days later he "walked about searching all over the town" for "necessary accoutrements as a Corsican for the Stratford Jubilee." During a tour of the Continent, Boswell in 1765, then twenty-five, had got to know quite well Pasquale di Paoli, leader of the Corsican rebellion against the Genoese. In 1768, a year before the Jubilee and five years after his fateful introduction to Samuel Johnson, he published his *Account of Corsica,* a book so successful that it was at once translated into Italian, French, German, and Dutch, and its author dubbed in England "Paoli Boswell." In the meantime Paoli had so well discouraged the Genoese that they had sold Corsica to France. The Corsican rebels fought their new masters bravely until they were forced to succumb to superior numbers in 1769. Boswell's appearing as an advocate of Corsican independence will seem unusual only to those unfamiliar with the man. Obviously he thought the conflux at Stratford of so many notables an excellent occasion for giving public support to Corsican independence and for advertising both his book and himself.

He managed to get everything he needed for the Jubilee into his traveling bag, with the exception of his musket and a staff he had come upon accidentally in Cheapside. It was "a very handsome vine with the root uppermost, and upon it a Bird, very well carved." To the inquiries of the proprietor of the shop he responded, "Why, Sir, this Vine is worth any money. It is a Jubilee Staff. That Bird is the Bird of Avon."

AT FIVE O'CLOCK in the morning of Wednesday, September 6, worshipper and intended scoffer alike were awakened in their cramped quarters at Stratford by the booming of cannon to announce the opening of the Jubilee. But this was not all. "Immediately afterwards, the principal ladies were serenaded under their windows by a number of young men, fantastically dressed, belonging to the theatre" with a song accompanied by hautboys, flutes, clarionets, guitars, and other instruments.

"The whole town being roused by these performances," the Corporation established Garrick in his office of Steward, a ceremony involving the delivery to him of two more pieces of the true Mulberry Tree: a medal on which was carved a bust of the Bard "richly set in Gold," and his wand of office. They made a short oration, to which Garrick replied handsomely as he fastened the medal about his neck, whence he never again removed it during the days of the Jubilee. At the conclusion of this business the town bells, as prearranged, began to clang out, and the cannon were fired anew.

Everyone was perforce awake by now, in time for the public breakfast held at nine o'clock in the Town Hall, now called "Shakespeare's Hall." After breakfast the company filed, at half-past ten, into the church to hear Dr. Arne's oratorio, *Judith*, though a good many were at pains to miss this pleasure. Arne was a very able composer, but many who heard the excellently sung work politely expressed their confusion as to what an oratorio on Judith could have to do with a Shakespeare Jubilee. The question was never answered.

The oratorio concluded, Garrick, marching at the head of the singers, conducted the audience from the church. The nobility and gentry entered their coaches and chaises; the others followed on foot. The procession thus made its way to the amphitheatre, while the singers, to the accompaniment of instruments, sang a chorus so timed that at these lines the singers were passing by the house where Shakespeare was born:

14

Here Nature nurs'd her darling boy.

. . . .

Now, now, we tread enchanted ground,
Here Shakespeare walk'd and sung!

At three o'clock a sumptuous ordinary was laid in the amphi-
theatre. The band began to play, and Joseph Vernon, tenor at
Drury Lane, waving a cup fashioned of wood from the Mulberry
Tree, sang lustily a composition of Garrick's:

Behold this fair goblet, 'twas carv'd from the tree,
Which, O my sweet SHAKESPEARE, was planted by thee;
As a relic I kiss it, and bow at the shrine,
What comes from thy hand must be ever divine!
All shall yield to the mulberry-tree,
Bend to thee,
Blest mulberry,
Matchless was he
Who planted thee,
And thou, like him, immortal be!

. . . .

The genius of Shakespeare outshines the bright day,
More rapture than wine to the heart can convey,
So the tree which he planted, by making his own,
Has laurel and bays and the vine all in one.
All shall yield to the mulberry-tree, etc.

Then each take a relic of this hallow'd tree,
From folly and fashion a charm let it be;
Fill, fill to the planter, the cup to the brim,
To honor the country, do honor to him.
All shall yield to the mulberry-tree, etc.

There were many stanzas to this masterpiece. After one or two,
everyone got the hang of the thing and joined Vernon and Garrick in the chorus, "All shall yield to the mulberry-tree"—a sentiment Mr. Sharp must gladly have concurred in.

By seven it was time for an intermission. After tea and coffee,
the company retired to prepare for the night's assembly.

Boswell, meanwhile, was determined to create a sensation,
but had arrived late and mud-stained. En route he had found no

post chaise to be had at Woodstock because of the crowds which had preceded him. He hired a couple of horses. "I had no boots," he records, "and only a short great coat which I had borrowed of a Postilion, and it rained pretty thick." Farther on, however, he found a conveyance, and arrived at Stratford between twelve and one. One look at Stratford and he was happy. Luckily finding a small room, he went on to the church. "I was exceedingly dirty; my hair hung wet about my ears; my black suit and the Postilion's grey duffle above it, several inches too short in every way, made a very strange appearance. I could observe people . . . whispering about me."

The assembly and ball began at nine o'clock. The whole town was illuminated, drums were beating, and "a tumult of perfect satisfaction everywhere predominated." Meanwhile some of Angelo's fireworks were set off. In the Rotunda minuets were danced until midnight, when they were succeeded by country dances. At about three in the morning all retired. But Boswell had quitted the ball long before that. He had gone just "to be able to tell that I had been there." Utterly fatigued, he went back to his little room, where he informed his landlady, "Perhaps I might retire from the world and just come and live in my room at Stratford."

Thursday, the second day of the Jubilee, upon which he was to read the Ode he had especially composed for the ceremonies, was anticipated by Garrick as the most joyful day of his life.

But things began to go badly at once. Upon rising in the early morning, he found it was drizzling outdoors. Alas for the pageant upon which he had expended so much money! It was to include characters from all of Shakespeare's leading plays. Little Angelo, on holiday from Eton, was to be Ariel; his father was to represent Antony; Mrs. Yates was to appear as Cleopatra, fanned by Cupids. Not knowing what the plans would be, many of the performers put on their costumes; but Garrick's fellow-manager insisted that it was no weather for a procession: "All the ostrich feathers will be spoiled."

16

Moreover, Garrick's face was in a sad way. The local barber, still not sober from Wednesday's potations, had given him a deep and nasty gash that ran from the corner of his lower lip to his chin. Mrs. Garrick was busy for hours applying astringents to stop the bleeding.

By eleven o'clock it was obvious that the pageant would have to be abandoned. Many of the aristocracy had arranged not to arrive until this second day, so when they did reach Stratford it was in torrential rains. By noon the amphitheatre was packed, since obviously nothing was possible in the way of entertainment out of doors.

Though Shakespeare's statue was destined for the Town Hall, it was present today in the gallery of the Rotunda, behind and above where Garrick was seated, prior to reading his Ode. The high-backed chair in which he sat inhibited his histrionic intentions. It was not easy to gaze over it up at Shakespeare's statue with concentrated and awed affection, while the assemblage waited, and at the same time look natural, both of which Garrick was trying his best to do.

The Ode was the product of much labor on Garrick's part. He had been concerned to make its length appropriate to the importance of the occasion, without sacrificing the lightness which his audience would require. To aid the effect, he had hit upon the novel technique of using Dr. Arne's music as an accompaniment while he recited the verses. The Ode, interrupted for variety by a series of Airs, with words by Garrick and music by Arne, began:

> To what blest genius of the isle,
>   Shall gratitude her tribute pay,
>   Decree the festive day,
> Erect the statue, and devote the pile?
>
> Do not your sympathetic hearts accord
>   To own the "bosom's lord?"
>   'Tis he!—'tis he!—that demi-god!
>   Who Avon's flow'ry margin trod,
>   While sportive Fancy round him flew;

Where Nature led him by the hand,
Instructed him in all she knew,
And gave him absolute command!
'Tis he—'tis he!—
"The god of our idolatry!"
To him the song, the edifice we raise;
He merits all our wonder, all our praise!

. . . .

Prepare! prepare! prepare!
Now swell at once the choral song,
Roll the full tide of harmony along;
Let rapture sweep the trembling strings,
And Fame, expanding all her wings,
With all her trumpet-tongues proclaim
That lov'd, rever'd, immortal name!
SHAKSPEAR! SHAKSPEAR! SHAKSPEAR!

These last lines formed the first Chorus. Swiftly latching on to the idea, the enthusiastic assemblage shouted with vigor that lov'd, rever'd, immortal name, "SHAKSPEAR! SHAKSPEAR! SHAK-SPEAR!"

The first Air, now intervening, paid tribute to the Bard as "Nature's glory"; unlike Alexander, Shakespeare had no need to sigh for new worlds to conquer; he invented new worlds and creatures of his own.

There was an alarming note of the infelicitous about the sixth Air, with its address to the "soft-flowing Avon," by whose "silver stream" the Matchless Bard was wont to dream. Outside, the soft-flowing Avon was rising over its banks, and becoming a serious threat. The rain continued torrential.

The final passage of the Ode appealed to the Bard to smile upon his native land. The concluding lines remarked that "we ne'er shall look upon his like again!" and the last Chorus observed that "HIS name . . . shall never, never pass away."

It would be reasonable to suppose that such words heralded a welcome intermission. Not at all. Garrick now delivered in prose an encomium on the Bard, near the conclusion of which he demanded to know if there were any present who had ever been moved as much by other scenes as by the scenes of Shakespeare. "If there be any, speak! for him have I offended."

Nor was this the end. For now the latter-day Brutus asked, "Ladies and gentlemen, will you be pleased to say anything for or against Shakespeare?" Here, as scheduled, the comedian Tom King, he of the "large, dog-like eyes," arose from the audience, took off his overcoat, and revealed himself dressed in a suit of blue and silver, Macaroni style. He had, he averred, a great deal to say against Shakespeare. King carried off his disparagement of the Bard so well, accusing him of being a ruffian who exercised tyrannical sway over everyone's will, that many took him seriously. He was hooted down and almost thrown out, until the laughter of the better-informed set matters right.

Garrick next addressed the ladies in a poetic epilogue, which exhorted them "to support the reputation of a poet who was so remarkable for upholding the dignity of the female character." During this part of the entertainment certain benches began to give way, and Lord Carlisle narrowly escaped being killed when a door fell on him.

By now the audience was not sorry that it was time for the three o'clock public dinner and the 150-pound turtle they were to consume. At five, the diners heard new songs and catches.

Boswell did not attend the public dinner. He had begun some verses for the Jubilee and went back to his room to finish them. When they were completed he ran with them to Garrick, read them to him, and was praised for them. The poem, "Verses in the Character of a Corsican at Shakespeare's Jubilee," began:

> From the rude Banks of Golo's rapid Flood,
> Alas! too deeply ting'd with patriot Blood—
>
> . . . .
>
> Behold a CORSICAN!

Gratified with Garrick's approval, Boswell took his forty-six lines to a printer. "He brought me a proof to the Masquerade Ball about two in the morning." But the final copy was not ready for the author to distribute in his Corsican attire.

Meanwhile the torrent of rain had not abated. It appeared to young Angelo "as if the clouds in ill-humor with these magnificent doings, had sucked up a superabundance of water, to shower down upon the finery of the mimic host; and that the river gods had opened all the sluices of the Avon to drown the devotees of their boasted bard. . . . An old lady of fashion . . . looking up at the welkin, exclaimed, 'What an absurd climate!'"

After dinner it proved almost impossible to get to the Rotunda for the great Masquerade. Angelo says that "the floods threatened to carry the mighty fabric off. The horses had to wade through the meadow, knee-deep, to reach it; and the planks were stretched from the entrance to the floors of the carriages, for the company to alight. Such a flood had not been witnessed there in the memory of man." As for the fireworks of Angelo senior, scheduled for eight o'clock on the other side of Avon, the rockets refused to ascend, and the surly crackers "went out at a single pop."

Nevertheless, the Masquerade Ball proceeded in good spirits. Three celebrated beauties, Lady Pembroke, Mrs. Bouverie, and Mrs. Crewe, were dressed as witches; there was a shortage of masks, and everyone was charmed by the contrast between the deformity these three feigned and their own beauty. There were a shepherdess, a Dame Quickly, a Dutch sea captain, numerous sailors, a jockey, and a Devil who "was inexpressibly displeasing." Lord Grosvenor was resplendent in oriental garb. Kendrick as Shakespeare's Ghost stalked the Rotunda, shivering "as though he had passed the last four and twenty hours on the cold marble." Boswell appeared in his Corsican habit "with pistols in his belt and a musket at his back: in gold letters in the front of his cap, were the words PAOLI, and VIVA LA LIBERTA." He also wore daggers in his belt, and carried the staff topped by the Bird of Avon.

Not having copies of his verses to distribute among the thousand present, Boswell began to recite them:

> From the rude Banks of Golo's rapid Flood,
> Alas! too deeply ting'd with patriot Blood—

but he was howled down. Everyone had heard enough that day, and Boswell was forced to desist. However, with his usual good nature, he seems to have recovered rapidly from the slight, and recorded that his "bosom glowed with joy" at the sight of so brilliant a company. He had indeed only one reservation: "But I could have wished that prayers had been read or a short sermon preached. It would have consecrated our Jubilee."

The rain continued to pour down all Thursday night, and on Friday, the third and last day of the Jubilee, it was raining still. There could be no Pageant. Despite the mud, a race was run for the Jubilee Cup at noon at Shottery Race-ground. The site, Garrick's advertisement had assured the world, was perfect; the stream, the hills and woods, and "the verdant lawns" formed "a scene too delicious for description." There were five runners. The Jubilee Cup, engraved with Shakespeare's arms, was won by a Mr. Pratt, a groom who declared he knew nothing about drama in general or the Bard in particular.

In the late afternoon the rain at last ceased. Many people anxious to make sure of their departure, left as early as possible, but a great many more were compelled to stay on because of the shortage of horses and vehicles. In the evening there was an assembly at the Town Hall, where Mrs. Garrick danced a minuet that evoked comment for its grace, and joined in the country dances. These ceased at four o'clock, and thus closed the Jubilee.

Boswell left on Saturday morning. But first he presented a copy of his poem to Garrick. Though exhausted and disappointed in the extreme, Garrick generously read the lines aloud then and there. Whereupon Boswell, out of pocket, asked him for a loan; after a weak attempt to avoid parting with any more money, the actor fetched five guineas from his wife and handed them to Boswell.

DESPITE GARRICK'S NOTORIETY for being close with money and having a good head for business, he had lost a small fortune on his Stratford venture. But that autumn he recouped his losses by presenting a musical pageant called *Jubilee* at the Drury Lane. An immense success, it broke records for more than forty successive nights. Here the people of Stratford were represented onstage, some as country simpletons, and here at last the grand Pageant was nightly seen, consisting of "all the principal characters to be met with in Shakespeare's plays; with a large and highly ornamented triumphal car, in which two persons, representing Melpomene and Thalia, with the Graces" were "drawn by six persons habited like satyrs, with attendants carrying emblematical devices and insignia." The statue, his gift to Stratford, was borrowed and brought to the Drury Lane; in front of it Garrick had the pleasure of reciting his Ode and hearing the audience join in the Chorus to shout

> That lov'd, rever'd, immortal name!
> SHAKSPEAR! SHAKSPEAR! SHAKSPEAR!

At the end of the season, the statue was returned to Stratford and set in its destined niche in the Town Hall.

The success of the Drury Lane *Jubilee* obliterated the fiasco of the Stratford one—made it, indeed, in retrospect, seem to have been a great triumph—and Shakespeare Worship was now solidly established and ready for every kind of embellishment.

But it is seriously to be doubted that the age worshiped the Bard with any true appreciation or for the right reasons. Garrick, for instance, who did so much *for* him, did, like all the other neoclassical adapters, quite as much *to* Shakespeare. Consider, for instance, his complacent mangling of *Hamlet*. Like the Olivier cinema version in our own time, Garrick's cut out the voyage to England and the execution of Rosencrantz and Guildenstern (the Olivier version omitted that pair entirely). Garrick, like Evans in his second American production, omitted too the Gravediggers and the funeral of Ophelia. In the Garrick *Hamlet,* the Prince bursts in upon the King and the court; Laertes reproaches him with the deaths of Polonius and Ophelia. Both young men reach a point of exasperation, the King interposes: he had ordered Hamlet to England and declares he will no longer put up with this rebellious behavior. Claudius threatens the Prince with his wrath. "First," cries Hamlet, "feel you mine"—and he at once stabs Claudius. The Queen now rushes off stage, crying to be saved from her son. Laertes finds the moment opportune for stabbing Hamlet with a mortal wound. Horatio is about to turn on Laertes, but is restrained by Hamlet, who says that Laertes was directed "by the hand of Heaven" to administer "that precious balm" for all of the Prince's ills. Next we are told that Gertrude has fallen into a trance; Hamlet begs that she may be granted an hour "of penitence ere madness ends her." He then joins the hands of Horatio and Laertes, and commands them to join their talents to "calm the troubled land."

Garrick's sincere adoration of Shakespeare is beyond question. What can have impelled him to violate *Hamlet* with the invention of this drivel is beyond answering. All that can be said in his defense is that so many others had been and were doing the same sort of thing. It is curious that an epoch which made so much fuss about "taste" should have been so frequently guilty of examples of the most execrable kind. This was not the only crime visited by Garrick upon the plays, but in itself it speaks eloquently for the fact that Shakespeare's high priest in the eighteenth century had a very limited comprehension of the magnificence of the god of his idolatry. If this was true of Garrick, what was to be expected of others who succumbed to Shakespearolatry?

The year after the Jubilee, Garrick, on the grounds of health, politely declined the offer to follow up with a second Jubilee at Stratford. Nevertheless, he advised the town to hold a yearly festival on or near the Bard's birthday. He suggested such entertainments as he himself had presented, but added: "Let your streets be well paved and kept clean, do something to the delightful meadow, allure everybody to visit the *Holy-land*. . . . Let it not be said . . . that the town which gave birth to the first genius since the creation is the most dirty, unseemly, ill-paved wretched looking place in all Britain." Garrick would not soon forget the mud of Stratford.

There was not to be another Jubilee for the rest of the century. But Stratford was never again the same. Inspired by the great event, a Stratford wheelwright, John Jordan (1746–1809), had turned poet by inditing some verses to the Steward of the Jubilee:

> By Garrick led, the grateful band,
> Haste to their poet's native land. . . .

Encouraged by sudden emergence into fame, Jordan followed this with more ambitious efforts, without repeating his success. The Jubilee, however, had set its seal upon him, and he took on the role of local poet, collector and vendor of Shakespeareana, and self-appointed cicerone to Shakespeare's town. By 1780 he completed his *Original Collections on Shakespeare and Stratford-on-Avon,* which Mark Noble found too confused to publish. Ten years later he had completed another volume of the same kind, *Original Memoirs.* By that time he had become well known to Stratford pilgrims. Edmund Malone, last of the great eighteenth-century editors, began corresponding with him in 1790 on matters of genealogy and the stories connecting the Bard with Sir Thomas Lucy and the deer-stealing legend.

Now that Shakespeare was safely enshrined as England's leading literary divinity, his worshipers were suddenly confronted with an intolerable vexation. Boaden put the problem in words whose cadences and admixture of stateliness and exaggeration make them sound like the very voice of the age: "It was a subject of infinite surprise to the admirers of Shakspeare's genius, to observe from age to age, that while discoveries very material to our knowledge of the period in which he lived, occasionally occupied the press, yet that with respect to himself little could be known;

and all the effusions that friendship or business must have poured from his pen . . . ALL, as if collected together in one mass destroyed BY AUTHORITY, had vanished away, and were entirely lost to posterity. This wonder was increased by our knowledge that he had neither lived in obscurity nor died in want." Shakespeare, Boaden continues, had been patronized by Elizabeth, James I, Essex, Southampton, and the two Pembrokes, had lived "in the closest intimacy" with Jonson and his friends, yet "not a single letter can be found subscribed with his name." The logical conclusion was that "some affectionate hand" had collected the Bard's papers and that on any day "a rich assemblage of Shakspeare papers would start forth from some ancient repository, to solve all our doubts, and add to our reverence and our enjoyment."

Small wonder, then, that William Henry Ireland should feel encouraged to unveil such a repository, and win the blessings of his countrymen by solving all their doubts and adding to their reverence and enjoyment. Small wonder, too, that the half-educated Jordan should enjoy a vogue and an authority among visitors to Stratford by sole dint of his being native to the Holy Land. Who could tell to what treasures the merest hint, the merest scrap of legend might not lead?

When Malone came on his researches to Stratford he naturally met Jordan, who greeted him with an affecting bill of complaints. "Alas, I am unnoticed by the world," Jordan wailed to Malone, as though it were natural he share the Bard's glories, "oppressed with affliction, and wrecked with despair; the anchor of hope has totally forsook me; I am dashed by the waves of a boundless sea of trouble, sorrow and misery, which brings to my mind an expression of Shakespeare, that

> Misery trodden on by many,
> Being low is not relieved by any."

(Sublime lines which Shakespeare omitted incorporating into his plays.) Malone was much touched by this speech, which might easily have come right out of the pages of some sentimental popular romance, and he was therefore further treated by Jordan to the story of the Crab Tree, which under the wheelwright's patronage was now vying for esteem with the story of the Mulberry Tree. But let Jordan tell the tale in his own inimitable words and spelling:

"Our Poet was extremely fond of drinking hearty draughts of English Ale, and glory'd in being thought a person of superior eminence in that proffession if I may be allowed the phrase. In his time, but at what period it is not recorded, There were two companys or faternitys of Village Yeomanry who used frequently to associate at Bidford a town pleasantly situate on the banks of Avon about 7 miles below Stratford, and Who boasted themselves Superior in the Science of drinking to any set of equal number in the Kingdom and hearing of the fame of our Bard it was determined to Challenge him and his Companions." After some difficulty in catching up with the challengers, Shakespeare and his fellows held the contest with them, "and in a little time our Bard and his Companions got so intollerable intoxicated that they were not able to Contend any longer and accordingly set out on their return to Stratford. But had not got above half a mile on the road e'er they found themselves unable to proceed any farther, and was obliged to lie down under a Crabtree which is still growing by the side of the road where they took their repose till morning when some of the Company roused the poet and intreated him to return to Bidford and renew the Contest he declined it. . . ."

Within a few years of Malone's exchange with Jordan, the apple tree would be cut down to furnish a rival supply of cups, boxes, and other ware, produced in quantity as astonishing as those products of the true Mulberry Tree. Jordan also gave Malone (for a price) the "original" manuscript of a ballad on Sir Thomas Lucy of the deer-stealing myth: Malone knew by the script and the language that the piece was a forgery, and he reprinted it as such.

The day of the Mulberry Tree was, however, far from over.

Malone was introduced by Stratford's young vicar, James Davenport, to an ancient alderman of the town who, as a lad, had eaten of the fruit of the true Mulberry: the boy's father had been Gastrell's neighbor, and the mulberries had dangled invitingly over the wall. Overwhelmed by his Stratford experiences, Malone too burst into song:

> In this retreat our Shakespeare's godlike mind
> With *matchless* skill survey'd all human kind. . . .

In London John Boydell (1719–1804) was busy adding to the Matchless Bard's glory. Born in Shropshire, Boydell came to London and built himself a fortune there by his engravings of small landscapes and bridges. In 1782 he became alderman of Cheap, and in 1790 lord mayor of London. It was in 1786 that he began publishing a series of prints illustrative of Shakespeare, after paintings commissioned by him, all the work of English artists. Almost every one of the most celebrated painters of his day painted canvases for him, and he opened a gallery in Pall Mall to house his paintings. This ambitious project took a number of years. There were 34 paintings in his Shakespeare Gallery in 1789, 65 in 1791, 162 in 1802—of that number 84 were very large pictures. He had employed the talents of thirty-three painters and two sculptors, among whom were Reynolds, Romney, Fuseli, Barry, Opie, West, and Angelica Kauffmann. All of his artists were paid handsomely.

Meanwhile the mania for collecting Shakespeareana was in full swing. After the Jubilee, Mrs. Harte, who had married a descendant of the Bard's sister Joan, began to do a thriving business at the Birthplace selling relics. Horace Walpole had seen a chair in which the Bard was said to have sat near the fire. In 1785 the Honorable John Byng, who figures importantly in our story as a close friend of Samuel Ireland's, bought a slice of it as well as the lower crossbar. Visitors, though more and more numerous, seemed unable to exhaust the supply of mulberry articles in Sharp's shop.

But for that fact Samuel Ireland, who had been an intimate of those pioneer Shakespearolatrists, Garrick and Macklin, counted himself only lucky when he arrived at Stratford in the summer of 1793 with his dull-witted son, William Henry.

TWO

A Gullible Pair in Tow

❊ ❊ ❊ ❊ ❊ ❊ ❊ ❊ ❊ ❊ ❊ ❊ ❊ ❊ ❊ ❊

SAMUEL IRELAND, although self-taught as an artist, had had gratifying success with several books copiously illustrated by himself: *A Picturesque Tour through Holland, Brabant, and Part of France* and, in sequel, two more books of *Picturesque Views* on the rivers Thames and Medway. Inevitably he thought it high time to add the Upper Avon to the latter series. Even if Avon's gentle meanderings were through country less attractive than it is, "The honor it derives from having produced our immortal Shakespeare 'so divine in reason! and in faculties so infinite, the paragon of the world!' would alone have been sufficient" to induce him to aspire to be its historian. The misquotation from Shakespeare (Ireland was forever reading him, yet never troubled to check before rushing into print) is as characteristic of the middle-aged antiquarian as his tendency to mistake the meaning of the Bard's lines. His proneness to these errors, however, is no qualification of the sincerity of Ireland's enthusiasm. With him the Matchless Bard was an appetite, a feeling, and a love which haunted him like a passion.

So in the summer of 1793 he arrived in Stratford with his unpromising eighteen-year-old son, William Henry (whom he preferred always to call "Sam"), and put himself and his heir in the hands of the "Stratford Poet," as he was now called, the old scoundrel Jordan.

During their visit Jordan had no cause to complain longer that "the anchor of hope" had "forsook" him or that the misery which had been "trodden on by many" was "not relieved by any." For he brought the Irelands to places where Samuel Ireland was easily induced to make purchases from which Jordan must have collected sizable percentages. Father and son were delighted with him. Samuel, as his book when it was published eloquently would prove, swallowed everything the Stratford Poet told him. And years later his son William Henry in his own autobiography spoke of "this civil inoffensive creature" as "a very honest fellow" who had "a spark of the Apollonian fire"; nor had the ex-wheelwright "been idle on the score of Shakespeare," for he had made "frequent visits to the neighboring villages and ancient houses, endeavoring if possible to glean any new anecdote or traditionary tale." Jordan's scrip, the Irelands found, was filled with many such anecdotes and tales.

The very first place he took them to, opposite the inn where they were staying, was Sharp's shop. They were overjoyed to find its proprietor "in possession of the remains of the mulberry tree, together with tobacco stoppers, busts, wafer seals, & c., all carved from the wood." Ireland bought "some of these bagatelles, and a goblet which had certainly been carved many years back" and for which he "gave an adequate price." When after his death Ireland's private collections were sold at auction in 1801, two of the purchases were listed in the catalogue as:

"A toothpick case cut with vine leaves and the arms of Shakspeare made of the mulberry tree.

"A goblet made of Shakspeare mulberry tree and mounted in silver." (This goblet brought six pounds, a higher price than Hogarths and Van Dycks sold for at the same auction.)

Next the pilgrims were taken to the church, which alone kept Ireland "a resident at that place for a week." "It would be impossible," his son records, "for me to describe the thrill which then took possession of my soul" on entering Stratford Church. His father at once began making sketches for the engravings of the various monuments to grace his book. While the father was occupied for a considerable time, being an artist "very particular in his delineations," William Henry strolled about the premises. On coming back to where his father was drawing the scene before him, the boy noticed a door opposite. It was the entrance to the charnel house. "I pushed it open, when the largest collection of human bones I had ever beheld instantly struck my regard." He called to his father, who immediately reflected upon the impression such a place must have had on the Bard's exquisite sensibilities: "It was by no means improbable that they inspired him with a horror at the idea of so many remnants of the dead being huddled together in a vast heap"; it was for some such reason that the Bard had caused "to be carved on the stone which covers his grave (being to the right of the charnel-house door, and directly under his bust), in order to deter any sacrilegious hand from removing his ashes," the celebrated epitaph cursing the man who should move the poet's bones from their resting place.

Since Samuel Ireland's speculations, there have been many others upon this epitaph far more absurd than his, particularly on the part of those who dispute Shakespeare's authorship of his own works. It is odd that it never occurred to him or to later commentators that few men manage to provide the lines carved on their tombstones or to superintend the disposition of their remains. It is quite conceivable that Shakespeare's ghost would have been struck no less with the force of novelty upon reading the epitaph than with exasperation at its literary inadequacy.

The moment of discovery permitted Samuel the opportunity to reveal his own limited appreciation of the Bard. The closeness of the charnel house to the grave, he decided, "was particularly calculated to make a forcible impression upon such a mind as that of Shakespeare's, and may probably have given birth to that striking exclamation, at which, however just the composition, humanity recoils, and the soul thrills with horror: *Chain me with roaring bears / Or shut me nightly in a Charnel house,*" etc. Typically Samuel singles out one of the most embarrassingly inept moments of *Romeo and Juliet* for awed admiration. It is strange, too, that he did not pause to ask himself how Shakespeare could have been inspired by the proximity of the charnel house to his grave some twenty years before he was buried in it! Young William Henry, on the other hand, felt that the proof that "our bard had a great antipathy to the removal of the relics of the dead," was to be found in Hamlet's speech over Yorick's skull.

The time not occupied in going from site to site under the guidance of old Jordan was enthusiastically dissipated by father and son in talk about Shakespeare. "Not one hour was spent," William Henry records, "but in the favorite pursuit; while the conversations at our dinners and suppers were still of Shakspeare, the immortal and divine Shakspeare."

At the Bard's Birthplace they found part of the premises still occupied by a descendant of the poet's sister Joan. This worthy was busily engaged in "the humble occupation of a butcher. His father, Thomas Harte . . . informed me that when a boy he well remembered having, with other boys, dressed themselves as Scaramouches (such was his phrase) in the wearing apparel of our Shakespeare."

In the kitchen, of which Samuel "proceeded to make a correct drawing," since "it is more than probable our great poet must have frequently been seated" in it, there had stood an old oak chair which, he was informed, had for many years received nearly as many adorers as the shrine of the Lady of Loretto. This relic had been purchased in July, 1790, by the Princess Czartoryska, who was first told it was not for sale. Because the old oak seat had been blessed with the Bard's *derrière*, the Princess had rapturously consigned her own to it for a space, and upon departing from the Birthplace left a handsome tip to old Mrs. Harte. Four months later, still avid to possess the sacred oak, she sent an agent to Stratford to acquire it at no matter what price. The

Hartes weakened and parted with their treasure for twenty guineas.

Part of the original premises of the Birthplace was now a public house, in a lower room of which Samuel noted a plaster relief over the chimney, inscribed with the date 1606, and placed there "possibly by the poet himself." It was enough for Samuel that this relief "held a conspicuous place in the dwelling house of who is himself the ornament and pride of the island he inhabited," and so he made a drawing of this representation of David and Goliath.

Upon the younger Ireland the Birthplace made so lasting an impression that within a few years, when he heard that the Birthplace was to be sold upon the death of old Harte, he applied to the Stratford attorney in charge of the estate for its purchase. A correspondence ensued between the two, but soon the bubble of William Henry's glory had burst, and negotiations were dropped. For then he was more actively concerned, perforce, with providing himself with the day's bread and butter.

Father and son were of course anxious to see what was left of New Place. At its site they listened much moved to the account of how Macklin and young Garrick had sat under the Mulberry Tree, whose ghost still hovered over them. There followed the tale of Gastrell and his hated ax, perpetrator of a "sacrilegious act merely to avoid the earnest importunities of the frequent traveler, whose zeal might prompt him to hope that he might meet inspiration under its shade."

Poor Gastrell! He surely earns some measure of sympathy for what he endured before leveling the Tree, when one reads Philip Hamburger's hilarious account of the sufferings of the Langdon family in Elmira, New York. Mark Twain, whose wife was a Langdon, had worked in a small octagonal study on the grounds of Quarry Farm during the summers he spent in Elmira. For years after Twain's death the Langdons were subject to every inconvenience. "Young couples turned up at all hours, demanding

to be married in the study." Some of these people had read Mark
Twain, some intended to read him; some stole small objects,
others carved their initials in Twain's worktable. Perhaps most
unbearable of all, "large numbers of sightseers fell to their knees
in the study and made damn fools of themselves." Small wonder
that by 1952 the Langdons had had enough. They did not demolish the study, but instead donated it to Elmira College, on whose
campus it now stands. It is fair to assume that Gastrell's provoca-
tion must have been far greater.

Opposite to New Place was the Falcon, a public house, whose
sign "was first set up as a compliment to Shakspeare, whose crest
of cognisance . . . was a Falcon." In the Bard's time the owner
was Julius Shaw, carpenter and undertaker by trade, who was
supposed to have been "the person who buried him. Shakspeare is
said to have had a strong partiality for the landlord, as well as for
his liquor."

As one listens to these tales of Jordan and other Stratfordians,
one gathers that Shakespeare could scarcely have had time to
write those plays which are the pride of Stratford. They must have
written themselves. Nor could he possibly have been in London,
seeing to their production or acting in them or in other plays. He
was too busy in Warwickshire, where, if he was not sitting on an
oak chair in the kitchen of the Birthplace or agreeably holding his
own Ann upon his knee in Shottery, he was occupied in paying
little visits to his neighbors, drinking deeply of good ale or
stronger spirits, or else engaging in Gargantuan drinking contests.
Mr. Hamburger reports similarly of Mark Twain in Elmira. Despite the fact that Clemens during his summer days there was
busy working on *Tom Sawyer, Huckleberry Finn, Life on the
Mississippi,* and *A Connecticut Yankee,* Elmirans today are divided into two groups: those who were engaged in or who know
people who were engaged in forever "bumping into him in the
streets of Elmira," where he was always to be seen with a stogie
in mouth or hand, and where he was daily to be heard saying in-

comparably funny things; and those who were spectators to or who know people who were spectators to the sight of Twain, always to be seen through "the big front windows of old downtown hotels," sitting in the lobby, "big as life," with a stogie in mouth or hand, his feet in the window, and obviously in the act of saying incomparably funny things. Both groups agree that he was never without his stogie or his incomparable jokes, and no member of either group can remember a single one of them.

AND NOW OCCURRED the experience that was to alter the whole course of William Henry's life. Thus far, despite the delirium of rapture with which Samuel had been following in Shakespeare's steps, he was still deeply frustrated in his paramount desire: to acquire something, anything—any scrap of parchment with Shakespeare's own handwriting on it. Though probably more intense than most of the Shakespearolatrists, Samuel was not alone in this fervent wish. Boaden, as we have seen, was to state eloquently what seemed so great a mystery to his age, though it is none to ours, that all of Shakespeare's papers "had vanished away." Samuel was untiring in asking questions about where Shakespearean documents might conceivably be found, and must have pestered Jordan to rack his ingenuities. At length old Jordan satisfied him, bringing him the corroboration of some of the oldest Stratfordians: upon the demolition of New Place "all the furniture and papers were removed to the ancient mansion of the Clopton family," a mile away.

Clopton House was, therefore, highly important to see, and at once. The current tenant was a Mr. Williams, gentleman-farmer, "rich in gold and the worldly means of accumulating wealth," as William Henry describes him, "but devoid of every polished refinement." This judgment is fair enough, but it appears that Williams was also something of a practical joker who could not resist amusing himself at the expense of the two innocents who had come in worship of the Bard. Indeed, it may be conjectured that rascally old Jordan had arranged in advance with Williams and his wife the little farce which they proceeded to enact for the Irelands. Certainly the whole episode was calculated to lend massive credibility to Jordan's fund of cock-and-bull stories; and Williams reveals himself in it to have taken a coarse delight in the credulity of the unsophisticated. If this guess is right, Jordan and the Williamses were unknowingly taking upon themselves the role of Fate in the life of William Henry. That day young Ireland had good reason never to forget, and his recollection of it could hardly have been more vivid.

Mr. Williams on their arrival, he tells us, invited them into a small, gloomy parlor, where Ireland senior explained the motive of his visit: a wish to ascertain whether "any old deeds or manuscripts were then existing in any part of the mansion." Whereupon Williams exclaimed: "By God, I wish you had arrived a little sooner! Why, it isn't a fortnight since I destroyed several basketsful of letters and papers, in order to clear a small chamber for some young partridges which I wish to bring up alive! And as to Shakspeare, why there were many bundles with his name wrote upon them. Why, it was in this very fire-place I made a roaring bonfire of them."

Ireland senior's face exhibited his horror at this information. He tried to suppress his anguish as Williams spoke. Suddenly, "starting from his chair, he clasped his hands together, exclaiming, 'My God! Sir, you are not aware of the loss which the world has sustained. Would to heaven I had arrived sooner!'"

This was a rewarding beginning, and Williams now called to his wife in the adjoining room, and she came into the parlor, "My dear, don't you remember bringing me down those baskets of papers from the partridge-room? And that I told you there were some about Shakspeare the poet?"

Mrs. Williams had heard her husband's discourse to the Irelands, and replied: "Yes, my dear. I do remember it perfectly well and, if you will call to mind my words, I told you not to burn the papers as they might be of consequence." She was not only a co-operative wife and an adept at listening behind doors, but apparently also a woman who could not miss the opportunity to impress her visitors with the general superiority of her sex in matters cultural.

Unable to give up all hope, Samuel, tortured to think how the most lavish of all his desires had been so nearly within grasp, begged to be allowed to inspect the partridge room. Williams (gleefully, we may imagine) consented. Alas! the room contained nothing but partridges.

Still unwilling to resign himself to so crushing a defeat, Samuel now asked whether he might be allowed to go over the whole house. Williams obligingly ordered two lanterns to be fetched, and the search began in earnest. "Every chamber underwent the strictest scrutiny." As the visitors moved from room to room, they found them all furnished with ancient pieces and hangings. In the cockloft were piles of moldering antiques; "among the rest was an emblazoned representation on vellum of queen Elizabeth, the wife of Henry VII, as she lay in state in the chapel of the Tower of London, after having died in childbed." Williams presented this to Ireland as "a *picture* which was in his opinion of no service because, being on vellum, it would not do *to light the fire*." Samuel's face must have been a study as two conflicting emotions strove for mastery over him: pleasure at his new acquisition and misery over this proof of Williams' indifference to the past. Williams, no doubt, made the offering which he held so lightly merely to sharpen the edge of Ireland's unhappiness over the pretended disappearance of the manuscripts.

The prime object of the house's inspection went unrewarded. "As to Shakspearian manuscripts, not a line was to be found."

The Williamses must have had a merry time of it when bumbling old Ireland left. That he had the stamina to continue his researches after Clopton House testifies to the staunchness of his determination to leave no pebble unturned.

The narrow margin by which his father had missed a treasure-hoard beyond price and the bitterness of his disappointment lay heavily upon young William Henry. If only he himself could bestow upon the old man the gift of but one so-yearned-for manuscript!

But Samuel Ireland had the rest of the Upper Avon to sketch for the sake of his book. Besides, there was still Ann Hathaway's Cottage to see at Shottery. He had a particular purpose in view in going there. Old Mr. Harte at the Birthplace in Stratford had told him of "an old oak chair that had always in his remembrance been called Shakespeare's Courting Chair" and also of "a purse that had been likewise his, and handed down" to the present inhabitants of the Cottage. It was doubtless Jordan who had convinced him that "this account was authentic, and from a wish to obtain the smallest trifle appertaining to our Shakespeare, I became a purchaser of these relics."

The occupants of the Cottage were poor folk, and they substantiated the authenticity of both chair and purse. The purse was some four inches square, "wrought with small black and white bugles and beads," the tassels of the same materials. (This item when sold at Ireland's auction in 1801 brought two shillings.) There was also an ancient bed—Ann Hathaway's? The old woman to whom these articles belonged, "had slept in the bed all her life" and resolutely refused to part with it at any price which Ireland offered. Her stand convinced him that he "had not listened with too easy credulity to the tale she told" concerning the articles which he did purchase. She also informed him that during the Jubilee she had sold to Garrick a small inkstand and a pair of fringed gloves which the Bard used to wear. (Some day someone is going to write an impressive book documenting the ease with which the rustic innocent can swindle the city sophisticate.) Shakespeare's Courting Chair wherein "our bard used to sit . . . with his Ann upon his knee," was presently placed in Samuel Ireland's study.

Before they quitted Stratford, Jordan also took them for a ramble to Bitford; on the road he pointed out the famous Crab Tree, and gave them his own misspelled manuscript of the story connected with the Mulberry's rival. Samuel made a "very correct drawing" of the tree, since he heartily agreed with the late Thomas Warton that "the meanest hovel to which Shakspeare has an allusion interests curiosity and acquires importance"; wherefore the "tree that has spread its shade over him and sheltered him from the dews of the night, has a claim to our attention."

So ended the visit to Shakespeare's native country. And so began the meteoric career of William Henry Ireland. After their return from their tour, William Henry tells us, their experiences in and about Stratford had taken such root in his mind that he was "more partial than ever to the pursuit after antiquities of every description, and more particularly to everything that bore the slightest affinity to our bard." His father's predilection for the name of Shakespeare seemed also to have been increased by the visit. His encomiums were unceasing.

But Williams' wicked joke at the Irelands' expense boomeranged. Samuel kept in touch with Jordan at Stratford, and doubtless often reverted to his anguish over the burned basketfuls of Shakespeare papers. Jordan, in turn, relayed the tale to Malone, who apparently took it as seriously as had Ireland, for he wrote to Williams' landlord, Wyatt, to protest the right of a tenant to burn his landlord's papers. Wyatt looked into the matter, to Williams' annoyance. Presently Jordan was writing to Ireland that Williams "would have wrote to you himself but he is so averse to scribbling that he almost dreads the thought of putting pen to paper. . . . He was rather out of temper about the papers he told us he had destroyed." Williams made the excuse that in point of fact Wyatt was in possession of all Clopton papers, and that his conversation with Ireland was strictly his own business.

That judgment was to prove far from the truth. Had it been otherwise the story we have to trace would not have occurred.

The experience at Clopton House had left its mark, and Samuel Ireland sighed more profoundly and more often than ever for the possession of a Shakespearean manuscript. "He would frequently assert," his son writes, "that such was his veneration for the bard that he would willingly give half his library to become possessed even of his signature alone." William Henry had no desire to own half his father's library before the hour when it might become his by inheritance. But he was consumed by the wish to gratify his father's ardent ambition.

This he was able to do a year later, on December 16, 1794, at eight o'clock, in the Ireland home, in the presence of the entire family.

THREE

Father and Son

❀ ❀ ❀ ❀ ❀ ❀ ❀ ❀ ❀ ❀ ❀ ❀ ❀ ❀ ❀ ❀

As an object of study Samuel Ireland remains faintly exasperating. Just when you think you have the contours of his character clearly delineated, some new detail or minor fact obtrudes to blur the outline, the figure loses its form and you find yourself beginning all over again the process of reconstructing him. Certainly his contemporaries were even more confused about him. Some of them violently asserted that he was the prototype of a shrewd Svengali masterminding the activities of a weak-minded son; some avowed that he was himself the perpetrator of misdeeds for which he allowed the boy to assume the guilt; and others stoutly defended him as a sort of simple-minded dupe of William Henry. His son's confessions and his own publications strongly tend to prove him the victim. But even that interpretation must be modified by certain incontrovertible facts. If undeniably naïve in some matters, he was as undeniably acute in others. If he was his son's victim, he was so because of his own fanatical desire to be duped. He appears to have been almost childlike in his innocence, yet there was more than a little of the sophisticate in his make-up. Greedy he assuredly was, not demonstrably for money, but greedy, as are fanatical collectors, for objects for his collections.

Everything connected with his origins he deliberately shrouded in mystery. He never permitted himself the revelation of a hint as to his lineage. He apparently first began by studying architecture, and in 1760 was awarded a medal by the Society of Arts. In 1765 one of his drawings was hung at the Society's exhibition. Three years later he became an Honorary Member of the Royal Academy of Arts. Years after that, in 1784 he exhibited a view of Oxford at the Royal Academy. He seems to have taught himself to draw, etch, and engrave. Though all his work lacks the stamp of true professionalism, during the last two decades of his life he turned out a considerable number of engravings. His earliest large-scale undertaking (1780–85) was a series of plates which he etched after the works of Hogarth and J. H. Mortimer.

Meanwhile, in 1768 he gave up architecture to start in business as a weaver of silk at 19 Princes Street, Spitalfields. There, presumably, the four children which were known as his (two of them very possibly were) were born, and there he lived in sin with his housekeeper, Mrs. Freeman. His enemies insisted that he dealt also in prints and drawings, though there is no reason to believe that he trafficked in the sale of other than his own productions.

His true vocation in life was that of a collector. His ever-increasing passion for accumulating antiques was less the product of worship of beauty than a sort of lower-middle-class veneration for great names. For although his collection of Hogarths became one of the very finest in England, and although he could boast the possession of some paintings by Rubens and Van Dyck, he treasured no less his large assortment of grim odds and ends, and it is likely that his proud display of them must have lent the Ireland home something nightmarish in feeling. In May, 1801, when his effects were sold at auction after his death, his collection included: a dress and carpet from Otaheite; the seer cloth of a mummy at Rotterdam; part of Wyclif's vestment; part of a cloak belonging to Charles I; a pair of "very curious brown leather boots"; a leather shoe supposed to have been worn by Lady Lovelace of Charles I's court; a garter worn by James II at his coronation; a crimson velvet purse given by Henry VIII to Ann Boleyn; a leather jacket supposed to have been Oliver Cromwell's; a cloth jacket which belonged to Sir Philip Sidney; an emblazoned banner of the Bard's patron, Lord Southampton; a pocket fruit knife which belonged to Joseph Addison; a silver box with an embossment showing the Ghost's first appearance to Hamlet, once the property of Addison too; three Roman rings; a lock of Edward IV's hair, procured when the tomb was opened at Windsor; a gold ring containing the hair of Louis XVI of France. Besides other similar curiosities (whose authenticity may very well be held suspect), he owned a number of plaster heads, including those of Jonson, Shakespeare, and Dryden (the last two painted), and several models, such as the one of the Westminister monument to Shakespeare. In addition to these, and to the paintings, drawings, engravings, and miniatures, Samuel was constantly adding to a large library of books which were prized less for their contents than for their ancient dates.

For the first time in English history fortunes were to be made in the eighteenth century by the sale of antiquities, and Ireland was an eager purchaser. The taste and refinement paraded by the entourage of the Restoration court had now become attributes not only of the aristocracy but also of all such citizens as had time, inclination, and income to cultivate them. The Court was no longer the center of intellectual and artistic stimulation; it was superseded by London, the hub of industry. Trade with the East, and with India particularly, was amassing great fortunes for the merchant class. As their leisure increased, men of the middle class were more than willing to further Addison's dream of bringing culture out of the universities and into the homes of the merchants and the coffee-houses of London. The gracious Georgian buildings which Londoners chose for their dwellings show they had learned to combine elegance with comfort. It was for them that the brothers Adam, Chippendale, Sheraton, and Hepplewhite designed much of the world's most beautiful furniture, and

Josiah Wedgwood his lovely china. In the middle of the century the Wilton and Axminster factories had begun to turn out handsome unseamed carpets; and the walls of many houses were paneled with damask silks in exquisite colors or decorated with charmingly designed wallpapers. William Hickey gives us a glimpse into the gracious living of those days by his account of the home life of a man, Smith by name, whose income was two thousand pounds a year: "He had a noble house upon the border of the river . . . entertaining his numerous friends with a warmth and a cordiality that never was exceeded. . . . After a liberal quantity of the best port and madeira, which followed an excellent dinner, himself and guests adjourned to the billiard table, or Bowling Green, according to the weather, or the season of the year. From either of those amusements they went to the drawing room, where tea and coffee being served, music filled up the space till ten, at which hour supper was served, and at eleven everybody retired to their homes, or if his guests for the night, to their chambers, where every comfort awaited them."

That, as Mr. Spectator particularly wished, this new enthusiasm for culture expressed itself most of all in a thirst for books, the career of James Lackington (1746–1815) eloquently demonstrates. The son of a journeyman shoemaker near Wellington, who was more often at the bottle than at his last, young Lackington was an itinerant vendor of meat pies at the age of ten, at fourteen was bound apprentice to a shoemaker at Taunton, and a few years later worked as a journeyman at Bristol and other towns. By this time he had become a Methodist, and although he had not learned to write, he composed a number of street ballads. In 1773 he came to London, it is said with but a half crown in his pocket. In 1774 he opened a combined bookstall and shoemaker's shop in Featherstone Street; his beginning stock was a sack of old theological books purchased for a guinea, and a few bits of leather. A loan of five pounds from Methodist friends enabled him to expand, remove to other quarters, and concentrate on bookselling. Lackington & Company brought out its first catalogue of books in 1779, listing 12,000 volumes. A catalogue of the next year advertised 30,000 books. He was soon buying entire libraries, and presently occupied a very large shop on a corner of Finsbury Square, named "The Temple of the Muses." A great circular counter stood in the middle of the shop, and a wide staircase ascended to the "lounging-rooms," and the first of a series of circular balconies containing books. The higher one mounted the cheaper and shabbier were the volumes. By 1791 Lackington estimated that he was selling 100,000 volumes a year at an annual profit of four thousand pounds. He never pretended that his interest was in the books themselves.

Samuel Ireland's dealings were chiefly in his own drawings and engravings, and involved none of the appurtenances of a tradesman. He operated from his house in Arundel Street, where the Ireland family had moved around 1782. In 1790 they moved to 8 Norfolk Street, Strand. His own purchases were made at small cost from the bookstalls and seedy shops of odds-and-ends which he frequented regularly, or from the great houses of noblemen and gentry who happened to be in need of ready cash. He was not, of course, averse to parting with an occasional find if the price were huge enough or the purchaser of exalted connections. By degrees he became a welcome figure among numbers of the aristocracy and the highly placed because of their eagerness either to sell or to acquire.

But his own acquisitiveness dictated his keeping most of his finds for himself, and his feverish attachment to his collections was a danger to his perspective. Horace Walpole, engaged in issuing a pamphlet limited to forty copies, which he was preparing at Strawberry Hill, complained that Ireland had bribed the engraver to sell him a print of the frontispiece, which Ireland then etched himself. Walpole concluded that Ireland "will sell some copies as part of the forty." It is more likely that the collector of Arundel Street went to the trouble of buying the print merely to add to his collection. He did not make an engraved copy for sale, but merely etched the design and struck off a couple of examples of that for himself. These etchings were never published by him, and were sold at auction after his death as part of his collection of etchings. Nevertheless, the proceeding, however motivated, was less than honest, and Ireland's reputation has long suffered because of it, for it has always been brought up to fortify suspicions about his role in the incredible operations of his son.

Having enviable connections among the exalted, Ireland in 1789 made an autumnal tour of Holland and surrounding territory with a view to publication, and in the next year issued his handsomely printed *Picturesque Tour through Holland, Brabant and Part of France,* in two volumes, copiously illustrated with engravings from drawings made by him on the spot. (In 1796 it had a second edition.)

Reading his respectable and enthusiastic comments, you irresistibly think of him as an earlier Mr. Pickwick, kindly and fussy, right out of the pages of the Dickens-to-be. But just as you are confirmed in this resemblance, you are brought up short by his eighteenth-century sophistication, and Samuel Ireland begins to slip out of focus.

What is the difficulty? Is it because the atmosphere of the closing years of that century is beginning to thicken with the qualities we think of as Victorian, while still retaining enough of eighteenth-century skepticism, that Ireland escapes definement? Is it because he was so much the man of his age that you cannot satisfactorily conceive of him as entirely either a figure out of Hogarth or, on the other hand, a character out of Dickens? After all, the year of his tour was the year of the fall of the Bastille.

Certainly the tone of this *Picturesque Tour* eludes categorizing. At Amsterdam he is sorry to have missed by one night a Dutch *Hamlet* which he is assured is much superior to the original English. But he has not forgotten our Bard is Matchless:

"Judge what improvement the elegant and sublime passages of our immortal bard can derive from the gutteral rumblings of the Dutch language!" He is told that the Dutch use many mechanical aids in their performances. Thus, in the scene in Gertrude's closet, "when the hero starts at the imagined* appearance of his father, his wig, by means of a concealed spring, jumps from 'the seat of his distracted brain,' † and leaves poor Hamlet as bare as a Dutch willow in winter." Yet on the very next page you read with some astonishment: "We visited one of the Musico's or licensed Brothels. Our stay was but short, the ugliness and impudence of the women soon causing us to make a precipitate retreat. The number of these houses is incredible." There are a fiddler and harper present, playing until dawn, and everything is seen through immense clouds of tobacco smoke. "I am told it is not uncommon to meet a sober citizen and his wife . . . introducing a virtuous young woman, their daughter, merely to show the horrid tendency of immorality. . . . The situation of these wretched females is lamentable beyond description: immured within the walls for life, and only permitted to breathe a purer air one day in the year. . . . But somewhat [sic] too much of this."

Had Samuel Ireland been a creation of Dickens he would hardly (at least to a reader's knowledge) have visited a brothel, would certainly never have recorded the visit for the world to read. On the other hand, granted the impossibility that he could have made such a visit and then recounted it, a Dickens' Samuel Ireland would surely have described it with just such an air.

At Antwerp he sounds like the Samuel Ireland who will soon be visiting Stratford. He goes into raptures over the chair in which once sat the "divine Rubens"—who, however, is not Matchless—and who might very well have been puzzled to hear himself called "divine." "Such is the veneration for this great

---

* Ireland's "imagined" affords a clue as to the un-Shakespearean manner in which *Hamlet* was presented in his day.

† Another choice example of Ireland's addiction to misquoting his adored Bard.

painter, that many of the brass nails have been drawn out of the chair to make into rings as precious relicks."

At Paris he conjures up the scene of the taking of the Bastille a few months earlier. The rejoicing then must have formed a picture "at that happy moment of the dawn of liberty more strongly to be felt by the mind of sensibility than is in the power of language to express." The next sentence, however, with its unheralded vein of rationality, records a fact that the rapture of the world over the event has generally chosen to ignore: "I do not learn that more than four or five prisoners were found at the taking of this place." It is true: when the terrible Bastille, symbol of the tyranny of the old order, at last fell, it was found to hold a mere half dozen prisoners!

The trip to the Continent also had its practical side. En route Samuel stopped at Amiens to leave his fourteen-year-old son William Henry, who had been failing miserably in his studies in England, at a school in Picardy in the expectation that there he might at least learn the French language.

When *A Picturesque Tour* was published it gave further evidence of the alternations in Ireland's personality. The book was dedicated, of all people, to Captain Francis Grose, the "antiquarian Falstaff," friend of Robert Burns. Grose's elephantine figure is said to have been matched by his appetites. It was characteristic of him that one of his major efforts was the compilation of a dictionary of slang replete with definitions of the foulest obscenities, and generally read by the bucks of the day. He was never without his ribald jest or his scatalogical anecdote. Burns wrote a rollicking epigram about him in which Satan declines to carry Grose off because he makes such "a damnable load."

Ireland's work was so much of a success that the next year he moved to spacious quarters in the Strand, and took the house at number 8 Norfolk Street as more suitable to his increasing importance as well as to his ever-swelling collections of old books, prints, and antiques. During the ensuing years he continued the

48

series begun with *A Picturesque Tour* with his accounts of the countryside bordering on the Thames (dedicated to Earl Har-court), the Medway (dedicated to the Countess Dowager of Aylesford), the Avon (dedicated to the Earl of Warwick), and the Wye—all profusely illustrated by him.

After the Medway Tour had appeared he issued a fourth vol-ume which again beclouds his character, *Graphic Illustrations of Hogarth, from Pictures, Drawings, and Scarce Prints in the Au-thor's Possession* (1794). Despite the attribution, some of these pictures are unquestionably not the work of Hogarth, but those which are form a rich and varied collection and fully prove the excellence of the Ireland treasury. Why then did he include a number which were patently counterfeit? Remembering the affair of the Walpole pamphlet, his enemies branded him a deliberate humbug, though what his motives could have been in a deception or what he could have hoped to gain from trickery no one can suggest.

Angelo junior complicates the question by describing Ireland as having been "an able hand in detecting pretenders and quacks." By way of illustration he tells a story of a party, one Sunday evening, at the home of the notorious Dr. De Manne-duke, practicer of "animal magnetism," who lived stylishly in Bloomsbury Square, and obtained a fortune by practicing on the credulity of the *beau monde.* The Sunday night *conversaziones* at his elegant drawing rooms were well attended for several seasons. While the Doctor twiddled his fingers before their faces, young women and old would faint, weep, laugh, and sigh at his direc-tion; nor were the men less gullible, for they too "were played upon in a like manner, until worked up to a *crisis,* they grinned, or sobbed, or stared, or languished, as though they were possessed."

Samuel Ireland was unknown to the Doctor when he ap-peared at one of these gatherings and volunteered as an object of one of the experiments. "Ireland was seated beneath a girandole; all eyes were fixed upon him, and credulity was on tip-toe to behold the paroxysms in which he would be thrown. The doctor began his incantations, made a thousand strange gesticulations, uttered all his metaphysical jargon, worked his fingers in mystical forms, and in short exhausted all the trumpery of his art, but in vain; for his patient, determined not to be conjured or seduced out of his reason, laughed his attempts to scorn. The doctor, finding his efforts vain, complimented him, by declaring his nerves proof against all excitement: 'Excepting,' added Ireland, 'that of laughter,' when he, and all the company joined in bursts of risibility, and Dr. de Manneduke retired in confusion."

Here would certainly seem to be the skeptical eighteenth-century man of the world. Some facets of Samuel Ireland's make-up do invite the notion that he owned a strong capacity for sorting the facts and a conscientious need for taking the pains to put them down. His drawings and engravings, for example, though for decades highly cherished by collectors, are almost depressing in the careful precision of their detail; their very want of imagination seems to bespeak forthright clearheadness.

But, as we shall see, the proof is abundant that Ireland was anything but a cautious man. It is to be doubted that he believed his spurious Hogarths other than genuine. How could the possessor of so splendid a collection have been hoodwinked into adding to the larger number of his legitimate Hogarths even a few bastards? The question assumes him to have been a man of perfect taste and authority. To answer it you have only to counter with another one. Ireland's worship of Shakespeare so nearly approximated a religion that readings and quotations from and discussions of the Bard's holy text were as much of a daily ritual as readings from the Bible in other households. Why then did he so consistently misquote the Bard?

As for Ireland's drawings and engravings, they are in truth remarkable for their apparently calm preoccupation with scenic detail. Nevertheless, after viewing plate after plate, one becomes aware that the method has its tricks too. Whenever the human form does enter upon the landscape, it is always seen from so great a distance that it is obvious that no skill was required in dotting the minuscule figures and in losing them in the uninspired exactitude of the setting. Human figures, when they are there, seem rather the setting for the landscape. If this is not a hint of subterfuge, it is at least a clever masking of technical inadequacy. The engravings and the séance at Dr. De Manneduke's notwithstanding, Ireland was less of an eighteenth-century rationalist than an agitated little chipmunk of a man. The wonderful collection of true Hogarths may be attributed less to the exquisiteness of his taste than to his eager desire to accumulate what was reverend to own. The false ones were added, it is safe to assume, through the same impulse. Rather than a deliberate humbug, he was, I believe, recurrently a pathetic blunderer—a man whose ready enthusiasms, as we have seen from his being a dupe of the Williamses, quickly annihilated his sense of proportion, never at any time very active.

The difficulty of focusing his character will remain, however. The very tissue of his private life is a web in which the respectable is curiously interwoven with the unconventional, the pious with the profane. During and before the years which concern us, he had been presenting to the world Mrs. Freeman, his mistress, as his housekeeper, Though he has regularly been spoken of as a widower, with the implication that his three surviving children were the offspring of a dead mother, the truth was not that simple. In a generally overlooked entry in his diary, the painter Joseph Farington recorded: "Mrs. Freeman who lives with Ireland, and is the mother of the children, had, it is said, a fortune of £12,000, and is of a good family. Her brother is now living in London in great circumstances, but disowns her." Farington was unable to discover her maiden name. "Ireland behaves very ill to her," he continues. "The children for many years bore the name of Irwin; and it was at the birthday of one of them, when many persons were invited . . . that it was signified by Mrs. Freeman that the young people were to be addressed by the name of Ireland. They had passed as her nieces."

There is no reason to doubt the honesty of this account. Farington was no gossip, was not malicious like Walpole. Moreover, it satisfactorily explains a host of rumors which later flourished about the Irelands, and which, without the Farington entry, make no sense at all.

As a matter of fact, Mrs. Freeman's maiden name was Anna Maria de Burgh Coppinger. It is significant that the elder of Ireland's two daughters was named Anna Maria; had she been the daughter of another woman (assuming that a Mrs. Samuel Ireland ever did exist), the coincidence would be too great. From a poem of Mrs. Freeman's it seems clear that she had been at one time a mistress of the Earl of Sandwich, one of the most unashamedly depraved and notorious rakes of the era. That would account for a highly placed brother's breaking with her; her unmarried status in the Ireland home would have aided nothing in effecting a reconciliation. Her earlier attachment to Sandwich would also explain Ireland's never marrying her. Eighteenth-century morality (and in some quarters, twentieth-century morality too) would have been shocked at the notion of one man's marrying another man's cast-off mistress. Doubtless such a possibility never entered Mrs. Freeman's own mind. *Mr.* Freeman (like the deceased *Mrs.* Ireland) was probably a polite myth, with possibly a private pun involved in the adoption of the Freeman name. It is also significant that the Ireland children seem never to have been baptized, for no records of their baptism have ever been found in any of the churches of the various neighborhoods associated with them.

Mrs. Freeman was a woman fairly well educated for her sex in those days. She is the author of a number of poems and plays, and published at least one book, *The Doctor Dissected* (1771). Her plays were sometimes enacted by children at the Ireland house.

The eldest of the three surviving Ireland children was Anna Maria, who dabbled in oil painting, engraving, and etching, and who was married in December of 1795, a time in which her father and her brother were at the pinnacle of their fame, to Robert Maitland Barnard, of East India House. The younger daughter, Jane, was quite skilled in the painting of miniatures. In 1792 and 1793 her work was exhibited at the Royal Academy, and in 1795 she made a miniature of her brother William Henry, the only surviving son of the house, who had been named after Bolingbroke.

William Henry had been the younger of male twins. The elder, named Samuel, had died in his youth. His name, after his death, was bestowed upon William Henry by their father, who always called him "Sam." Indeed, William Henry often signed himself, "Samuel Ireland, Junior," or "S. W. H. Ireland."

Probably all the children were illegitimate. But for reasons of his own, Ireland allowed the understanding to become general that the girls had been born in wedlock to a mother now dead. As for William Henry, the youngest of his offspring, he permitted mystery to shroud the boy's origins. The Irelands' great foe, Edmund Malone, asserted that the lad was illegitimate, the product of a liaison which his father had had with a Mrs. Irwyn, a married woman separated from her husband. (Malone, no doubt, had become confused by rumor because *all* the children had once been called "Irwin.") William Henry, Malone deposed (without investigating the declaration himself), had been baptized as W. H. Irwyn at St. Clement Dane's in 1777—but no such record has ever been found in the register of that parish. Though William Henry throughout his life gives that year as the date of his birth, his father's testimony is that he was born two years earlier. William Henry never tired of underlining his youthfulness during the brief period of his glory, though if 1775, the likelier date, is the true one, his activities surely appear precocious enough.

Without committing himself on the subject of a putative Mrs. Irwyn, William Henry certainly entertained serious doubts about his legitimacy as well as about his parentage—subjects his father insisted upon keeping in the dark. It is indeed odd that no one has troubled to ponder how much these doubts had to do with his need to immolate himself in a blaze of fame. His inner anguish over the matter might well have been a cardinal motive for his conduct.

At one point he was apparently convinced that he was the son of Mrs. Freeman and her (imaginary) husband, Mr. Freeman, for in a letter of December 13, 1796—to be quoted hereafter—he signed his name as "W. H. Freeman." Again in January, 1797, we find him expressing every doubt that he is either Samuel Ireland's or Mrs. Freeman's son, and reminding his father that he had been promised that upon achieving his majority there would be a dispelling of the mystery concerning his birth, and that that promise still awaited fulfillment. Surely these yet unsettled doubts account for the cryptic quality of the opening lines of his *Confessions* (1805), published when he was about thirty: "As the period of my infancy can be productive of no satisfaction to the public, it will be sufficient for me to say that I was born in London." More than that he was never willing to say.

THE ELDER IRELAND rode his hobbyhorses joyously, and provided the tamer nags for the decorous sports of his well-conducted household. In his late fifties William Henry was to recollect those days with warm affection. He speaks of old Ireland as "a gentleman gifted with the most open heart and liberal sentiments," whose "assortment of pictures, prints, and drawings, was universally extolled; his library well selected. . . . Among the strongest of his predelictions, my father entertained an unbounded enthusiasm for the writings of Shakspeare: four days, at least, out of the seven, the beauties of our divine dramatist became the theme of his conversation after dinner; while in the evening, still further to impress the subject upon the minds of myself and sisters, certain plays were selected and a part allotted to each." After these readings there always ensued Samuel's enthusiastic comments on Shakespeare's genius—for him "Shakespeare was no mortal but a divinity"—and amidst these Ireland would frequently declare that "to possess a single vestige of the poet's handwriting would be esteemed a gem beyond all price, and far dearer to him than his whole collection." At these outbursts young William Henry was always present, "swallowing," as he says, "with avidity the honied poison."

Despite the air of middle-class respectability that settled upon the household doings of the Irelands, Samuel had close attachments with a world not so respectable, the free and easy world of the London theatres. (One remembers how in the twentieth century Emma Borden, after standing loyally by her sister during her trial for the ax-slaying of their parents, thereafter broke irrevocably with her because Lizzie had become friends with a prominent Boston actress whom she had invited to their home.) One of Ireland's most intimate friendships was with Thomas Linley, proprietor of the Drury Lane, and his family, and because of this the Irelands had free access to the theatre and behind the scenes. Not surprisingly, William Henry early in life "acquired a great fondness for theatrical pursuits," as he phrased it with characteristic pomposity. He adored the private theatricals in which he took part, and he never forgot the performance of *The Gentle Shepherd* at the house of Sheridan in Bruton Street, "at which were present a large party of the nobility." All the roles were enacted by young people. Though William Henry's part was a trivial one, that fact "did not diminish the zest" he felt, and the occasion only rendered his "predilection for theatrical pursuits even more determined."

As a child he loved making pasteboard theatres, while he nurtured an overpowering aversion to all forms of study. In consequence he was held by his schoolmasters and, inevitably, by Ireland senior as incorrigibly stupid. He seems almost to boast of his childhood dullness: "When at Mr. Shury's academy at Ealing, I was so very backward that once on going home for vacation, I was made the bearer of a letter from Mr. Shury wherein he acquainted my father . . . that I was so stupid as to be a disgrace to his school, and that as he found it impossible to give me the least instruction, he would much rather I should not return after the holidays, as he . . . conceived it was no better than robbing Mr. Ireland of his money." Another school was tried in Soho Square. There occurred an event which must have had some influence in a later choice of William Henry's. The students gave a performance of *King Lear.*

His constitution was so delicate at this time that his father deemed it expedient to send him off to the country. All efforts at educating him, however, proving of no avail, William Henry at the age of fourteen (or, as he would have it, twelve), was taken by his father, after a tour of Holland and a sight-seeing visit to one of its bordellos, to France to study there. He managed to master the French language with considerable proficiency, and never lost his fluency in it. Later in life that skill served him well. He remained in France for three years, which he accounted the happiest period of his life. When his father came to bring him back to England, he was loth to go. "As if a presentiment had hung over me, I would fain have continued there for years." On his return to England he could scarcely speak English. For some time, he says, "my conversation was so loaded with Gallicisms as frequently to render my meaning incomprehensible."

If he was reluctant to quit France it may very well have been chiefly because that meant returning to his father's house. While there is no reason to think that Samuel Ireland was either an unkind or a severe father, there is also every indication that he was far from an affectionate one. Even for that epoch, when the very air was charged with sentimentality, William Henry was certainly a remarkably sentimental boy. He must have been the victim of chaotic emotions as a result of his conviction, inevitably fortified by his father's postponing a revelation of the facts, that he was illegitimate. He must have felt both wounded and pleased with the wound which set him apart from others; but he must assuredly have been constrained in his father's presence. Throughout all his later confessions there persists the note of a frustrated love for his father. At least in France he was placed at a distance from the daily reminder that his father had no warmth to bestow upon him. There is a chilling formality about the way Samuel Ireland refers to his son in print, even during the years when he had every incentive to feel closest to him and immensely proud of him; and for the rest of his life William Henry more usually than not refers to his father as Mr. Samuel Ireland or Mr. Ireland rather than "my father." It is not, I believe, that the older man in any way discriminated against his son; it is only that whatever love he had to expend was lavished upon his antiques and old books.

Shortly after the boy's return his father decided that his son should be articled to a conveyancer in chancery (i.e., apprenticed to a lawyer who prepared documents for the conveyance of property), one William Bingley, at New Inn.

At home William Henry was drawn into the agreeable round prescribed by his father's program for the cultural life. If he found himself hindered at first by having almost forgotten his native tongue, the best cure for that was the nightly rehearsals of scenes from the plays of, naturally, Shakespeare, in which Ireland senior took the principal role and the other parts were assigned to Mrs. Freeman, his sisters Anna Maria and Jane, and himself. There were, of course, the discussions of Shakespeare over dinner and after the readings as well, but in these William Henry, by his own admission, preferred to be an auditor rather than a participant—an attitude that could only confirm his father in the view of the English schoolmasters that his son was a dull, stupid boy. A man like Samuel would, without meaning to do so, have tended to ignore such a lad.

But William Henry did not cease trying to please. Following

his father's example he concentrated on early English writers, and became particularly enamored of Chaucer and the old romances. These led him to a fondness for old armor. He began to collect helmets, breastplates, gorgets and the like; "and any part of the suit which was deficient I, like a second Quixote, made up for with pasteboard." His bedroom became an armory.

Proud of his father, but lacking any real communication with him, he found an outlet in moonstruck fantasies. "I have often sighed to be the inmate of some gloomy castle; or that having lost my way upon a dreary heath, I might, like Sir Bertram, have been conducted to some enchanted mansion. Sometimes I have wished that by the distant chime of a bell I had found the hospitable porch of some old monastery, where, with the holy brotherhood, having shared at the board their homely fare, I might afterwards have enjoyed upon the pallet a sound repose, and, with the abbots, blessing the ensuing morn, have hied me in pursuit of fresh adventures."

It is characteristic of him that he should have had so much to say about such a scene and nothing about the adventures. William Henry seems to have had very little need of the animal exertions common to boys, not even in his imaginings. On the contrary, there is something unnaturally pietistic about his youthful thoughts, as though under suitable direction he might easily have become a psalm singer. It has been said with some truth that everyone tends to identify Shakespeare with himself; to this inclination young Ireland was, as we shall see, no exception. To Shakespeare the young man was going to attribute his own prayer-meeting proclivities. It may very well be—the notion is consistent with the picture—that Samuel Ireland was responsible for that sort of emphasis in the nightly reading of the volume of Shakespeare's plays. The fact that he had for so long been living in sin with Mrs. Freeman in no way ruled out his love of Sunday-school platitudes or the air of moral rectitude with which he faced the world.

But there was one other book which was to conjoin with the volume of Shakespeare to have a prepotent influence on William Henry's destiny, a novel called *Love and Madness*. Its author, Herbert Croft (1751–1816), a parson in Essex, wrote copiously in order to sustain his taste for luxurious living. He is now remembered, if at all, for the biography of Edward Young which he contributed to Johnson's *Lives of the Poets,* of which piece Burke has said that it was but a poor imitation of Johnson: "It has all the nodosities of the oak without its strength."

It was a sensational murder—connected with another of the mistresses of that Lord Sandwich who had cast off Mrs. Freeman —which gave Croft the idea for his most popular work. James Hackman entered the army as an ensign at the age of nineteen. Invited to Sandwich's house at Hinchinbroke, he fell madly in love with Sandwich's current mistress, Martha Ray, already the mother of several children by his Lordship, though young enough to be the old lecher's daughter. She was very pretty and had a lovely voice; there was even some talk of her going on the stage. At twenty-three Hackman was promoted to lieutenant, but in a few months left the service to prepare himself for the church. In February, 1779, when he was twenty-six, he was ordained. But there remained only a few months of life to him. All this time he had been unsuccessfully proposing marriage to Miss Ray, despite her relationship to Sandwich. On April 7, 1779, in a fit of despair he waited for her as she was leaving Covent Garden Theatre. As she was about to step into Sandwich's carriage, at the side of the theatre's arcade, she was touched upon the shoulder. Turning around, she was shot dead by Hackman. The young clergyman immediately placed another pistol to his own head, and shot himself. His wound did not prove fatal. Hackman also tried to dash out his brains with the butts of his pistols, but he was too weak to succeed in that. During his trial he maintained that his intention had been to kill only himself, and that he had shot his beloved on a sudden impulse. He was nevertheless found guilty of premeditated murder, and hanged on April 19.

The younger Angelo attended the hanging. His account of his experience on the following day sheds light upon a century that never wearied of self-praise for its sensibility and fastidious taste. "I met my friend W. Lacey . . . and on our way home, as we were passing by the Old Bailey, curiosity prompted us to go to Surgeon's Hall, where the body was taken for dissection. Having been placed on a large table, an incision had been made in the stomach, and the flesh was spread over on each side. On leaving the place we retired to Dolly's Chop House. Our first dish was *pork chops*, and the sight I had witnessed produced such an impression on my mind, that not only did I reject them in disgust, but I have never been able to eat any since."

Boswell, still collecting material for his great biography of Johnson, not only attended the trial but also rode to the hanging with Hackman. He reports that the young murderer's having had two pistols occasioned a fierce contention between Johnson and Beauclerk three days before the hanging, though there were few people in the world of whom Johnson was as fond of as Topham Beauclerk, a man whose graceful conversation mirrored a wide range of knowledge and observation. Johnson argued that Hackman's possession of two pistols was proof that he had meant to shoot two persons. Beauclerk objected that a wise man who intended to shoot himself would have two pistols, to be sure of ending his agony if the first failed of its purpose; Beauclerk was able to cite two examples of this precaution. In the second instance the extra pistol was found lying beside the suicide. "Well," said Johnson triumphantly, "you see here one pistol was sufficient." Beauclerk dismissed the observation with, "Because it happened to kill him," and added that he knew more about this suicide than Johnson did. Dinner went on agreeably for a while. Suddenly Johnson abruptly asked Beauclerk, "How came you to talk so petulantly to me as, 'This is what you don't know, but what I know'? One thing *I* know, which *you* don't seem to know, that you are very uncivil."

Beauclerk retorted, "Because *you* began by being uncivil—which you always are." (Johnson confessed later that he had thought over the matter before objecting to Beauclerk's words, and decided to make an issue of them only because there were present two strangers, men of the world, and he did not want them to imagine that they could take the kind of liberties with him which Beauclerk had taken.) The contention lapsed again until the talk was of Hackman's violence of temper. Johnson then said, "It was his business to *command* his temper, as my friend, Mr. Beauclerk, should have done some time ago," and appended, "No man loves to be treated with contempt." Beauclerk bowed to Johnson and replied handsomely, "You have known me twenty years, and however I may have treated others, you may be sure I could never treat you with contempt." Johnson considered the apology ample.

Croft lost no time in capitalizing on the misfortunes of the subject of this quarrel, and the year after the murder published *Love and Madness* with the subtitle *A Story Too True; in a Series of Letters between Parties Whose Names Would Perhaps Be Mentioned Were They Less Known or Lamented.* The novel is related in a series of letters, to be sure, and there is something outrageous in the tone of factuality maintained, as though these were the actual missives exchanged between Hackman and Martha Ray. To heighten that impression, the hero figures as H. and the heroine as M.

The book was enormously popular, and went through seven editions. That it should have been openly esteemed in the Ireland household is fairly strange. She had been in earlier days a mistress of Sandwich herself; it is odd that Mrs. Freeman should have been willing to participate in the frequent recitals from the pages of that novel, or that Ireland should not have preferred to avoid the book altogether. It is even possible that some of the Ireland children were actually his Lordship's. How could either adult have borne to hear the novel? Was it an exquisite form of self-torture for Mrs. Freeman? Was it on Ireland's part a piece of quiet sadism? Or was she vindictive enough to revel in the sufferings of a rival to the old rake's affection? And was Ireland merely indifferent to her former connection—or, perhaps, even rather proud of it in his middle-class way? In any case, the Irelands got to know *Love and Madness* very well. It was allowed to share honors with the Bard in the evening sessions of reading aloud at the Ireland home. William Henry was so much taken with it that he pored over it by himself. It was to prove for him a Circe's cup.

The book is full of the sentimental drivel which was *à la mode* to an age that adored Saint-Preux and Werther, but its prose, like most of the prose of that century, is basically good—though marred by its false sentiment. Sentimentality, the indulgence in emotion for the sake of the emotion, and at the opposite pole from true sentiment or compassion, always ends by turning moral values topsy-turvy. *Love and Madness,* whose sacredness became only second to that of Shakespeare's with William Henry, must have worked effectively to pervert his sense of right and wrong. His father innocently aided the process if, like his contemporaries, he doted on the silliest passages as particularly sublime.

The main outlines of Hackman's blighted love affair with Sandwich's mistress, faithfully followed by Croft, afford enough opportunities for inflated emotion. Not content with these the author added to them copiously. H. confesses to M. that his passions are as "wild as the torrent's roar," that the element of which he is formed is fire, that in his brain he has a burning coal. Real men have never been wild enough for his admiration; he therefore prefers the creations of fiction—men like Othello—"but he should have put *himself* to death in his wife's sight, *not* his wife." He has no taste for comedy: "Give *me*, I say, tragedy, in the world as well as in the theatre." Yet as he writes her, "behold, I am as weak as a woman. My tears flow."

There is a fine exhibition of sentimental rot at one point in the novel. The lovers have exchanged views on a contemporary mur-

der case in which the wife and her lover killed the husband.
Though they agree that the woman must have been a savage, H.
declares, "Yet their feelings, when she and Aikney were at the
gallows . . . must have been exquisite." Crime, William Henry
may have felt as he lingered over the passage, when viewed with
such exaltation was capable of a kind of grandeur.

Not the least significant aspect of Croft's novel, so far as William Henry's future is concerned, was the author's strange attrac-
tion, clergyman though he was, to the careers of forgers. To his
contemplation of their courses he brings the perverted sympathies
of the approved sentimentalist.

His first reference is to James Macpherson, who palmed off his
anemic inventions as translations from the Gaelic of the old bard
Ossian. These ludicrous productions, confected to suit the tastes
of the age, had an incredible popularity everywhere. They had
succeeded in banishing Homer from Goethe's youthful heart, and
were still to become Napoleon's favorite bedside book (comprehensible only on the supposition that the Little Corporal suffered
from insomnia), and the question of their authenticity was still
furnishing a lively battleground. Since Werther had translated
Ossian for his beloved Lotte into German from Macpherson's
English, why should not H. send the volume to his beloved M.?
Nothing was more fitting for the nurture of a wild and illicit
passion.

As he read, William Henry must have been deeply impressed
with the fact that so interesting and soulful a creature as H.
does not care whether or not the Ossian poems *are* Macpherson's
forgery. If the world so much admires the work, all the more
credit to Macpherson if it *is* his fabrication. There are so few,
H. reflects, who can judge poetry anyway, and there is therefore
no point in publishing one's own verses. To such judgments a
sentimental youth like William Henry could only assent. It was
undeniable, as Croft reminded his reader, that the ill-fated
Chatterton had been granted at least some attention while he

was operating as a forger. Once he attempted to appear as the author of his own work there was nothing left for that rare genius but suicide!

Presently H. is concerned with the fate of another forger, William Dodd (1729–1777). Known as the "macaroni parson," Dodd had risen to the post of chaplain, was tutor to the Earl of Chesterfield, and because of his sermons had become very popular with the world of fashion. He was the author of a number of works, including *The Beauties of Shakespeare*. Living far beyond his means and sorely pressed by creditors, he forged the name of his former pupil to a bond for £4,200. The deception was discovered almost at once, and Dodd returned £3,000 with a promise to add £500 immediately. He was almost certain that Chesterfield would not permit his being punished, but he was mistaken. His old student would do nothing for him. Despite the efforts of admirers, who included Samuel Johnson—Johnson, among many other kindnesses to him in his hour of need, wrote a letter in his behalf to the King—Dodd was executed.

H. is present to see the last of poor Dodd, and reports that "the scene was affecting," as he describes it with much emotion and detail. How many of the spectators, he wonders, have asked themselves "whether this wretch really deserved to die more than we?" With what tender emotion, William Henry may have noted, did Croft enwrap the vision of these luckless forgers!

And now comes the section of *Love and Madness* which was to be most fateful for William Henry. M. has asked H. to correlate what he has been able to gather concerning the boy wonder, Chatterton, prince of all forgers! This gives Croft the opportunity to insert a long passage of thirty-three pages on the career of Chatterton, a subject which has nothing whatsoever to do with his novel. Nevertheless, Croft's account is the most graphic of all contemporary narratives of the ill-fated young poet, for he had taken the trouble to do personal research on the boy's career.

64

Thomas Chatterton (1752-1770) was born four months after his father's death, in a poverty-stricken house that nestled in the very shadow of the church of St. Mary Redcliffe, which had been built in Bristol in the fifteenth century. His only escape from squalor and his chief intellectual stimulation were found within the walls of that old church. For seven years he attended the dreary charity school, where nothing was taught but the three R's; at night, however, he secretly feasted on *The Faerie Queene* and the Elizabethan lyrists, as well as Chaucer, Lydgate, and dictionaries of early English. It was the sight of the handsomely illuminated letters of some old manuscripts discovered in ancient chests in the loft of the church which first inspired him to read. By the time he was eleven, he had written "Elinoura and Juga," a poem he penned on a piece of old parchment; to a schoolfellow he presented it as a relic of the Middle Ages. His friend was so successfully hoodwinked that young Chatterton was tempted to try the hoax on his teacher, who was equally taken in. From then on he began to "discover" innumerable literary antiquities, which he was busy manufacturing during feverish hours of the night in his garret room. About the historical figure of William Canynge, lord mayor of Bristol, young Chatterton created his own fifteenth-century Bristol, in which the leading personality was one "Thomas Rowley," presumably a poet-monk and confessor to Canynge. Besides his dictionaries Chatterton put to such good use the inscriptions on the tombs that the citizens of Bristol were enchanted to find their genealogies traced in the "discovered" Rowley manuscripts. Encouraged by their credulity, the boy produced a number of historical documents glorifying Bristol and its families. In 1767 he entered the employ of an attorney, in whose office he had even more time for his literary forgeries. He began to send copies to Horace Walpole and the publisher Dodsley. Walpole, who prided himself on his talents as a medievalist, at first was very much interested in what he believed to be the recovery of works of a forgotten poet. But when his friend Gray, a sounder scholar, pointed out to him the impossibility of Chatterton's claims, Walpole was furious at having been duped, and turned on the boy in a most brutal style.

Disgusted with the limited prospects of Bristol, Chatterton determined to try his fortunes in London. To free himself from the shackles of legal study, he worked hard at convincing his employer that he was insane, was released, and set out for London in high hopes. There, he wrote like a true eighteenth-century hack, but his editors and publishers were in no hurry to pay him for his work. After starving for a few months he decided that death was better than defeat or charity; he took a dose of arsenic, and died while he was still but seventeen. The *Rowley Poems* were not published until 1777, only two years before Croft began writing his novel.

In the long passage devoted to Chatterton in *Love and Madness* Croft is certain that the boy was the author of all the poems attributed to Rowley. He gives an account of the family and education of the lad, whom William Henry must have been impressed to see dubbed "our Bristol Shakespeare." H. has only praise for a youngster who could throw a bit of Latin into his forgeries, even though no Latin had been taught him at the charity school. He has scathing words for the people of Bristol who, because they accepted Chatterton's poems, "fondly imagined themselves the patrons of genius." The post-mortem sale of the poems brought rewards to everyone but their author and his family.

Croft had gone to Bristol to seek out Chatterton's relatives, and in his novel there now follows a letter which he obtained from the dead poet's sister. By way of preface, Croft writes: "For Chatterton's sake the English language should add another word to its dictionary; and should not suffer the same term [i.e., forgery] to signify a crime for which a man suffers the most ignoble punishment, and the deception of ascribing a false antiquity of two or three centuries to compositions for which the author's name deserves to live for ever."

This passage must have made an indelible impression upon William Henry's sympathetic mind—he, like Chatterton, wasting his genius in a lawyer's office! In fact, he later says concerning *Love and Madness:* "The fate of Chatterton so strongly interested me that *I used frequently to envy his fate, and desire nothing so ardently as the termination of my existence in a similar cause.*" (Italics mine.)

"Strange-fated Chatterton!" Croft continues. "Hadst thou possessed fewer and less eminent abilities, the world would now give thee credit for more and for greater." And now Croft delivers a judgment that must have burned itself upon the mind of the susceptible young Ireland [italics mine again]: "Most readily I admit that, if Chatterton be an imposter—i.e., *the most wonderful human being I firmly believe him*—he imposed upon every soul who knew him. *This, with me, is one trait of greatness.*" Even after his death Chatterton's sister and mother continue to believe that all the Rowley poems came out of an old chest. How wonderful that this genius could steadfastly keep his great secret! Let any man try not communicating to a single individual for a whole year one single scheme or circumstance respecting himself. "Let him try how it is to lock up every thing, trifling or serious, sad or merry, within his own solitary breast. There are easier tasks.— This boy did it during his whole life. . . . That Chatterton should wrap his arms around him, stand aloof from the whole world, and never lean upon a single individual for society in his schemes . . . *is with me almost more wonderful than the schemes.*" Such a faculty is worthy a great general.

Next comes the letter to Croft written by Chatterton's sister, with all its misspellings intact—to be able to print such a document was a great scoop for Croft—and in it William Henry found more than one parallel between himself and the dead genius. The sister reports that Chatterton "was dull in learning" as a child. (That surely echoed in William Henry's breast: he had not forgotten the exasperation of his teachers and his father. Surely, he may have thought, this itself must be a sign of true genius.) By slow degrees the boy began to learn, until after his eleventh year, his sister writes, "he wrote a caterlogue of the books he had read to the number of 70. . . . He had been gloomy from the time he began to learn, but we remark'd he was more chearfull after he began to write poetry. Some saterical peicis we saw soon after. . . . He was a lover of truth from the earlyest dawn of reason. . . . When in school . . . his master depended on his verasity on all occations." And Chatterton had never lost his goodness: "Confident of advancement he would promise my mother and me should be partakers of his success." (William Henry's father and sisters were, indeed, in no need of his financial aid. But it still might be possible to match Chatterton's goodness by bestowing upon his father, himself no doubt a bastard by birth and thereby as pathetic in his own way as Chatterton, greater gifts than those promised by the Shakespeare of Bristol.) "His hours in the office was from 8 in the morning to 8 in the evening. He had little of his masters business to do, sometimes not 2 hours in a day, which gave him opportunity to pursue his genius." (Again the likeness! William Henry, articled too to a lawyer, had plenty of leisure time in the offices to pursue his fancies.)

The letter concluded, Croft continues with details of the young poet's life in London. He was, naturally, incomprehensible to all who met him. Croft, determined to surmount forgery with the halo of genius, rejects—what was the fact—the possibility that Chatterton took arsenic because of absolute want. He computes that the suicide took place four days after a new moon—a statistic of mystical import. Who can argue the motives for "self-destruction of such a being? The motives for everything he did are past finding out." A boy like Chatterton, Croft concludes, is a greater benefactor of humanity than was ever Alexander the Great, who was brilliant only in destruction. Chatterton's deception was an innocent one; what he accomplished was truly god-

68

like. If he had been Apollo himself temporarily incarnated, the deity could not have come to earth "with more credit to himself."

So, William Henry could reflect, a notable writer like Croft could hold a literary forger greater than the destructive Alexander; his crime was innocent, his accomplishment godlike; his deed was worthy of Apollo himself. With what avidity must young Ireland have drunk deeply the praises of this great-souled, honest, proud, courageous, and godlike youth who had demonstrated his genius to the popular novelist by dint of his being able to deceive the world!

After these pages on Chatterton, *Love and Madness* quickly proceeds to H.'s murder of M. The concluding passages of the novel are written by a friend detailing H.'s last hours, and ending —to the great satisfaction of the Irelands—"Rest, rest, perturbed spirit!"

HAVING SURRENDERED HIMSELF to the hectic pages of *Love and Madness*, William Henry was ready to start out on the road which lay irresistibly and invitingly before him, whether or not he was at first conscious of the fact. Chatterton had become for him a chevalier *sans peur et sans reproche*, in whose gallant path it was but logical for genius to follow.

While his inner being was preparing itself for the great attempt, his conscious mind was already giving evidence of what was fomenting. Almost immediately he composed a sentimental acrostic on Chatterton:

> C omfort and joy's for ever fled:
> H e ne'er will warble more!
> A h me! the sweetest youth is dead
> T hat e'er tun'd reed before.
> T he hand of Mis'ry bow'd him low;
> E'en Hope forsook his brain:
> R elentless man contemn'd his woe:
> T o you he sigh'd in vain.
> O ppressed with want, in wild despair he cried
> "N o more I'll live!" swallow'd the draught, and died.

A less than promising beginning for one who was yet to match his talents with those of the Matchless Bard.

Like Chatterton, William Henry began, too, to write imitations of medieval poetry. One example he retained in his possession for years: an acrostic on Chaucer written "in the style of John Lydgate," a chief master of Chatterton. It began:

> Con I yn rythms thilke clerke's fame make knowen,
> Hondlynge so poorlee thys my quille . . . ?

The spelling here is sane in comparison to William Henry's later efforts (though possibly it was subsequently altered by its author before publishing it among his confessions), but he already demonstrates that unshakable worship of Chatterton which caused him to play the latter's sedulous ape in orthography. William Henry preferred imitating a bad imitation to going for his spelling and vocabulary to the old poets themselves, though they were accessible enough on his father's shelves.

Yet, even if he seems to have paid scant attention to their contents, he was already an enthusiast for ancient books—at least, an enthusiast, like his father, for acquiring them. "As Mr. Samuel Ireland was very partial to antiquities of every description," he tells us, "and particularly old books, I had hourly opportunities of remarking the satisfaction which the possession of any rarity gave Mr. Ireland. . . . In consequence I became a follower of similar pursuits. . . . Nothing gave me so much gratification as exciting Mr. Ireland's astonishment on my production of some rare pamphlet which chance or research had thrown my way." Like his father he had taken to haunting old bookstalls and out-of-the-way shops where such finds in those days still could be made. One of his father's friends, a well-known collector who frequently called at Norfolk Street, was delighted with William Henry's discoveries and encouraged him to continue his hunt for rarities.

Meanwhile the nightly readings of the Bard of Avon continued, as did Ireland senior's encomiums. "These very frequent praises lavished on our poet," William Henry says, "led me to the perusal of his matchless works: and although silent myself on the subject, I nevertheless paid the greatest attention to every statement made by Mr. Ireland."

We are now quite familiar with what the most frequent statement was. Then, in the summer of 1793 came the visit to Stratford, and the appalling "disclosure" by the rogue Williams at Clopton House that several baskets full of Shakespearean documents had just been consigned to the flames. That such priceless treasures could have been so wantonly destroyed haunted Samuel Ireland, but it also raised in him a renewed conviction that somewhere specimens of the Bard's handwriting could be found, if only one knew where to look for them.

Chatterton, the Matchlessness of the Bard, the burnings at Clopton House, and his father's unceasing declarations that he would willingly sacrifice his entire collection for one scrap of Shakespeare's script—William Henry was rather slow to ignite, but his father's purchases in and about Stratford had made it evident that the elder Ireland was not. Within a year the task of a dutiful son, who happened also to be a genius, was at last obvious. For months he had been searching through all the old deeds in his employer's chambers in the mad hope that chance might throw his way some document bearing Shakespeare's autograph. It had become his heartfelt wish to be the one to make good the burning desire of his aloof and somewhat mysterious father. Such a gift would surely at one stroke banish the cloud of illegitimacy, cancel the years of disappointment over his unfitness as a scholar, and, if anything could, cause a warm spring of love to gush in his father's heart. But alas! The old parchments in the Bingley office yielded no such treasure. By now the only employee there, William Henry, when he should have been at his post, had next tried the stalls of merchants of old paper and parchment without luck. There was nothing to do but supply the deficiencies of Fortune himself.

Could he manage to bring off such a labor of love successfully? To make certain, he first tried an experiment. Some months earlier he had picked up a small quarto tract containing a set of prayers, written by a gentleman of Lincoln's Inn, and dedicated to Queen Elizabeth. The woodcut border on the margins of each page, the vellum binding, and the gold stamp of Elizabeth's arms on the cover suggested to the boy that "it had very probably once belonged to the library of that queen." He decided to *make* it a presentation copy from the author. Diluting ink with some water, he wrote a dedicatory epistle on a piece of old paper and thrust it between the vellum cover and the end paper, which had become unglued. As a further precaution William Henry dropped in on Laurie, a bookbinder known to him, whose shop was two minutes' walk from Bingley's chambers, and showed him the fabricated letter. "I told him with a smile that I had just executed it and was desirous of seeing how far Mr. Ireland would accredit it." Laurie was of the opinion that it would pass; but one of the two journeymen who were also present at this little scene told William Henry that he could furnish him with a mixture that would look much more like ancient ink than the specimen on the letter. Delighted to hear this, the lad asked the man to do this for him. The journeyman mixed together three different liquids used by bookbinders in marbling the covers of calf bindings; when the journeyman wrote his name with this ink it was very faint. "However, on holding it for a few seconds before the fire, the ink gradually assumed a very dark brown appearance." Paying the man for his trouble, William Henry wrote the dedicatory letter over again, and then presented it with the book to his father.

It is not surprising that Samuel Ireland had no suspicions about the epistle. His son had been bringing home numbers of old books from the stalls, and there was nothing fraudulent about the book itself. The copy could have once belonged to Elizabeth, and therefore there was small reason to doubt the letter. He might have wondered why she should have inserted it between the end paper and the cover, but Samuel Ireland was an enthusiast, not a reflective scholar. He was only too willing to declare the letter genuine, to congratulate his son, and to spur him on in his Elizabethan searches.

The boy made one further experiment with his "ancient" ink, a phial of which the journeyman had given him. At an old broker's shop he found a terra-cotta relief head of Oliver Cromwell, whose leather jacket was prominent among Samuel's earlier collections. It was the work of a young sculptor now safely dead. To the back of the relief William Henry affixed a piece of paper on which he had written a legend stating that the head had been given by Cromwell himself to John Bradshaw, lord president of the court which condemned Charles I to death. (Young Ireland was obviously unaware of the fact that Bradshaw had been an outspoken opponent of Cromwell, and that an intense dislike had existed between the two Puritans.) When the boy brought the head home, it was shown "to several persons eminent for their knowledge in sculpture." They agreed it was "a very striking resemblance" and that it was clearly the work of the celebrated Abraham Simon, who made models of leading Parliamentarians during the Protectorate of Cromwell.

These then were the experts! Though William Henry wrote in self-justification and there is more than a residue of Croft's judgment on Chatterton in what he says, it must be conceded that there is simple truth in his later comment: "If the model had been produced as the performance of the young man who really modeled it, a slight commendation would have passed upon his merits by those very persons who attributed it to Simon. . . . Either it possessed merit or it did not. If it did . . . the young artist was certainly a rising genius as a modeler: if it did not possess sufficient spirit, it was the name of Simon being annexed which made it pass current." (Such indeed proved to be the case with that quite brilliant twentieth-century forger who deceived the world with a number of new Vermeers.)

Obviously, with the father he respected so much as well as

73

with that father's antiquarian friends, it was only the age of a work which counted, not its quality. His own efforts at verse went unencouraged—after all, they were the work of someone still alive. An old piece of paper—or, just as effectively, one that appeared to be old—was more to be prized than the effusions of modern genius. Croft was right. Of what use would it be to make a career of writing under one's own name? Chatterton was given a hearing so long as he masqueraded as Rowley and no longer. Only the antique could move his father, and what alone could raise him to the heavens William Henry knew only too surely.

Well, the ink had proved itself.

The great event he had now in readiness required a worthy prologue. On December 2, 1794, he made a dramatic announcement to his father. About ten days ago (later he added that this had occurred at a coffee-house) he had made the acquaintance of "a gentleman of fortune, who was from my conversation given to understand that I had a great predilection for everything like antiquity." The gentleman, being of magnanimous cast, had urged him to drop in upon him at his chambers. There William Henry would find no end of old documents which the family had possessed for a long time. His new friend, who had no interest in old papers, assured him that he would be welcome to anything of interest to himself which he might find.

A morning was arranged for the visit, but on reflection William Henry decided that the other man was merely ridiculing him, so he let the day go by. But some mornings later as he happened to be passing by the gentleman's chambers, he yielded to an impulse to visit him then and there. After a gentle reproof at young Ireland's failure to keep the appointment, the gentleman greeted him warmly and led him into an adjoining room. There he found a huge chest (Chatterton had had *his* chest) filled with papers and documents, many of which were tied up in bundles and numbered. In but a few minutes William Henry had found a deed signed by none other than the Matchless Bard!

William Henry left it to his father to conceive the delirium of delight into which the discovery lifted him. Trembling with excitement, he had brought the document back to his new friend, who was much astonished to find that he had such a thing in his possession. But "having promised me everything I should find worthy my notice, he would not be worse than his word, and desiring only that I would make him a fair transcript in my own handwriting, he told me the deed was at my service."

Bursting with excitement Samuel Ireland begged his son to tell him more about this incredibly generous gentleman. And where on earth was this marvelous document?

But ah, there were provisos. The gentleman absolutely refused to have his name or place of residence known, and the boy had been obliged to take a solemn oath that he would never reveal them to any living being, not even his dear father.

Yes, yes. Samuel Ireland was familiar enough with the whims of the aristocracy, and experienced in not questioning them. But what about the deed, the deed—since it had been given to his son as a gift?

Oh, about that there was no need to fret. It would be necessary to wait a week or two until the deed had been copied out for the kind gentleman. Just now he had been required to leave town for a little to see after an estate in the country. As soon as he returned the copy could be made, and the document would belong to William Henry.

It was a hard thing to wait to see, but Ireland must have felt that not much was being asked of him in having to master his impatience. In the interim William Henry was able to bask in the light of his father's anticipatory approval.

At last on December 16, 1794, exactly two weeks later, at eight o'clock at night, young Ireland walked into the drawing room of his father's house, where his sisters and Mrs. Freeman were sitting with Ireland senior, put his hand in his bosom, and dramatically extracted a document. Handing it to his father, he cried, "There, sir! What do you think of that?"

The elder Ireland slowly opened the parchment with tremulous hands, studied it a long time, examined the seals carefully, folded the document again, handed it back to his son, and said solemnly, "I certainly believe it to be a genuine deed of the time." The deed was a mortgage made between Michael Fraser and his wife on the one hand, and on the other John Heminge and William Shakespeare.

William Henry, celestially happy, thrust the parchment back into his father's hand immediately. "If you think it is so," he said, "I beg your acceptance of it."

Samuel Ireland at once took the keys to his library out of his pocket and extended them to his son. "It is impossible for me to express the pleasure you have given me by the presentation of this deed," he said. "There are the keys of my bookcase. Go and take from it whatsoever you please. I shall refuse you nothing."

Deeply touched, already rewarded, the boy returned the keys. "I thank you, sir. I shall accept nothing."

His father rose from his chair, and went to fetch a scarce tract from among his books, William Stokes' *The Vaulting Master* (1652), which he insisted that William Henry have. He had priced it at £3.3s., a high price then for a book, but a considerable reduction from the value of his entire collection, which he had often expressed a willingness to exchange for such a document as his son had bestowed upon him. But William Henry never reflected upon his father's lack of generosity—not at a later date, nor then. He was far too much elated by the sensation he had caused.

FOUR

Shakespeare "en Caisse"

THAT WILLIAM HENRY's first Shakespearean forgery was motivated solely by a desire to please his father is proved, if by nothing else, by his total suppression of every impulse to be original. No personal crotchets, no vibrations of fancy were allowed to intrude. His father's desire, at this time, was comparatively modest: to possess a specimen of Shakespeare's signature. It was simply to supply that signature that William Henry's first Shakespearean counterfeit was undertaken.

Apparently he got the idea from reading in Johnson and Steeven's Shakespeare of the mortgage deed formerly in the possession of Garrick. First he made a tracing of the facsimiles of Shakespeare's signature to his will and to this mortgage deed as printed in the volume. Next he cut off a piece of parchment from the end of an old rent-roll belonging to his employer's large collection of old deeds and documents. He selected a deed from the reign of James I, and then attempted to imitate its style of penmanship for his forgery. When the document was written he affixed Shakespeare's signature and, to make it seem the work of another hand, inscribed Michael Fraser's with his left hand. Copying the heads of the authentic mortgage deed from the Shakespeare volume, he scrupulously employed the terminology of his model, writing with the ink purchased from the bookbinder's man. This document, in consequence, is of little interest to read; the only significant thing it contained was the all-important signature of the Bard. A brief excerpt will suffice here:

> . . . they the said William Shakespeare and John Hemynge have demised leased graunted and to ferme letten and by these presents do demise grant and to ferme lett unto the said Michl. Fraser and Elizabeth hys Wife all those his two Messuages or tenements abutting close to the Globe theatre by Black Fryers London. . . .

Thus far everything went easily enough. Unlike Chatterton's, William Henry's materials were convincing. The parchment and terminology were of the right period; the ink would dry to a color equally authentic. But the seals posed a real problem. He knew that Jacobean seals were affixed to narrow strips of parchment which were pendent to the signatures. These strips annexed, he first tried melting down in a shovel seals cut from some old deeds. But the wax was too old and crumbled instead of softening. He therefore hit upon the device of paring an old seal down the back with a heated knife, careful not to crack the seal during the operation. Next he scooped out a cavity with a penknife behind the seal's impression, placed the strip of parchment there, and heating some wax less ancient, placed it within the cavity, thus giving the seal a back. However, since the front and back of the seal, because of the difference in age of the waxes, were of different colors, he again moistened the seal before the fire, rubbed soot and coal ashes over it, and thus managed fairly to obliterate the variations in color.

The journeyman who had supplied the ink had shown him that though pale when applied to paper, it gradually took on an antique brown when held before a fire for a few seconds. William Henry therefore held all his parchments before the fire after he had written them. "Their scorched appearance originated in [this way] . . . and as I was constantly fearful of interruption, I sometimes placed them so near the bars as to injure the paper;

which was done in order to complete and conceal them as speedily as possible from any unexpected person who might come suddenly into the chambers."

Their scorched look, it turned out, was all to the good. For a time, indeed, the marks of the excessive heat were to raise new questions about the origin of the manuscripts. But just when the collection of William Henry's forgeries was nearing its fullest, his father "was credibly informed by persons who had known Mr. Warburton, that a fire happened at his house in the neighborhood of Fleet Street about thirty-six years before, that destroyed all his effects, amongst which were many books and manuscripts. Many of these papers were shrewdly surmised to have been the writings of Shakespeare: so that when that circumstance was stated to me, who was anxious to catch at any substantiated fact which might apply to the papers, I consequently stated 'that the world, I trusted, would no longer entertain a doubt as to the validity of the papers, as their burned appearance was now accounted for by their having been rescued during the conflagration of Mr. Warburton's property.'" This suddenly invented pedigree for the forged papers operated to validate their authenticity. Apparently it did not trouble William Henry, his father, or anyone else that linking them with the important Warburton collection was tantamount to annihilating the tale of their having been for ages in the possession of the family of the "donor" of the manuscripts to William Henry, the anonymous philanthropic gentleman.

Samuel Ireland was no sooner the delighted owner of the mortgage deed than he applied for confirmation of its authenticity to his young friend Sir Frederic Eden (1766–1809), son of the governor of Maryland. Though not yet thirty, Sir Frederic was a brilliant success in the world of finance, chairman of the Globe Insurance Company, and a serious student of economics. At the time he was engaged in writing *The State of the Poor,* a classic in its field. He was also the author of a humorous poem, *The Vision,* and a cultivated dilettante in literature. Though no Shakespearean, he did have a hobby for old seals. He came at once to Norfolk Street in a ferment of enthusiasm. After carefully examining the document he pronounced it indisputably genuine. Then, studying the seals, the one under the signature of Shakespeare, he decided, represented a quintin. (The quintin, as William Henry obligingly explains, "was used by the young men in order to instruct them in the art of tilting on horseback with the lance. . . . An upright beam was firmly fixed in the earth, at the top of which was a bar placed horizontally, moving on a pivot. To a hook at one end of the bar was hung a large iron ring; while from the other extremity was suspended a large bag filled with sand. The object of the tilter was to unhook the ring and bear it off upon the point of his lance when at full gallop.") "As this amusement seemed to bear so great an analogy to the name *Shakespear*, it was immediately conjectured that the seal must have belonged to our bard; and from that moment the Quintin was gravely affirmed to be the seal always used by our monarch of the drama."

Thus, unintentionally, William Henry was adding to the biography of Shakespeare. The truth is that in cutting this seal from an old deed at his employer's, he never bothered even to look at the impression. He confesses that had he looked at it, he would not have recognized the quintin, "a machine of which I had never heard until after the delivery of the deed."

Sir Frederic directed Ireland senior to a drawing of a quintin in John Stow's *Survey of London* (1598). Samuel was the more enraptured. Nothing was easier to grant than that Shakespeare should have cleverly hit upon the machine as a device, a quibble on his name.

Numerous people flocked to Norfolk Street to see the deed, and all agreed that it was valid. "After the lapse of some few days, it was hinted that in all probability many papers of Shakspeare's might be found by referring to the same source." Greedy for more spoils, Samuel pressed his son. Basking for the first time in his life in his father's favor, William Henry obliged in a few days with another legal document. While keeping safely within the confines of legal formalities, he permitted himself a little daring in the composition of this forgery. Shakespeare is here promising to pay his good friend John Heminge five guineas (like the true gentleman he was—anyone less well bred would have made it five pounds) as a reward for taking "great trouble" in transacting some unidentified business for him at the Globe Theatre as well as for other "trouble" in going down to Stratford on some affair which is likewise unspecified. It is not clear why Shakespeare should have felt obliged to pay a good friend for services rendered; it is even less clear why he should have felt it necessary to sign an agreement before making such a payment. But to the Irelands, with their thoroughly middle-class values, these questions were apparently unimaginable.

To this document William Henry thoughtfully added John Heminge's receipt for the five guineas, paid exactly one month later. Whatever is to be said about the forgeries, it must be acknowledged that William Henry was untiring in the endeavor to do his best, according to his own lights, for the Bard. Here he was proving that Shakespeare had possessed the most important of all middle-class virtues, responsibility in matters financial—or as William Henry himself phrased it far more elegantly: from this document "it was generally conjectured that Shakspeare, in addition to his other good qualities, was very punctual in all pecuniary transactions." What nobler virtue can a man own?

Nevertheless, Shakespeare may be supposed to have had a drink or two before writing the agreement, for he was strangely careless in the spelling of the name of his native town:

One Moneth from the date hereof I doe promyse to paye to my good and Worthye Freynd John Hemynge the sume of five Pounds and five shillings English Monye as a recompense for hys great trouble in settling and doinge

much for me at the Globe Theatre as also for hys trouble
in going downe for me to statford Witness my Hand
Wm Shakspere

September the Nynth 1589
    Received of Master Wm Shakspeare the Sum of five
Pounds and five Shillings good English Money thys Nynth
Day of October 1589
Jno Hemynge

The young forger was unaware that no such promissory note had
ever come down from Shakespeare's day.

It seemed sensible to William Henry to use his left hand in
signing Heminge's name. This trifling detail, at a most crucial
moment, was to raise questions of shattering proportions.

In passing, it is interesting to note in this document a phrase
to which William Henry was addicted. In the Shakespearean forgeries we are forever encountering the "trouble" or "pains"
which someone has undertaken in performing an office. Both
words also appear frequently later in William Henry's own *Confessions.*

Samuel Ireland's appetite was now raging for bigger and better things. The lad grew bolder. A friend of his father's spoke
often of Southampton's reputed "bounty" to Shakespeare, and
was heard to enlarge on how much "light" would be thrown upon
the relationship of patron to poet if only some document could
"be discovered denoting the sum so given by his lordship."

Like Chatterton young Ireland had all the leisure in the world
at his employer's chambers to manufacture his forgeries. The opportunity had been widened by the dismissal of the only other
employee, so that the boy was alone and free for a far more ambitious undertaking. He penned a letter of thanks to Southampton from the Bard himself, and another letter of graceful acknowledgment from the noble patron. Liberated from the shackles of legal form, the youthful forger was at last able to draw

upon the reservoir of fancy, "merely committing my thoughts to paper in the disguised hand as they occurred to my mind." Since he feared that some document might any day be unearthed revealing an exact sum donated by Southampton—like his elders William Henry lived in daily anticipation of the recovery of authentic Shakespeareana—he thought it wiser not to mention any specific amount of money.

Shakespeare's letter done, he was about to fold it up when a horrible thought struck him. Since the Bard was supposed to have sent this letter to his patron, how could it have come back to Shakespeare's possession? A little cogitation, however, solved the difficulty: to the top of the letter he affixed the words that should signify this was but a transcript of the original, made by Shakespeare to keep among his records:

> Copye of mye Letter toe hys grace offe Southampton
> Mye Lorde
> Doe notte esteeme me a sluggarde nor tardye for thus havynge delayed to answerre or rather toe thank you for youre greate Bountye I doe assure you my graciouse ande good Lorde that thryce I have essayed toe wryte and thryce mye efforts have benne fruitlesse I knowe notte what toe saye Prose Verse alle all is naughte gratitude is all I have toe utter and that is tooe greate ande tooe sublyme a feeling for poore mortalls toe expresse O my Lord itte is a Budde which Bllossommes Bllooms butte never dyes itte cherishes sweete Nature ande lulls the calme Breaste toe softe softe repose Butte mye goode Lorde forgive thys mye departure fromme mye Subjecte which was toe retturne thankes and thankes I Doe retturne O excuse mee mye Lorde more at presente I cannotte
>> Yours devotedlye and withe due respecte
>> Wm Shakspeare

Here the eager forger's own lifelong distaste for punctuation is in evidence, as are his personal preferences in spelling. His affection for *toe* for "to" will hereafter remain constant in the forgeries. The surplusage of consonants *à la* Chatterton—*notte, Bllossommes, fromme*—found here is the burgeoning of what will eventually become a kind of madness with him.

The sentimental contents, of course, do not read even like a travesty of Shakespeare; there is no hint of the Bard in them beyond a clouded distillation of some of his lines.* The letter is, of course, purely eighteenth century in its inflated emotion. "My lord, more at present I cannot," is an echo from the conclusion of a note from M. to H. in *Love and Madness*.

When it came to writing Southampton's response to the Bard, William Henry, unaware that specimens of his lordship's handwriting were extant, wrote that too with his left hand. All who viewed the page were rather astonished at the miserable scrawl of his Lordship; all would have been more astonished if they had seen the neat and careful hand which Southampton had actually written.

Deare William

I cannotte doe lesse than thanke you forre youre kynde Letterre butte Whye dearest Freynd talke soe muche offe gratitude mye offerre was double the Somme butte you woulde accepte butte the halfe thereforre you neede notte speake soe muche on thatte Subjectte as I have beene thye Freynd soe will I continue aughte thatte I canne doe forre thee praye commande mee ande you shalle fynde mee

Yours
Southampton

Julye the 4

To the Globe Theatre Forre Mastr William Shakspeare

* This bud of love, by summer's ripening breath,
May prove a beauteous flower when next we meet.
Good night, good night! as sweet repose and rest
Come to thy heart as that within my breast!—*Romeo and Juliet*, II, ii.

If Shakespeare, in the exquisite confusion of his brimming emotions, had been fairly vague about everything except those emotions, Southampton was not indefinite. Naturally, delicacy would have exempted *him* from mentioning the precise sum involved. But his feelings for Shakespeare and his appreciation for the splendor of his character are sufficiently stated. William Henry was once more assigning to the national idol of literature such qualities as could but endear him further to the faithful.

But there is something touching too in these sentimental outpourings when we recollect that they came from an emotion-starved boy. He was, no doubt, addressing Southampton with all the fervor with which he had never dared approach a father who had always held him in mild derision. No doubt, too, he was being addressed, as the author of that letter, in return by his lordship with a gratifying and enveloping warmth such as had never radiated from Mr. Ireland.

With these two letters William Henry may be said seriously to have embarked upon his brief and perilous career. They "were deemed highly curious and valuable, and the style of Shakespeare's was applauded beyond measure." What was he to think but that he had caught some of the sparks of Shakespeare's genius? Had he not permitted his father's scorn of his talents to end in self-depreciation? What he had composed was at once accepted not only as the Bard's, but as the Bard at his best. If everyone was so easy to take in, and so eager to be taken in, why should a young genius, appreciated by neither father nor teachers, curb his flights? Why bother to seek recognition for one's own gifts? Remember Chatterton!

Now that brilliant luminary of Bristol was being grudged no admiration, no love, no sympathetic tears by William Henry's elders. It was but a few years ago that Chatterton had been exposed, and now he was being hailed as another Shakespeare, another Milton, cut off before his harvest had fully ripened. Croft's exaggerated estimate of him in *Love and Madness* was far from unique; everyone more or less agreed that Chatterton's having been a forger somehow was a proof of his genius.

Nor was his the solitary example of the century to indicate to daydreaming William Henry that a fraud who aimed high might achieve not so much notoriety as fame. Perhaps the most celebrated hoax of the time was that perpetrated by George Psalmanazar (d. 1763), whose true name is even today not known. Born in the south of France and educated to become a brilliant Latinist, he made a number of attempts at various professions on the Continent. Suddenly he decided that he would pass as a Japanese who still practiced the religion of his native land. To complete the picture he began to live on roots, raw flesh, and herbs, and he next constructed, to top the deception, a new language for himself. For this he invented an elaborate alphabet and grammar; the symbols of this exotic tongue ran, as in Hebrew, from right to left across the page. He then assumed the name Psalmanazar, taking it, with an absence of logic that disturbed nobody, from the name of the Assyrian prince, Shalmaneser, who appears in the Book of Kings. He also contrived a form of worship which, he said, was *de rigueur* in Japan: it involved his facing the sun both at its rising and its setting, and the incantation of gibberish in verse and prose. These prayers were written out by him in their full length in his fabricated alphabet and inscribed in a book which he decorated with figures of the sun, moon, and stars. He managed completely to deceive even a Walloon clergyman.

But William Innes, chaplain to a Scottish regiment, penetrated the pretense at once. Innes saw in the young man an opportunity for profit to them both. He publicly baptized Psalmanazar as a Protestant, and then sent an account of the deed to the Bishop of London, to whom he described his convert as a native of Formosa (Formosa being far more unfamiliar to Englishmen than even Japan), who had been abducted by Jesuits and carried off to France. The youth, Innes went on to explain, had refused baptism, and had fled from his persecutors to Germany. Luckily

Innes had rescued him from the Papists by making him see that he could be saved only as a Protestant. The story was immediately credited, and Innes was urged to bring his exotic friend to England, where he would be welcomed.

Psalmanazar arrived there in 1703, when he was in his early twenties. He caused a great sensation everywhere he appeared. To the Bishop of London he presented his "translation" into Formosan of the catechism. With Archbishop Tillotson he conversed in flawless Latin. It is not surprising that the clergy started a fund to maintain him and to enable him to continue his studies. His unfailing personal dignity won credit for him all around. Although Formosa belonged to China, he was able to convince all hearers that they were wrong: it was a province of Japan's! A Jesuit missionary, happening to be in London then, just freshly returned from China, debated his contentions publicly, but Psalmanazar prevailed. Soon his society was courted by the aristocracy and notabilities of the age. At Oxford he spent six months, and was there besought to teach Formosan to a selected group of gentlemen and ladies. These he charmed by averring that it was no sin to eat human flesh, though he was willing to admit that the practice was not conformable to the best manners.

At Innes' suggestion he wrote a full account of his early life—in Latin. This, translated into English, was published in 1704. Its many attacks on the Jesuits were naturally applauded, with the reign of James II fresh in memory. Its full relation of the language, clothes, religion, and politics of Formosa was considered a sheer delight. The book was a great success.

Soon, unfortunately, Innes was appointed chaplain-general in Portugal, and thus left Psalmanazar to manage the hoax alone. By 1708 he was being ridiculed, and he found it expedient to retire from public notice. Four years later, when induced to revive his Formosan pretensions, he met with scant approbation. At length he decided to settle down to the drudgery of literary hackwork. But he seems to have paid no penalty for his earlier deceptions, probably because of the austerity of his life and the regularity of his habits. He did, it is true, steadily consume alarming spoonfuls of opium—but that habit was not then looked on as morally reprehensible. It is clear that he won an ever-increasing respect from those who knew him. In 1747 he confessed (though anonymously) to his fraud, and the rest of his life was lived in the midst of considerable veneration. Johnson assured Mrs. Piozzi that Psalmanazar's "piety, penitence, and virtue exceeded almost what we read as wonderful in the lives of the saints." He in fact admitted often seeking out the man: "I used to go and sit with him at an alehouse in the city." Johnson, who habitually thundered his convictions at anyone and everyone, nevertheless so much reverenced Psalmanazar that, as he confessed, "I should as soon think of contradicting a Bishop."

Among celebrated frauds, the most successful was still alive. It had been established among the discerning that James Macpherson was himself the author of the rubbish he had issued as translations of the bard Ossian—though many refused to face the evidence. Thousands all over western Europe fanatically adored reading him. Macpherson's bold (and, to us, transparent) deception had in no way interfered with his being an international bestseller.

Even in the realm of Shakespeareana, the respectable had not withstood temptation. Lewis Theobald (1688–1744) was one of the truly great editors of Shakespeare; some of his emendations rank as the most brilliant ever proposed. Nevertheless, he presented as a lost play of Shakespeare's a tragedy which was aptly entitled *The Double Falsehood*. It was acted at the Drury Lane in 1727. There was but a single manuscript extant, and this Theobald said he had purchased at considerable cost. The work is certainly based upon an old play, and parts of it are by either Massinger or Shirley; but most of it is unquestionably of Theobald's own composition. Even a Theobald was not above attempting a monumental hoax!

With such examples and incitements present to his mind, why should a lonely boy like William Henry scruple to prove his genius in some similar way? Besides, he could already boast of working on a higher moral plane than other celebrated pretenders. His latest inventions—had they not added to the personal stature of the Bard? Those mementos carved from the inexhaustible supplies of the Mulberry Tree and the Crab Tree—what did they do more than pander to the satisfaction of their purchasers? Whereas he was rescuing Shakespeare from the mists of obscurity into which the lack of personal records had cast him, and doing his task so well that everyone recognized the sound of Shakespeare's voice through his pen. There was something almost occult about his success. Moreover, Mr. Samuel Ireland was now looking upon his heir in a new light, with something closely approximating respect. That alone was reward enough.

The next endeavor—its author thought of it as such—showed that William Henry had thrown all caution to the winds. He heard from his father and his father's friends more and more of the treasures which *must* lie awaiting discovery in his benevolent friend's collection. "Being thus urged forward to produce what really was not in existence, I then determined on essaying some composition in imitation of the language of Shakspeare."

What magnanimous document should he next produce—one which could be calculated most greatly to incandesce the figure of the Bard? No piece of gossip was more generally deplored in solid English circles than the whisper that Shakespeare had possibly been a Papist. In substantiation of that noxious view there existed two items: "the bigoted profession of faith found at the birthplace of Shakspeare, and said to have been written by John Shakspeare, our poet's father," unmistakably Catholic in its tendency, and "the language made use of by the Ghost in Hamlet as to purgatory & c." A true Ireland, William Henry was repelled at the very notion that Shakespeare could be so construed. Having himself "the most rooted antipathy to everything like superstition and bigotry" (except, of course, of a Protestant variety), he determined to decide the case for Shakespeare by writing for him a profession of faith such as could have been written only "by a sincere votary of the protestant religion."

The Profession of Faith was written on a sheet of old paper from the outside of a bundle containing accounts from the days of Charles I. Knowing nothing of Elizabethan watermarks, William Henry carefully selected paper without any mark at all.

A few days after the unveiling of the Southampton letters he told his father that he had found the Profession of Faith, and lauded it as one of the sublimest compositions his eyes had ever viewed. Indeed, it had had on him the effect of perfectly convincing him "of the truth of the New Testament and the existence of Jesus Christ." He also knew beyond doubt that Shakespeare was "a true Christian"—i.e., anti-Papist. So matchless was the Profession of Faith, the boy averred, that he had learned it by heart and was now repeating it "every morning and evening in his prayer."

A few days later the joyful father was rewarded by the presentation of the manuscript itself:

> I beynge nowe offe sounde Mynde doe hope thatte thys mye wyshe wille atte mye deathe bee acceded toe as I nowe lyve in Londonne ande as mye soule maye perchance soone quitte thys poore Bodye it is mye desire thatte inne suche case I maye bee carryed to mye native place ande thatte mye Bodye bee there quietlye interred wythe as little pompe as canne bee ande I doe nowe inne theese mye seyriouse Moments make thys mye seyriouse professione of fayth and which I doe moste solemnlye believe I doe fyrste looke toe oune lovynge and greate God ande toe hys gloriouse sonne Jesus I doe alsoe beleyve thatte thys mye weake and frayle Bodye wille retturne toe duste butte forre mye soule lette God judge thatte as toe hymsselfe shalle seeme meete O omnipotente and greate

God I am fulle offe Synne I doe notte thynke myselfe
worthye offe thye grace and yette wille I hope forre evene
the poore prysonerre whenne bounde with gallyng Irons
evenne hee wille hope for Pittye ande whenne the teares
offe sweete repentance bathe hys wretched pillowe he then
looks ande hopes forre pardonne thenne rouze mye Soule
ande lette hope thatte sweete cherisher offe alle afforde
thee comforte alsoe O Manne whatte arte thou whye con-
sidereste thou thyselfe thus greatlye where are thye greate
thye boasted attrybutes buryed loste forre everre inne
colde Deathe. O Manne whye attemptest thou toe searche
the greatenesse offe the Almyghtye thou doste butte loose
thye labourre more thou attempteste more arte thou loste
tille thye poore weake thoughtes arre elevated toe theyre
summite ande thence as snowe fromme the leffee Tree
droppe ande disstylle themselves tille theye are noe more
O God Manne as I am frayle bye Nature fulle offe Synne
yette greate God receyve me toe thye bosomme where alle
is sweete contente ande happynesse alle is blysse where
discontente isse neverre hearde butte where oune Bonde
offe freyndshippe unytes alle Menne Forgive O Lorde alle
oure synnes ande withe thye grete Goodnesse take usse
alle to thye Breaste O cherishe usse like the sweete Chick-
enne thatte under the coverte offe herre spreadynge Wings
Receyves herre lyttle Broode ande hoveringe oerre
themme keepes themme harmlesse ande in safetye

Wm Shakspeare

To lend verisimilitude to this fantastic undertaking William
Henry in penning it was at pains to employ as many of the
"twelve different letters contained in the christian and sir names
of Wm. Shakspeare" as possible, and also "many capital *double-
yous* and *esses*," all of which he made conform to the letters in
Shakespeare's authentic signature. Nevertheless, as he later ob-

served, "had any person minutely compared the style of writing therein produced with those manuscripts which were penned after I had acquired a facility in committing to paper the disguised hand, he must instantly have discovered the difference, which was indeed . . . obvious."

As for the contents of the Profession of Faith, to anyone who knew his Shakespeare, how could it have passed as either the creed or the composition of the creator of Hamlet, Lear, Othello, Desdemona, Beatrice, Imogen, or Prospero? What would Falstaff have said to this psalm singer? The ludicrousness of foisting this pietism on Shakespeare should have awakened the common sense of the dupes of this nineteen-year-old adolescent. The absurd perversion of the Scripture's beautiful image into "the sweet Chicken" should in itself have been enough.

But Samuel Ireland was convinced by the manuscript and the high poetry of the style. This was the most astonishingly priceless of all the finds yet—still it was almost too good to dare believe in without the certification of authorities greater than himself. Who more suitable to consult than the eminent Doctors Joseph Warton and Samuel Parr?

Joseph Warton (1722–1800), described by Johnson as a "very agreeable man," though not much of a poet was a learned and perspicacious critic. He had written some thoughtful essays on *The Tempest* and *King Lear,* but was most justly respected for his *Essay on Pope,* which proved the superiority of the riotous imagination of the Elizabethans to the "correctness" of eighteenth-century poetry. A great and ceaseless talker, he was an intimate of Johnson, Burke, Garrick, Reynolds, and Bishop Percy. Cowper was delighted beyond measure by Warton's approval, and exclaimed, "The poet who pleases a man like that has nothing left to wish for."

As for Samuel Parr (1747–1825), who was twenty-five years younger, with a square, athletic, rather short figure and a massive head, he seems to have imposed himself upon his contemporaries more by his energies and great sociability than by any remarkable personal talents. He had once taught Sheridan at Harrow. Ordained in 1769, he continued the stout Whiggism of his youth through life, and was a firm supporter of "that devil" Wilkes. In 1771 he started a rival school at Stanmore, where his students were encouraged to compose English verses instead of classical ones—but "at risk of flogging if the English were bad." He encouraged the boys in literary discussions, cricket, and prize fighting—not astonishing in a man who himself was always in the midst of some controversy. Hot and capricious in temper, he could ignore public opinion. When he chose to ride through town "in high prelatical pomp," seated on a black saddle and carrying a long ivory-headed rod, the townsfolk laughed at him openly; at other times he stalked through the streets "in a dirty striped morning gown." Presently he gave up the school, went to Colchester, quarreled with the trustees there, moved on to Norwich as headmaster (1779), and at that place published his first work, a volume of sermons. In 1785 he changed his residence to Hatton, where he spent the rest of his life. Accepting only a few pupils, he devoted himself to building a fine large library. With his aversion to a peaceful life, he naturally was quite vocal in support of the French Revolution. Wherever he lived the atmosphere did not long remain tepid. For instance, on the Sundays following the sermons which Dr. Bridges was required to give at Hatton, Parr would take as his own subject the errors perpetrated by his superior. The author of various political tracts, one in elegant Latin, he precipitated himself by his radicalism into all sorts of quarrels. He got to be known as "the Whig Johnson." Boswell records that Parr was about to write about Johnson, between whom and Plutarch he discerned "forty points of similarity." Boswell was no admirer of the belligerent little clergyman, and observes that at a stimulating gathering his own pleasure was "checked a little by my perceiving in Parr less of orthodox acquiescence than in my opinion is becoming a clergyman." Notwithstanding, Parr had a vast number of friends, and was himself a warm friend, though very touchy and quick to take umbrage. His aggressive nature had won him wide repute by the time Samuel Ireland invited him to inspect Shakespeare's Profession of Faith.

Ireland senior was alone in his study when Warton and Parr arrived, but in a little while William Henry was summoned to answer their questions. "I confess I had never before felt so much terror, and would have almost bartered my life to have evaded the meeting: there was, however, no alternative, and I was under the necessity of appearing before them." He told them the tale of the unknown gentleman, his generosity, how the various documents had come to light, and the necessity of keeping the secret of his benefactor. One of the two learned doctors, William Henry could not later remember which, then said, "Well, young man, the public will have just cause to admire you for the research you have made, which will afford so much gratification to the literary world." The young forger bowed his head and maintained silence.

Enchanted at the condescension of these great men, the elder Ireland, inviting one of them to sit in Shakespeare's Courting Chair, now proceeded to read aloud from the manuscript. Warton and Parr listened in rapt silence, "paying infinite attention to every syllable"; William Henry, meanwhile, "continued immovable, awaiting to hear their dreaded opinion."

He was due for a shock. The reading ended, the vigorous Dr. Parr raised his head and exclaimed to Samuel Ireland: "*Sir, we have many very fine passages in our church service, and our litany abounds with beauties; but here, sir, here is a man who has distanced us all!*" (The fact that William Henry italicizes this outburst in his later *Confessions* would indicate how cardinal it was to his activities for the next year.) "When I heard these words pronounced," he reports, "I could scarcely credit my own senses." He did not know whether to smile or not. But as he left the study he could not help reflecting on the praise which had been "lavished by a person so avowedly erudite on the unstudied production of one so green in years as myself. On entering the back dining-room, which was contiguous to Mr. Ireland's study, I reclined my head against the window frame, still ruminating on the words I had heard . . . fired with the idea of possessing genius to which I had never aspired."

What, William Henry might well have thought as he looked out the window at the garden, his face flushed with exaltation—what were the achievements even of a Chatterton when matched with those of William Henry Ireland, a youth of uncertain birth, whose hasty effusions were deemed on highest authority to be worthy of the Matchless Bard? And how could this triumph be less than a beginning, a prelude to greater ones?

FIVE

With No Middle Flight

Everyone privileged to inspect the Profession of Faith and to hear Samuel Ireland's eloquent reading of it from the noble embrace of Shakespeare's Courting Chair, his preferred emplacement, was stirred to the depths of his being by the sublimity of its emotion and the profundity of its thought, and the verdict was unanimous that the composition could have been created only by the Matchless Bard. That it bore no resemblance to anything Shakespeare had ever written apparently occurred to no one. The physical appearance of the manuscript was convincing. And in that staunchly Protestant circle which considered the Roman Church the Symbol of Superstition and Bigotry (their own bigotry in so thinking was to them a symptom of broad-mindedness), there was a special gratification in connecting Shakespeare with the Protestant sentiments expressed in the Profession. William Henry, even a decade after his bubble had burst, never quite recovered from the notion that he had somehow done Shakespeare a permanent service. "Nor was my satisfaction a little heightened on finding that this effusion banished at once every idea of Shakspeare's catholicism from the minds of those whom I had frequently heard hazarding that opinion as to his religious tenets."

The universal enthusiasm provoked by the Profession shed an ever-brighter radiance upon young Ireland. His father's distin-

96

guished friends made him tell over and over the story of his meeting with the wonderful gentleman, his discovery of the first and later documents, and the inexhaustible possibilities of the gentleman's storehouse. Everyone stressed the likelihood that there must be untold treasures still awaiting disclosure to an eager world. His father's collector's avarice, having been awakened, developed the appetite of a tapeworm.

The endorsement of Warton and Parr, supplemented by all the attention of his father's intimates, became a heady wine to William Henry, and his imagination began to run riot. Soon he overwhelmed his father with the news that in the gentleman's country house he had come upon one of Shakespeare's great tragedies written in the Bard's own hand. Next, Sir Frederic Eden's identification of the quintin on the deed's seal became unexpectedly corroborated. Among the gentleman's possessions there had just turned up a carnelian seal with an intaglio of the quintin— the very intaglio employed in sealing the Fraser deed! His noble friend, of course, had promised that these two treasures should soon be his.

One day after dinner, a choice piece of lunacy suggested itself to William Henry. He calmly announced to his father his newest discovery, which at the appropriate time his noble friend would present to him: a portrait of Shakespeare—not just a head, but large as life and painted on board, a full-length portrait. This mad invention he had plenty of cause ruefully to regret, for from that moment his father gave him no peace in his anxiety to own it. Its possession, old Ireland declared, would settle beyond the hints of the most malicious the authenticity of the documents.

To divert his father's impatience the boy invented new extravagances. He promised him "two copies in folio of Shakspeare's works with uncut leaves." For these he was soon as "equally tormented as for the whole-length portrait of our bard." It is indeed almost awesome to consider the risks run by this reckless boy and the incredibly harebrained expedients into which he was forced.

It had been, it will be recalled, his practice in supplying ancient seals for the legal documents to scoop out a hole in the back of an old seal, hold the pendent strip to the hole, fix it in place with some freshly melted wax, and disguise the difference in color of the two waxes by smudging the result with soot. One time a viewer examining one of these documents, allowed it to fall from his hands onto Ireland's desk. The old wax with the impression was so brittle that it fell loose from the strip of parchment. A close observer would, of course, instantly have noted the differences in the wax. Quickly William Henry bound the two parts of the seal together with black silk. Had anyone unwound the silk the falsification would have been exposed immediately. Nevertheless, the document continued for a while to be shown without any questioning of the presence of the black silk. Worried that sooner or later someone would be curious enough to uncover the true state of the wax, William Henry told his father that the noble gentleman desired to look over the document again for an hour or so. The elder Ireland could hardly refuse the request. His son hastened to his employer's office, heated some fresh wax, riveted the parts together, and replaced the black silk around the seal. It might have been expected that Samuel Ireland would be astonished to find the seal whole again. He seems never to have unwound the silk himself. At all events, the seal was now safe for all newcomers.

Eventually the boy's supply of antique ink gave out. He knew the danger, but nevertheless applied to the same journeyman in Laurie's shop for more. For a shilling he bought enough for the rest of his projects.

As for old parchment, the pieces he could cut off from ancient documents were necessarily limited in number, and these he kept for the fabrication of legal matters. After searching in various shops, he found a bookseller named Verey in St. Martin's Lane who, for five shillings, permitted him to cut from all the folio and quarto volumes in his shop the blank flyleaves. Thus the boy had an ample store of old paper.

He did not feel free to use it indiscriminately. From the variety of watermarks current in his own day he surmised that they must have been subject to constant change since Shakespeare's. At first he therefore used only such old sheets as had no watermark whatever. Listening attentively to the discussions of his father's friends, he presently learned that some Elizabethan paper bore the watermark of a jug. He thereupon carefully sorted from the papers he had bought those with this distinguishing mark and used them, intermingling them with sheets which bore no mark.

Once while he was busy with one of his major inventions, a letter of Queen Elizabeth's, the charwoman who did the cleaning was present in his employer's chambers. He could not resist parading his accomplishment before her admiring eyes, and asked her whether she would not take the paper and its writing to be ancient. "She replied in the affirmative, adding with a laugh that it was very odd I could do such unaccountable strange things."

The boy had thus placed his security within possible jeopardy at the whim of at least four different people: Laurie, the bookbinder to whom he had shown the dedicatory epistle; Laurie's man, who had twice supplied him with ink; the charwoman at his employer's chambers—all three of whom were aware that he was forging documents—and Verey, who had sold him the large supply of old paper, and might easily have become suspicious of his young client's purposes. Any one of them could have undone him with a word. Yet, even though William Henry's Shakespearean fabrications were presently to be discussed widely in the London press for the better part of a year, not one of these four ever stepped forth to proclaim what he knew. Perhaps they had a better sense of humor than their learned contemporaries.

That young Mr. Montague Talbot had an extravagant one is a matter of record. Talbot, also employed by a conveyancer, had become William Henry's friend shortly after the latter had first been articled. Their common distaste for their employers' profession (shades of Chatterton!) formed a basis for chitchat, and Talbot was in the habit of dropping in on his companion when both their employers were absent from chambers. Soon William Henry was confiding his enthusiasm for antiquities, but Talbot had only lively mockery for them. His own passion was for the stage, an old love of the Irelands. Before long he was a constant visitor at William Henry's house, and made to feel welcome there.

It was while Talbot was out of town for a few weeks that William Henry had undertaken his earliest Shakespearean forgeries. Had Talbot been around he could not have concentrated on his labors without detection. On his return Talbot visited the Irelands and was permitted by Ireland senior to inspect the few documents already in existence. Having seen William Henry playfully imitate old script, Talbot at their next meeting laughingly assured his friend that he was certain William Henry had manufactured the papers his father had so proudly exhibited. His friend stoutly denied the charge, but Talbot, who thoroughly enjoyed the idea that there had been trickery, persisted in his conviction. Thereafter William Henry was compelled to keep a wary eye out against Talbot's unheralded appearances. "He frequently came in upon me so suddenly that I was with infinite difficulty enabled to conceal from his observation the manuscript on which I then chanced to be engaged." This was undoubtedly one of the reasons why the young forger for a while devoted himself to turning out brief inventions, such as playhouse receipts and memoranda of playhouse expenditures. Also, there was an advantage in fabricating these pieces of drudgery. He had been assured by his elders that "the more bulky the papers were, the more probable would their authenticity appear." Finally, supplying a stream of these was one way to placate his father's prodding to produce the full-length portrait, the carnelian seal of the quintin, and the two uncut folio volumes—none of which he could possibly bring into existence.

Among these brief papers were two connecting Shakespeare

with Leicester. It is to be noted that one of William Henry's favorite phrases, the taking of "trouble" or of "great trouble" reappears in each:

> Inne the Yeare o Chryste
>
> Forre oure Trouble inne goynge toe Playe before the Lorde Leycesterre ats house and oure greate Expenneces thereuponne 19 poundes Receyvedde ofs Grace the Summe o 50 Poundes
>
> Wm Shakspeare

> Forre oure greate Trouble inne gettynge alle inne orderre forre the Lorde Leycesterres Comynge ande oure Moneyes layde oute there uponne 59 Shyllynges Receyvedde o Masterre Hemynge forre thatte Nyghte 3 Poundes Master Lowinne 2 Shyllynges moure forre hys Goode Servyces ande welle playinge
>
> Wm. S.

The first of these had its own interesting little history. After "Chryste" in the headline William Henry had originally inscribed a date two years after Leicester's death, so careless was he of his facts. Learning by chance of the error he had made, and unwilling to destroy his labors, he tore off the corner of the paper, leaving it without a date. The receipt was considered none the less valuable because torn, and tended to prove that the Bard's "company of players must have ranked foremost in that day, it having been selected in preference to any other, by so renowned a favorite of queen Elizabeth as the lord Leicester." Moreover, the sum of fifty pounds was clearly an unusually immense sum for payment.

But one little fact none of the Irelands—least of all the forger himself—had at his disposal. Leicester died in 1588; Lowine, who was being rewarded for his "well playing," must have been incredibly precocious, for he was in that year only twelve. As for

Shakespeare, by 1588 as either player or author he had hardly begun his apprenticeship, and was as yet unknown in London.

As the number of these old papers of small accounts increased it was pointed out to William Henry that there was something unusual about them. Small slips of paper such as these had ordinarily been kept together by tying them up in bundles. He was anxious at once to make good the deficiency, but feared that the use of a piece of contemporary thread might betray him. Soon an opportunity presented itself. Samuel Ireland frequently went to the House of Lords to "hear his majesty's speech and be present when he was robed"; on one of these occasions, when William Henry accompanied him, "having to pass through some adjoining apartments . . . I observed that the walls of the chambers were hung with very old and multilated tapestry." It occurred to him that if he had a remnant of this ancient material he might unravel it and use the worsted to tie up his bundles of small slips. Accordingly, he mutilated one of the tapestries further by tearing off a piece that was hanging loose. Thereafter he had string enough for his needs. By the time of his exposure as a fraud there still remained a small square of tapestry not yet unraveled.

Another device for swelling the bulk of Shakespeareana without running too much risk of being interrupted by Talbot was the production of Shakespeare's Library. The generous gentleman who was his friend had in his country house, William Henry reported, innumerable books that had belonged to the Bard, and which had been annotated in Shakespeare's own hand.

William Henry, with his father's encouragement, had become quite adept at ferreting out old and even rare volumes—still to be found by the patient browser. Now, instead of presenting them to Ireland as great finds, William Henry tendered them as part of what had constituted Shakespeare's personal library. The volumes he produced were of more than casual interest. There were Carion's *Chronicles* (1550) in which Shakespeare had annotated the reigns of those monarchs dealt with in his own plays; the 1590 and 1596 quartos of *The Faerie Queene* in which the Bard's notes were so highly esteemed that one visitor to Norfolk Street offered Ireland sixty pounds for one of the volumes; a book on the Guy Fawkes affair, in which on the margin of the passage describing Fawkes' ascending the scaffold William Henry had inscribed a very feeling note "indicative of the philanthropy of Shakspeare," and added as a postscript, "Hee hadd beene intreatedd bye hys freynde John Hemynges to attende sayde executyonne, butte thatte he lykedde notte toe beholde syghtes of thatte kynde." Another of these volumes was Foxe's *Book of Martyrs,* with a woodcut showing Bishop Bonner scourging a man with rods; William Henry had been taught to hate "that bigoted minister of a more bigoted queen," Mary Tudor, and therefore wrote on that page in the Bard's hand twelve bitter lines beginning,

> O Bonnerr! thyne was fylthy witte,
> So harde the breeche of mann to hytte . . .

These verses helped banish whatever vestiges might remain of the notion that Shakespeare could have been a Catholic.

It is surprising to note that numbers of these books of the Shakespeare Library had been purchased by William Henry from White in Fleet Street and from Otridge in the Strand. Neither of them ever disclosed that the volumes which were supposed to have been the Bard's had, in point of fact, been lying on the shelves of their bookshops only a few weeks before—without any annotations.

More discoveries meant not the pacification of Ireland's greed, but only an acceleration of his importunities. Among the chief sources of annoyance was pressure for Holinshed's *Chronicles,* which William Henry in a euphoric moment told his father he had seen in the gentleman's country house. The boy searched everywhere for a copy with margins wide enough for the writing of marginalia. He had no luck. Wherefore, Holinshed joined the in-

taglio, the portrait, the two folio volumes, and other items promised, as material for Samuel's badgering his son. When was the
gentleman going to part with these treasures?

As the Shakespeare Library continued to increase, William
Henry's attempts grew bolder and bolder. In a very scarce edition
of Skelton, Shakespeare had become very impatient with "several
miserable stanzas" displaying the "filthy debaucheries" of one
Eleanor Rummin, and was moved to inscribe on the page an Epitaph concluding, "For earthly ale hath got thee ail in hell." Forgery, it would seem, in no way impaired the respectability William
Henry had imbibed at his father's house, where Samuel Ireland
lived with his mistress. Indeed forgery, if anything, was but operating as a spur to virtue and abstemiousness.

William Henry had already composed a number of Shakespearean comments which were awaiting the correct volume in
which to be inscribed in the Bard's hand; and in addition, a collection of complimentary acrostics—on Southampton, which cleverly authenticated the Southampton forgeries by its allusion to
that nobleman's donation to the Bard; on Elizabeth; on Mary,
Queen of Scots, in which the Bard's humanity caused his anti-
Papism to be forgotten; on Richard II; on Sidney—all of which
were intended to be revealed in a hitherto-unpublished "Crown
Garlande daintilye besette withe costlye Gemmes." Unfortunately, before the project could be carried through, William
Henry's hoodwinking of the public was a thing of the past.

The Shakespeare Library was soon to prove, when the Shakespearean manuscripts became an issue of public dispute, a significant prop to the whole fabrication. Francis Webb would presently point out, with an innocence demonstrative of how he had
been entrapped in the maze of William Henry's inventions, that
the annotations in the books which once belonged to Shakespeare
were obviously "the productions of the one and the same man."
Webb was so much enamored of their astuteness as to add, "The
most consummate wisdom, the most perspicacious ingenuity,

united with the most artful cunning and most indefatigable labor, could not have . . . forged such a series." The marginalia were all, Webb was convinced, highly characteristic of the matchless Bard. "I therefore think I see this immortal poet rise again to life, holding these sacred relics in one hand and hear him say, *These were mine:* at the same time pointing with the other to these important volumes, once his own, informing us that these were his delightful companions in his leisure hours."

Thus Shakespeare's Library for a while served William Henry's purposes better than he had planned, though each acquisition made his father only the more avaricious.

But life was beginning to be difficult because of the incursions of Montague Talbot. At the office, William Henry always kept one watchful eye upon window and door. One day, however, Talbot bent himself double and crept beneath the window at which William Henry was writing; unobserved he suddenly darted into the room, and before William Henry could hide the document which he was inscribing, seized his friend's arm. Talbot "by this stratagem became at once acquainted with the whole mystery." William Henry begged him to swear that he would never reveal the truth.

It must be said, in testimony to Talbot's loyalty, that he never at any time broke his promise—not even when he himself had become entangled in the web of William Henry's deceptions. Probably his sense of fun caused him to enjoy the hoax too much ever to expose it. But he was to go much further than was healthy for his own reputation in keeping faith with his friend.

Relieved of the strain of protecting himself against Talbot, William Henry felt free at last to follow up his great triumph of the Profession of Faith with worthy successors. He penned a financial agreement with Condell, who after Shakespeare's death had with John Heminge edited the First Folio, and one with Lowine, an actor in the Bard's company. According to his contract, Lowine is to be paid "the summe of oune Pounde ande ten

Shillings per Week" for his "services." Kind Shakespeare! In case of illness Lowine will not be obliged to perform "butte shalle more over receive the sayd Salarye" from Shakespeare. However, if Lowine should otherwise break any article of the contract, he will have to give Shakespeare a hundred pounds. Where a player would be likely to come by such a sum Shakespeare did not seem to care. Shakespeare, on his part, agrees to pay Lowine his salary every Saturday before midnight. Condell's contract has even more curious conditions: he is apparently never to perform in Shakespeare's own works, and he is to receive nine shillings less a week than Lowine, though his salary is still large.

These two contracts owe their existence to a belated awakening on the forger's part. Although the First and Second Folios of the Bard's plays were in his father's library, he was unaware that both editions on their first leaves print the names of some of the actors in Shakespeare's company. One day he happened to hear this fact referred to. Immediately he consulted the Folios, and soon thereafter began on these documents, which were written on parchment, to give them legal standing, and were sealed in a manner similar to the mortgage deed. For throwing "great light upon the theatrical affairs of that period," the contracts were immensely valued by Ireland's visitors. They also validated the "originality of the whole mass of papers produced." Original they were indeed! Even the payments allotted by generous Shakespeare to his fellow actors would have been in that period considered fabulous.

But fabulousness became the keynote of William Henry's endeavors from this time on. Having no full-length portrait of Shakespeare to give his father, the boy turned up one day with a drawing of Shakespeare's head executed upon old parchment. He had used as his model the Folio portrait, adding in the background Shakespeare's initials, a couple of antic heads, Shakespeare's arms, and in the corners Shakespeare's signature. It was wretchedly drawn, and not surprisingly Ireland ridiculed it as of "no consequence." Dazzled by his daily successes, William Henry was unprepared for this, his first, rebuff. Was he indignant at the slight and therefore determined that his father should swallow this hoax as he had swallowed all the others? Or did he merely fear that one forgery would topple all the others?

At any rate, the next day, he penned, as from Shakespeare to Cowley the player, a letter which presumably had accompanied the drawing and revealed it to be the subject of a merry jest or conundrum:

> Worthye Freynde
> Havynge alwaye accountedde thee a Pleasaynte ande wittye Personne ande oune whose Companye I doe muche esteeme I have sente thee inclosedde a whymsycalle conceyte whiche I doe suppose thou wilt easylye discoverre butte shoudst thou notte whye thenne I shalle sette thee onne mye table offe *loggerre heades*
> Youre trewe Freynde
> Marche nynthe   Wm Shakspeare
> Toe Masterre Richard Cowleye dwellynge atte oune Masterre Holliss a draperre inne the Wattlynge Streete Londonne

This letter changed Ireland's mind at once about the importance of the drawing. It had come from the Bard's own hand, and had been done as a *jeu d'esprit!* How precious! The "whimsical conceit" became in the Ireland circle "an object of learned investigation, but all to no effect." Many wise guesses were made but nothing was concluded. Which is not to be wondered at, since William Henry later confessed that when he had made the drawing he had intended no meaning of any kind. Nevertheless, letter and drawing revealed Shakespeare as a sociable, entertaining man—a good son of the eighteenth century. William Henry was doing more for him all the time! The very inscrutability of the conceit was further proof that it was genuinely the creation of the deepest of all human minds.

A few days later William Henry followed up his artistic triumph with another one. As he was walking along Butcher Row he saw an old drawing hanging up for sale; it was framed between two glasses to show both back and front. On one side was an aged figure in the clothes of a Hollander, on the reverse was a young man in dress of the Jacobean period. He purchased it and took it back to the office. On the side representing the old man he painted in a pair of scales, so that the figure could pass as Shylock's; on the other, he drew in one corner Shakespeare's arms, but carelessly reversed the spear, directing the point to the right instead of the left hand; on the opposite corner he inscribed "W S," along with the titles of a few of Shakespeare's plays. Then with Droeshout's print before him he altered the face of the young man to make it look as much like Shakespeare as he could. Replacing the glasses in the frame, he brought the work home to the Ireland house.

The colored drawing was an instantaneous hit. Though it was deemed a bit odd that he should be dressed as a Dutchman, Shylock was recognized at once. The young man was clearly Bassanio, and it was wonderful to see Shakespeare as cast in that role. (It is a role which he almost certainly never performed.) The drawing added another important item to the stock of biographical information on the Bard. The general conclusion was that this invaluable work must in all probability have "graced the green-room of the Globe theatre."

In order to place beyond cavil the authenticity of this new prize, Ireland consulted Mr. Hewlett of the Temple, an expert on old handwriting. With the aid of a magnifying glass Hewlett thought he could make out, at one corner of the drawing, faint traces of the name of John Hoskins, an artist of the time of James I. William Henry confesses that he himself was never, even with the aid of magnifiers, able to see anything looking like that name;

in his opinion Hewlett was misled by dint of the deeper black of the Indian ink of the background having sunk into some of the veining of the paper.

Almost daily William Henry had pampered his father with new discoveries he had unearthed among his noble friend's papers and in his library. But for the next few days the elder Ireland became concerned because his son returned home empty-handed. There was, however, good reason for this pretense of temporary defeat. For during those few days he was engaged in what was the grandest of his ventures to date—a love letter written by Shakespeare to his beloved Ann during the youthful days of courtship, as well as a love poem to her, both of these accompanied by a lock snipped from his own sublime head!

Dearesste Anna

As thou haste alwaye founde mee toe mye Worde moste trewe soe thou shalt see I have stryctlye kepte mye promyse I praye you perfume thys mye poore Locke withe thye balmye Kysses forre thenne indeede shalle Kynges themmeselves bowe and paye homage toe itte I doe assure thee no rude hande hathe knottedde itte thye Willys alone hathe done the worke Neytherre the gyldedde bawble thatte envyronnes the heade of Majestye noe norre honourres moste weyghtye wulde give mee halfe the joye as didde thysse mye lyttle worke forre thee The feelinge thatte dydde neareste approache untoe itte was thatte whiche comethe nygheste untoe God meeke and Gentle Charytye forre thatte Virrtue O Anna doe I love doe I cheryshe thee inne mye hearte forre thou arte as a talle Cedarre stretchynge forthe its branches ande succourynge smaller Plants fromme nyppynge Winneterre orr the boysterouse Wyndes Farewelle toe Morrowe bye tymes I wille see thee tille thenne Adewe sweete Love

Thyne everre
Wm Shakspeare

Anna Hatherrewaye

    Is there inne heavenne aught more rare
    Thanne thou sweete Nymphe of Avon fayre
    Is there onne Earthe a Manne more trewe
    Thanne Willy Shakspeare is toe you

    Though fyckle fortune prove unkynde
    Stille dothe she leave herre wealthe behynde
    she neere the hearte canne forme anew
    Norre make thye Willys love unnetrue

    Though Age withe witherd hand doth stryke
    The forme moste fayre the face moste bryghte
    Still dothe she leave unnetouchedde ande trewe
    Thy Willys love ande freynshyppe too

    Though deathe with neverre faylynge blowe
    Dothe Manne ande babe alyke brynge lowe
    Yette doth he take naughte butte hys due
    And strikes notte Willys hearte still trewe

    Synce thenne norre forretune deathe norre Age
    Canne faythfulle Willys love asswage
    Thenne doe I live and dye forre you
    Thy Willye syncere ande moste trewe

A decade later William Henry unaffectedly explains his motive and procedures: "As our great dramatist was married very early in life . . . I became desirous of introducing to the world one of his love effusions of that early period. . . . As the engraving of Shakspeare . . . represents our bard as having short straight and wiry hair, I selected a lock of a similar kind, then in my possession (which in my boyish days had been given me as a *gage d'amour*)." From an old vendor of parchments in Clare Market he had already bought some royal patents of Henry VIII, Mary, and Elizabeth, the great seals of which were affixed to the parchment with thick woven silk about four inches in length. He thought that one of the pieces of woven silk would lend an imposing air to the lock of hair, and in the accompanying love letter he emphasized the workmanship of the silk to intimate that it was the product of the Bard's own labor. When William Henry reflected on the many people who were dumbstruck at the lock of hair, people who were accustomed to inspecting grants and charters, "most of them having a similar twist" of silk, he was much astonished that no one remarked on the silk. As for the lock, small bits of it "were distributed into several rings."

Despite their silliness, the letter and poem evoked greater peals of praise than ever from Samuel Ireland and his friends. Both were found replete with "the utmost delicacy of passion and poetical spirit," by the enthusiastic editor of the *Oracle,* James Boaden—soon to become one of the Irelands' staunchest foes.

As William Henry's successes turned his head more and more, and as he was encouraged by the ignorance of the learned to think of himself as perhaps the Bard's equal in genius, he grew more and more reckless with his spelling. The letter and verses give token of an approaching lunacy in this respect. Though he had occasionally spelled wildly in the preceding forgeries, here the insane exaggerations began to assert themselves with alarming frequency. No longer content to add a final *e,* change an *i* to *y,* and double a consonant now and then, he began to indulge himself in quaintness: *dearesste, forre, thenne, themmeselves, itte, knottedde, gyldedde, thatte, fromme, winneterre,* etc. Nothing, in the long run, tended more to undo him than this orthographical extravagance.

The next project was equally bold and important. Its purpose was "to make our bard appear so much of consequence in his own time as to be personally noticed" by no less a person than Elizabeth herself. During the excited discussion of his discoveries, held in his father's library, he heard the Honorable John Byng, purchaser of the crossbar and a slice of Shakespeare's fireside chair at the Birthplace in Stratford, speak often of a letter supposed to have been written by James I to Shakespeare. Perhaps, Byng declared, that precious lost missive would be found among the anonymous gentleman's papers. That hope was expressed so often that William Henry thought the fabrication of such a letter would "be too obvious." He therefore decided on one from the Queen, in the preparation of which he was aided by an original autograph of hers, a facsimile of which he had easy access to in his father's collection. Never had Elizabeth been so informal as when addressing Shakespeare:

> Wee didde receive youre prettye Verses goode Masterre William through the hands off oure Lorde Chamberlayne ande wee doe Complemente thee onne theyre greate excellence Wee shalle departe fromm Londonne toe Hamptowne forre the holydayes where wee Shalle expecte thee withe thye beste Actorres thatte thou mayste playe before oureselfe toe amuse usse bee notte slowe butte comme toe usse bye Tuesdaye nexte asse the lorde Leicesterre wille bee withe usse
>
> Elizabeth R

> Thys Letterre I dydde receyve fromme mye moste gracyouse Ladye Elizabethe ande I doe requeste itte maye bee kepte withe alle care possyble
>
> Wm Shakspeare
> For Master William Shakspeare atte the Globe bye Thames

How good a friend to the Bard is her Majesty revealed! But not any better a friend than William Henry himself. This newest forgery shows how the Bard, though indifferent to the publication of his plays as well as to the preservation of his own manuscripts, was a most loyal subject of his Virgin Sovereign, and therefore careful to preserve this effusion of hers.

William Henry's ambition to cause Shakespeare to emerge as

a person of consequence in his epoch was at once achieved. Later so clearheaded about these manuscripts, the editor of the *Oracle* was at first as delightedly muddleheaded as everyone else; he declared that this letter proved that the old stories about the Bard's having to hold horses outside the theatre to earn his living when he first came to London were unadulterated and degrading nonsense—that Shakespeare was now proved to have been petted and spoiled, as he should have been, by the illustrious of his epoch—that as an actor he was, in short, now to be seen as the "Garrick of his age." (There is no evidence that Shakespeare was much of an actor. He did not have to be.)

There are, unhappily, a few inconvenient facts overlooked by the forger and his admirers. Elizabeth, lending a lovely touch of historical coloring to her missive, mentions Leicester—which necessarily dates the letter prior to 1588, the year of Leicester's death. At that time Shakespeare was only twenty-four, had been in London for not more than two years, and certainly had as yet had small opportunity to establish himself either as actor or writer worthy the notice of his queen. Moreover, the letter is directed to the Globe Theatre, which in 1588 was not yet in existence.

Concerning the contents there are at least two further objections. The Queen assuredly would never have called a player, no matter how gifted, her "good Master William." Nor is it likely that she would, for that player's sake, have penned the entire letter herself, addressing it, as Waldron later put it, "as if it were to be sent by the penny-post," instead of merely, as usual, writing only her royal name.

Some time before this William Henry had told Ireland that in his benevolent friend's old chest there reposed a handwritten copy of one of the tragedies. Our forger was operating at an almost incredible speed, but he preferred to postpone the arduous task of providing the text of a complete play in antique handwriting and spelling while triumphs could be won with brief expenditures of time and ingenuity. Besides, for his purposes he did not wish to use the Folio version of whichever play he would hit upon; he needed, he felt, a Quarto published during the Bard's own lifetime. Early in 1795 Samuel Ireland acquired a Quarto edition of *King Lear,* and William Henry was ready for one of his most outrageous creations.

A true son of the eighteenth century, William Henry was bound to improve on Shakespeare. He later calmly admitted: "As it was generally deemed extraordinary that the productions of Shakespeare should be found so very unequal, and in particular that so much ribaldry should appear throughout his dramatic compositions, I determined on the expedient of rewriting, in the old hand, one of his most conspicuous plays, and making such alterations as I conceived appropriate." Borrowing his father's copy, he brought it to his employer's chambers, where he worked at this ambitious forgery assiduously—with appalling results. The Second Quarto of *King Lear,* dated 1608, which he used as his basis is far from an ideal text, but the mayhem which William Henry visited upon Shakespeare's masterpiece by way of excisions, substitutions, additions, and confusions of meaning is truly beyond belief.

But the century was so well habituated to the violence done to Shakespeare's lines by his improvers and adapters, that many of the Bard's most fervent admirers were in no position to recognize the spurious. Since he avoided "the insertion of that ribaldry which is so frequently found in the compositions of our bard," William Henry's small public was all the more pleased. (Actually, Shakespeare's bawdry is almost maidenly when compared with that of his contemporaries.) The consequence of William Henry's *Lear* was the consensus that this "authentic" version from the hand of the master himself proved Shakespeare to be "a much more finished writer than had ever been before imagined."

It is a fact that the tamperings of the players with Shakespeare's text have sometimes found their way into the printed versions of his plays. Indeed, there are a couple of such passages, peculiarly inane, allotted to the Fool in this very play. But such interpolations are few, and the reader who knows his Shakespeare can identify them as readily as if they were printed in red ink. The passages which William Henry chose to delete are not of this order. Yet, ten years after the event he still writes of his vandalism as though he had been led by some supernatural intuition to purify the text of what he chose to consider spurious lines.

The most obvious eccentricity of William Henry's *Lear* is the spelling. For reasons best known to himself, though he had the Jacobean spelling before him in the Quarto, he let himself go mad. For example:

THE QUARTO PRINTS	WILLIAM HENRY SPELLS IT
in the diuision of the Kingedoms it appeares not	inne the divysyonne of the Kyngdomme itte appeares notte
acknowledged	acknowleggedde
Propinquity	Propinnequitye
Scythian	Scythyanne
region	Reygonne
clamour	clammourre
Princes	Prinneces
infirmities	Innefyrmytyes
Unfriended, new adopted	Unnefreynnededde newe adoppetedde
obseruation	Obserrevatyonne
brother	brotherre
indignation	Innedygnatyonne
friendship fals off, brothers divide	Freyndeshyppe dyvides ande brotherres are notte soe [a little example of W. H.'s improvement on the text]
villanous melancholy	Villaynouse Melanncholye
answered	annesweredde
leaue thy drinke and they whore	leave thye drynke ande thye hope [!]
Candle	Cannedelle
discernings are lethargy	dyscerrenynges are letharregye
perswaded	perreswadedde
untender	unnetennederre

And these are but a handful of expressions chosen at random from the earlier scenes of Act I!

When the discerning few presently pointed out the absurdity of the spelling, the *Lear* manuscript was parodied merrily in the press. The *British Critic* suggested that a passage from Lyly's *Euphues,* as printed in 1585, "There is no privilege that needeth a pardon neither is there any remission to bee asked where a commission is graunted," in the Ireland papers would have run, "Theyre isse noe pryvyledgde thatte needethe a parredonne, neytherre isse theyre annye permyssyonne toe bee askedde where a commyssyonne isse graunetedde." And the *Telegraph* invented an invitation from Shakespeare to a good friend: "Tooo Missteerree Beenjaammiinnee Joohnnssonn, Deeree Sirree, Wille youe doee meee theee favvourree too dinnee wythee mee onnn Friddaye nextte attt twoo off theee clockee too eatee sommee muttonne choppes andd somme poottaattooeesse, I ammm deeerree sirree, Yourre goodde friendde WILLIAME SHAEKSPARE."

But the mutilations visited upon the play itself are even more shocking. No one was more delighted with them than Samuel Ireland. When he published the documents for the world to enjoy, he said in his Preface that he considered "the recovery of the original" of Shakespeare's *Lear* "an important accession to the Literature of his Country." This version of the play shows our Bard in the native simple "undress" of style before other hands tampered with his work. The reader will note, Ireland observes, that every time this original text varies from the heretofore printed versions, he will find Shakespeare's "simple phraseology and sentences framed according to their natural order"; the alterations of others have resulted in "tumor" and gaudiness and "hardness." Ireland singles out passages from William Henry's version to show their superiority. Whereas the 1608 Quarto has for the Steward's speech in II, ii (*all italics mine*):

Tript me behinde, being downe, insulted, raild,
And put *upon him such a deale of* man

> That worthied him, *got* praises of the King,
> *For him attempting who was self subdued,*
> *And in the f1echuent* [misprint for "fleshment"] *of this dread* exploit
> Drew on mee heere againe,

the newly discovered manuscript reads:

> Tript mee behynde beynge downe insultedde raylde
> And putte *onne hymme soe muche o the* Manne
> That worthyedde hymme *ande gotte* hymme prayses o the Kynge
> *Ande forre the Attempt of thys hys softe subdud exployte*
> Drewe oune mee here agayne.

In the next scene the Quarto has Edgar plan to "*with presented nakednes out-face/ The winde,*" whereas William Henry–Shakespeare actually had written, "*inne Adam lyke Nakeddenesse* . . ." In the same scene the Quarto reads:

> I woud divorce *me* from thy mothers *toombe,*
> *Sepulchring an adultress,*

whereas the Ireland-Bard's lines were:

> I would divorce *thee* fromme thye Motherres *Wombe*
> *And say the Motherre was an Adultresse.*

Samuel Ireland left it to his readers to appreciate the "manly plainness and simplicity" of the Bard's true style. Moreover, as regards the superiority of William Henry's "original" version, Ireland "rests not so much on the several beautiful passages here given . . . as he does on the natural course of the dialogue and turn of thought." The reader will observe, Ireland is sure, how often the later versions have lost these qualities.

There are differences in William Henry's version much more remarkable for their silliness, though his father did not cite them to illustrate the power of this *Lear* "original." Of one of these William Henry remained very proud. It occurs during the last minutes of the play. In response to Albany's invitation to participate in the rule of the kingdom, Kent has two lines, his last in the tragedy:

> I haue a iuorney sir, shortly to go,
> My master cals, and I must not say no.

Our forger improved on the Quarto in this style:

> Thanks Sir butte I goe toe thatte unknowne Land
> Thatte Chaynes each Pilgrim faste within its Soyle
> Bye livynge menne mouste shunnd mouste dreadedde
> Stille mye goode masterre thys same Journey tooke
> He calls mee I amme contente ande strayght obeye
> Thenne farewelle Worlde the busye Sceane is done
> Kente livd mouste true Kente dyes mouste lyke a Manne

Ten years later William Henry justified this interpolation by saying that he could not "conceive such a jingling and unmeaning
couplet" as the Bard had actually written for Kent as "very appropriate." The sheer cheek of this meddling would be startling if
we did not remember that people as revered as Garrick had done
Shakespeare as much ill.

Every student of Elizabethan drama is familiar with the fact
that once a play had been written, it no longer belonged to the
dramatist but to the company for which he had composed it. To
keep the text out of rival companies' hands the owners of the play
were not anxious to see it in print. Like all his contemporaries
Shakespeare, particularly since he was part owner of his company, made no effort to have his plays published. Those that were
issued during his lifetime were printed without his consent. These
facts make the modest legend which William Henry inscribed at
the head of his version of the *Tragedye of Kinge Leare* very odd
indeed:

> Isse fromme Masterre Hollinneshedde I have inne
> somme lyttle deparretedde fromme hymme butte thatte
> Libbertye will notte I truste be blamedde bye mye gentle
> Readerres
>
> Wm Shakspeare

Shakespeare was indeed indebted to Holinshed for more than one
of his plots, nor had he ever scrupled to depart from him more
than a little. The superscription is strange from a man who gave

no thought to possible readers of his plays!

Young Ireland's *Lear* turned out to be the greatest triumph of all. Cried the editor of the *Oracle:* he had always suspected "the *licentious* passages" of the received texts, and now his suspicions "are confirmed by the original!—they are not SHAKSPEARE's, but the foisted impurities of buffoons." Others joined the general exultation that a "better Shakspeare" was now unveiled to the view of his worshipers.

It at first seemed natural to the boy to follow up this great *coup* with another like it. To *Lear* he had been directed as much by treasured childhood memories of its performance at his Soho school as by his father's purchase of the Quarto. But *Hamlet* was the most popular of the tragedies. Why should he not do as much for it as he had done for *Lear?* However, the manufacture of the manuscript of another complete play—in this case, Shakespeare's longest—suddenly appeared a "plodding business." Moreover, he was now in gratifying demand in the Ireland circle. The luscious pleasure of witnessing the awe and respect of his elders took time away from his labors of the moment. He contented himself, therefore, by producing a few stray leaves from the Bard's *Hamblette,* beginning after the "To be or not to be" soliloquy. There are a few speeches and the next leaf skips to the dialogue preceding the performance of the Mousetrap. Here he had the satisfying opportunity to expunge Hamlet's indecencies to Ophelia and her embarrassed replies. The leaf ends where the Dumb Show begins. The last leaf presents the murder of Polonius. Though brief, these few pages settled for everyone the Bard's "correctness as a writer," and "everything unworthy of our bard was laid to the charge of players and printers."

Reveling in his importance, William Henry permitted himself a brief intermission in the contrivance of his forgeries. Though the thousand questions put to him charged the atmosphere with threat, he was divinely happy. How long had it taken the lad to produce his imposing array of Shakespeareana? Considering the fact that everything was executed only during the free hours at his disposal at the conveyancer's chambers, and also that it took time for him to conceive the compositions, purchase the old paper on which to write them, find the ink and the string, repair the damage to the seal, and hunt for the various volumes of the Shakespeare Library, it would seem none too generous to allow him several years for all his inventions. The actual time he consumed is perhaps the most surprising aspect of the whole business.

He presented the first of the Shakespeare documents, the mortgage deed, to his father on December 16, 1794. The rest which we have thus far discussed, excepting the *Lear* (which was nearing completion) and the pages from *Hamlet,* were in Samuel Ireland's possession by the latter part of January, 1795. His son had amassed all of them in five or, at the most, six weeks.

The demonic rapidity with which these "discoveries" came to light was the most powerful cause of averting any suspicion that they could have been contrived. To have unearthed so much so rapidly would have been an accomplishment for an adult who had devoted all his time to rummaging in the noble gentleman's collection, and in shuttling back and forth from his London chambers to a house in the country. Even now, when the facts are beyond dispute, it remains almost inconceivable that one human being, boy or man, could have turned out that quantity in less than a month and a half. The lad's energies were as inexhaustible as the boughs of the Mulberry Tree.

SIX

Madness in Little Ones . . .

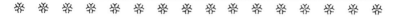

But what, during these six weeks, what of the wonderful anonymous gentleman, the donor of all these blessings?

Samuel Ireland was not the man to rest content with the gifts, particularly when the benefactor was a man of rank, without pressing his son for more specific information and, if possible, establishing personal relations with him himself. But to all his questions and those of his visitors the boy would reveal nothing more than that the gentleman could not be identified further than as "Mr. H."—did young William Henry hit upon this name because it was the designation of the hero of his beloved novel, *Love and Madness?*—and that Mr. H. "being possessed of a large fortune, and being well aware of the inquiries which must take place on the production of the papers, did not think fit to subject himself to the impertinent questionings of every individual who conceived himself licensed to demand an explanation concerning them; that he in consequence gave me the documents as mere curiosities, exacting at the same time a most solemn asseveration that I would keep his name for ever concealed."

Still the wonder remained for Ireland senior, who persisted in thinking of his son as essentially a stupid boy, as well as for Ireland's friends: why should these treasures come, of all people, to William Henry? To their middle-class minds giving away anything for nothing seemed to verge on the insane. To give away these priceless riches—and to a mere lad, not overbright! In order to silence these objections William Henry devised an explanation.

"I stated that during my research among the deeds of my friend I discovered one which established his right to certain property that had long been an object of litigation; on which account he conceived the giving me the Shakspearian manuscripts for the service I had rendered him." This did not account at all for the earlier gifts, but it allayed the doubts of the half-convinced. To nail down the matter the boy was inspired to fabricate another tall tale. Mr. H. had caused the Attorney-General to draw up a deed in which it was specified that all discoveries of Shakespeareana which might hereafter be made in Mr. H.'s store were to go to William Henry Ireland. Naturally, to protect himself from the importunities of the curious, this deed was always to be guarded under lock and key in Mr. H.'s possession.

Samuel Ireland was overwhelmed at Mr. H.'s nobility, and drawn to further reflections on his superior benevolence when William Henry soon thereafter related that a friend of Mr. H.'s, having been informed of the discoveries, had written to Mr. H. offering him £2,000 for the right to search for further finds in the precious chest. Mr. H. had thereupon left it to William Henry to decide. If the boy were agreeable, the friend could have whatever papers remained and young Ireland could take the £2,000. William Henry, naturally, had rejected the offer. The friend, not satisfied, had come in person to offer Mr. H. £2,500. Indignant at the vulgarity, Mr. H. had ordered his erstwhile friend out of the house.

Such inventions served only momentarily to quiet the elder Ireland's questions about Mr. H., and his anxiety to see the portrait, the carnelian intaglio, the folio volumes, and the Holinshed. Quite suddenly an opening presented itself for possible explorations on his own. William Henry had announced the most marvelous discovery of all, a heretofore unknown play by Shakespeare, written out in the Bard's own handwriting! The elder Ireland was just then preparing his *Picturesque Views* of the Avon for the press, and could not resist saying in the Preface that he had had "the singular pleasure of obtaining a treasure" which had thus far escaped "the most assiduous and active" researcher, and that the author of the present work intended "to lay before the public a variety of authentic and important documents respecting the private and public life of this wonderful man [Shakespeare]: one of his most affecting and admired Tragedies written with his own hand [i.e., *Lear*], and differing in various particulars of much curiosity and interest from any edition of that work extant, and at a future day to present a picture of that mind which no one has yet ever presumed to copy, an entire Drama! yet unknown to the world in his own handwriting." This was certainly counting his chickens before they hatched: the *Lear* had not yet been delivered, and the unknown play not even identified. Old Samuel could be as reckless as his son. It was only a duty, he continued, to make this disclosure in a book connected with the Avon, "on whose banks nature has in a happy and propitious hour teemed forth her proudest work."

Now it occurred to Ireland that it would be appropriate to send the proofs of his Preface to Mr. H. together with a request for permission to speak of the as yet undelivered and unknown play. This he did on the last day of January, 1795. In the accompanying letter, which he asked William Henry to deliver for him, he delicately reminded Mr. H. of that full-length portrait.

The occasion, fraught with danger, nevertheless opened new horizons to the lad. He was able to hand his father a prompt answer from Mr. H., quite beautifully written, praising the old man for "the genteel manner" in which the Preface had been sent, and for the pleasure afforded him in reading the proofs. He went on, did Mr. H., to settle a few matters which had been discussed in Norfolk Street: "For the portrait (though *I assure you* your son shall have it) for particular reasons as yet I wish to keep secret, but I may even say more it is a delicate business which remains alone in the bosom of your son for I will frankly own all he has yet said has been with my concurrence but he is acquainted with much more which I trust and am assured he has never mentioned. It may appear strange that a young man like myself should have thus formed a friendship for one he has little knowledge of, but I do assure you *Dr. sir* without flattery he is a young man after *my own heart* in whom I would confide and even consult on the nicest affair. In spring (with joy I say it) I shall hope for the Pleasure of seeing him, when I do assure you all shall be his own. As he seems to speak much of the Lear for *you,* and for which I still esteem him more and more, you shall in a short time have it not from *me* but through his hands." The gentleman further begged to be forgiven his "familiarity," but he confessed that he could not write more formally to "the father of one whom I esteem."

The script of this charming letter was elegant, though the bonds strengthening the ties among Mr. H., William Henry, and William Henry's Shakespeareana seem to have included a common distaste for punctuation and logical syntax. These were mild shortcomings when they were as true of the Bard as the other two. Moreover, Mr. H. kept his word: in a few days Ireland had the manuscript of *King Lear.*

Enchanted with this message, Ireland received another one the next day: "Excuse the liberty I have taken in addressing you a second time, it is merely to let you know the particular desire I have that your son should take himself one of the parts in the new play. . . . Should you wish at any time to communicate anything to me, I shall be always sure of receiving it through the hands of my Dear young friend." Though the new play had not even a name as yet, Ireland thought this matter over carefully, and concluded that William Henry might appear in it on opening night only.

A correspondence now began to flourish between Ireland and

the gentleman. William Henry permitted his friend to be his advocate on many matters in which he himself did not dare oppose his father. Mr. H., for instance, expressed surprise that Mr. Ireland could approve of the Ministry and its new taxes; Mr. H., for one, was resolved to use no more powder in his hair: "All who contribute their guineas for Powder give money for the support of the war. . . . My hair is now combed to its real color and will remain hanging loosely on my shoulders 'that Ladys may now perfume it with their balmy kisses.' [a reference to the Bard's letter to his beloved Anna Hatherrewaye] Besides, you cannot be an enemy to the manner in which our *Willy* wore his hair. Let me I beseech you see your son with flowing locks, it is not only manly but showing yourself averse to bloodshed." Like a true son of Britain, Ireland glowed with pleasure at the notice of a man of rank, but, also like a true son of Britain, he was ruffled at this meddling with his private affairs and political views. He was not going to be told how to raise his son. Though his views must have been fairly radical, to judge by his circle of friends, it was quite another thing to have them dictated by anyone else, no matter what his station. No Briton has ever tolerated that. He rebuffed the impertinence by failing to reply to it.

And now there were great doings in Norfolk Street. Early in February, 1795, Ireland decided that the collection was already extensive enough to justify parading it before the world. He opened his house for the public exhibition of the Shakespeare Papers, and the great and near-great thronged his library to see, and hear him read as he sat in Shakespeare's Courting Chair. One and all were satisfied that the documents were authentic.

No admirer was more fervent than James Boaden (1762–1839), later to be a fervent opponent, the editor of the *Oracle*, and a journalist, dramatist, and biographer. He was a man of considerable knowledge and charming manners, witty in his conversation, and with a large store of anecdotes. On February 16, he wrote in the *Oracle:* "By the obliging politeness of Mr. Ireland, of Norfolk Street, the conductor of this paper is enabled to gratify, in a general way, the public curiosity. To particularize would be fraudulent and ungrateful. Besides the Lear and Vortigern, there are various papers, the *domestica facta* of this great man's life, discovered." The letter "to the lady he afterwards married" is "distinguished for the utmost delicacy of passion and poetical spirit." The Profession of Faith is "rationally pious, and grandly expressed." As for the entire mass, "the conviction produced upon our mind, is such as to make all scepticism ridiculous, and when we follow the sentiments of Dr. Joseph Warton, we have no fear of our critical orthodoxy."

The danger of committing one's convictions to print! Boaden would shortly be eating his words, and he was making it more and more difficult for himself to do so. On February 21 his enthusiasm rose higher: "When we were favored with a sight of these invaluable remains, we promised the possessor that no sneering animadversions, written by those who had never seen them, should pass without reply, and probably reproof. One gentleman makes himself merry with a Profession of Faith from Shakspere; he shall be reduced at once to the plea of Ignoramus—there happens to be indisputable proof that this was the custom of the age, nay, that other members of the same family had done so." Among those who had never examined the Papers it had been rumored that an expert on Elizabethan handwriting was unable to decipher them. Boaden countered to this his readiness to prove his own acquaintance with Elizabethan script and his ability to read the Shakespeare Papers.

On February 26 Boaden called at Norfolk Street, expressed again his enthusiasm for the Papers, and the next day wrote Ireland a letter certifying a bit of Elizabethan history which they had discussed, and concluding, "this, or any deeper inquiry, will be but a poor return for the favor of your unreserved communication." On April 23, Shakespeare's birthday, Boaden said in his newspaper: "The Shakesperiana, which have been so luckily discovered, are now considered as genuine by all but those who illiberally refuse to be convinced by inspection." In short, no voice was steadier than Boaden's in his admiration of the forgeries. There had been, indeed, few to join in the dissent first raised on February 17 by the *Morning Herald,* which branded the Papers as false.

At the moment the discordant note was unheard in the chorus of enthusiastic praise. Francis Webb was speaking for the rest when he reminded the world that Shakespeare was truly unique, truly matchless, and that the Ireland Papers "bear indubitable proofs of his sublime genius, boundless imagination, pregnant wit, and intuitive sagacity into the workings of the human mind." These discoveries came either "from his pen or from Heaven."

It was inevitable with all the attention Norfolk Street was receiving that Boswell should appear there. He came on February 20. William Henry's account is certainly graphic. "The papers were as usual placed before him; when he commenced his examination of them; and being satisfied as to their antiquity . . . he proceeded to examine the style of the language from the fair transcripts made from the disguised handwriting. In this research Mr. Boswell continued for a considerable time, constantly speaking in favor of the internal as well as external proofs of the validity of the manuscripts. At length, finding himself rather thirsty, he requested a tumbler of warm brandy and water; which having nearly finished, he redoubled his praises of the manuscripts; and at length arising from his chair, he made use of the following expression: 'Well, I shall now die contented, since I have lived to witness the present day.' Mr. Boswell then kneeling down before the volume containing a portion of the papers, continued, 'I now kiss the invaluable relics of our bard: and thanks to God that I have lived to see them!' Having kissed the volume with every token of reverence, Mr. Boswell shortly after quitted Mr. Ireland's house." James Boswell, he of the insatiable curiosity, had had the crowning experience of a life given to the search for notable experience. Nor is it on record that he was ever put to the pain of disillusionment in these sacred relics, for he died but three months later, on May 19.

It did not take long, however, to swell the envious murmurs of the *Morning Herald*. Boswell, who was not going to have his joy ruined by the malicious, at once drew up a certificate vouching for the validity of the Papers (though he was in no way qualified to pass as an expert), and graciously gave it to Samuel Ireland. He in turn showed it the next day to Dr. Parr, who "exclaimed with his characteristic energy . . . that it was too feebly expressed for the importance of the subject, and begged that he might himself dictate" a formal statement. To this Ireland naturally agreed. Five days after Boswell's visit, on February 25 to be precise, the statement was issued. It included the signatures of some important men: "We whose names are hereunto subscribed have, in the presence and by the favor of Mr. Ireland, inspected the Shakspeare papers, and are convinced of their authenticity." Then followed these names: Parr; John Tweddell (1769–1799), a classical scholar, fellow of Trinity College, Cambridge—later he became involved in archaeological work at Athens, where he died, and was buried at his own request in the Theseum; Thomas Burgess (1756–1837), prebend of Durham Cathedral, and thereafter Bishop of Salisbury—he had been tutor and fellow at Corpus Christi College, Oxford, and was the editor of numerous classical works as well as an important Hebrew scholar and friend of the bluestocking Hannah More; Hon. John Byng, purchaser of parts of the Shakespeare Chair at the Birthplace and close friend to Samuel Ireland; James Bindley (1737–1818), book collector and leader of the Society of Antiquaries—he owned a valuable collection of rare books, engravings, and medals; Herbert Croft, author of *Love and Madness,* the novel which was partially responsible for William Henry's forgeries; Somerset (1775–1855), a young nobleman of William Henry's age, who had succeeded to the Dukedom in 1793, and was already an antiquarian and mathematician; Is. Heard, Garter King of Arms (1730–1833), antiquarian of great distinction; F. Webb (1735–1815), now secretary to Sir Isaac Heard and formerly a Nonconformist minister, one of the most enthusiastic supporters of the documents, and the author of miscellaneous writings; R. Valpy (1754–1836), headmaster at Reading School, known to be one of "the hardest floggers" of his day, despite which reputation he was loved by his students—his grammar textbooks were widely in use, he was an enthusiast for English and Latin poetry, and his adaptation of Shakespeare's *King John* was performed at Covent Garden in 1803; James Boswell; Lauderdale (1759–1839), Scottish earl, a leader of the Whigs, friend of leading French revolutionists, violent-tempered, shrewd, and eccentric; Rev. J. Scott (1733–1814), author of various poems, some satirical—he came to London when his parishioners in Northumberland tried to kill him for starting legal proceedings against them for the tithes; Kinnaird (d. 1805), seventh baron of that name, notable Whig; John Pinkerton (1758–1826), Scottish antiquary and historian, author of a book of "ancient Scottish ballads" soon proved to be largely his own compositions (a charge he readily admitted)—he was devoted to research, but was eccentric and prejudiced; Thomas Hunt; Henry James Pye (1745–1813), Poet Laureate, the feeblest England ever had, a decent man but totally devoid of poetic talent or feelings—Scott said of him that he was "eminently respectable in everything but his poetry"; Rev. N. Thornbury; Jonn. Hewlett, Translator of Old Records, Common Pleas Office, Temple (1762–1844), biblical scholar, well known for his profound knowledge of the Arundel marbles; Mat. Wyatt; John Frank Newton.

Such an imposing array of Believers, including scholars from every possible generation, was hardly calculated to induce modesty in William Henry or to suggest that he ought to desist from his efforts in the Bard's behalf.

Among those privileged to sit in the Shakespeare Courting Chair was John Taylor (1757–1832), first dramatic critic then editor of the *Morning Post,* and later purchaser of the *True Briton.* A frequenter of the Turk's Head coffee-house and a member of the Keep-the-Line Club, he was an intimate of actors, devotees of the theatre, and most of the literati of London. Wordsworth thought well enough of him to send him his poems. The author of much prose and facile verse, Taylor has left us some gossipy memoirs.

He was invited to inspect the Shakespeare Papers, though he considered himself unqualified to decide upon their authenticity. He went with a committee "of many very respectable and intelligent characters." They examined the documents and the Shakespeare Library, met William Henry, and heard from Albany Wallace, "an eminent solicitor," that the time was not yet ripe to disclose the source of these treasures. "At a future meeting a full explanation should be given."

Later, when it became known that *Vortigern* was to be produced, Taylor visited the Irelands again, this time in the company of an unidentified lawyer and John Gifford, a Tory pamphleteer and journalist. The three were to hear Ireland senior read the play so that "we might form some judgment as to its merits and authenticity." After tea had been dispatched, the reading commenced and "I requested to sit in Shakespeare's chair, as it might contain some inspiring power to enlighten my understanding, and enable me the better to judge. They laughed at my whim, but indulged me." During the reading, there was one passage which "Mr. Ireland admitted to be so quaint and unintelligible, that it would not be suitable to the modern stage." Ireland asked the lawyer and Gifford to suggest some alteration of the lines. "When they declined to propose anything, he asked me if I could suggest any modification of it. At this question I affected to start, and said, 'Good bless me, shall I sit in Shakespeare's chair, and presume to think I can improve any work from his unrivaled muse?' " *

It may well be asked how so many people who should have known better could have fallen prey to the deceptions of an adolescent. There are enough facts to account for the phenomenon. First of all, the parchments and papers *were* old, as were the impressions on the seals. Next, the color of the ink seemed right to the naked eye. The handwriting itself *looked* old. The spelling should have aroused suspicions perhaps; but it must be remembered that Elizabethan script was totally different from eighteenth-century handwriting, and would have required patient study to decipher it accurately. Samuel Ireland did not readily let the precious papers out of his hands, and in all probability the grateful viewer had to be content with looking at a given paper over its owner's shoulder. There must have been something of "The Emperor's New Clothes" here too; each certifier of the authenticity of the manuscripts made it more difficult for the next visitor to entertain doubts lest he prove his ignorance. For the most part, the enthusiasts were content to allow Ireland, royally seated in Shakespeare's Courting Chair (itself lending authority to the proceedings), read to them in a dramatic style suitable to the contents of the papers. It is significant that once he published the documents and his subscribers had the leisure to peruse them in print, the tide rapidly began to turn against the Believers.

But what of the content of the papers? Should not the Profession of Faith, all the letters, the poem to Ann Hathaway, and the absurd innovations in *Lear* (which were actually acclaimed as superior to the traditional texts)—should not any one of these, should not all of them taken together, have cried out their spuri-

---

* After the débacle, Taylor met William Henry one night at the theater. "To show me with what facility he could copy the signatures of Shakespeare, of which there are but two extant, and they differ from each other, he took a pencil and a piece of paper from his pocket, and wrote both of them with as much speed and exactness as if he had been writing his own name. He gave the paper to me; I compared the signatures with the printed autographs of the poet, and could not but be surprised at their accuracy."

ousness? Where was the feeling for Shakespeare on the part of these scholars and antiquarians, where was their esthetic judgment?

Let us not be too hard on them. Their resources were very different from those of modern professional Shakespearean scholars. Our contemporaries have available a vast amount of factual knowledge concerning Shakespeare's age which was not available to anyone in 1795, and surely even the most mediocre of twentieth-century commentators would, by the mere accumulation of data which has been pumped into him, have been protected against being taken in by William Henry's forgeries. For that the contemporary scholar would deserve no credit. On the other hand, if he were required to render a verdict based solely on his feeling for Shakespeare, the modern professional scholar might well be at a greater loss than those eighteenth-century gentlemen. He has been trained to avoid esthetic judgments. There is nothing he has been taught more to distrust than taste. Since modern scholarship has chosen to deny the validity of esthetic judgments, and thinks itself safe in relying upon dates above all other matters, the bulk of modern Shakespearean scholarship is merely vapid, esoteric, and false to the very fundamentals of literary creation. That William Henry's dupes were misled solely by the appearance of paper, parchment, ink, handwriting, and such external matters should not strike the modern Shakespearean critic as odd. These are precisely the sorts of proof which he holds infallible, and he would be the first to raise his eyebrows at anyone foolhardy enough to exclaim, "But Shakespeare *couldn't* have written that!" So far as the modern Shakespearean scholar knows, Shakespeare could have written *anything*, if the dates and external records indicate the possibility.

Thus encouraged, Samuel Ireland, without consulting his son, now decided out of hand to publish his treasure. Such a venture, he felt sure, would smoke out the reluctant Mr. H. On March 3 he wrote to him, via young William Henry, asking for more informa-

tion on the history of the documents for the Preface of his projected volume. Naturally, it was not a question of their authenticity, so far as he himself was concerned—there could not be "a
shadow of doubt in the mind of the candid." But there are people
of another stamp. Would not such declare that though the deeds
and even the plays might have fallen into the hands of John
Heminge, as a friend of the Bard's, "yet it cannot with the same
propriety be admitted that letters to his wife, his Profession of
Faith, and other circumstances of a domestic nature, should have
gone with them?" He did not wish to be understood as suggesting
the use of Mr. H.'s name; that was safe with him until death "if
required." Nevertheless, he confessed, "I yet flatter myself that I
may one day have the happiness and honor of personally being
acquainted with the Gent. who is with so much sincerity the
friend of my son." William Henry was at his wit's end as to what
to do about this letter.

Ireland's chief purpose in writing had been to know where he
would stand when the papers were published. But had he perhaps ruined matters for himself? Would the noble Mr. H. angrily
withdraw his offer of all the other wonderful treasures that had
been promised: the unknown original play, the full-length portrait, the intaglio, the Holinshed, the Folio volumes—and who
knows what other precious jewels? He and his friends had asked
William Henry again and again whether Mr. H. would consent
to have his gifts published, and the boy always answered, "They
were only given to me as curiosities; and by no means will the
gentleman agree to their being made public." To which his father
had recently replied, "If the gentleman be a friend of yours, why
does he set his face against a publication which it is admitted on
all hands would be productive of a fortune to you?"

This constant pestering began to make William Henry miserable, and for the first time he asked his father, "Supposing they
should not be really manuscripts of Shakspeare's?" His father
sneered at his son's ignorance. "If all the men of abilities living,"

he replied, "were now to come forward and severally attest that each had undertaken his particular part to produce these papers, I would not believe them." Already Samuel Ireland had canceled out any possibility that his son was bright enough to have had anything to do with originating the papers. As for the boy, he was now so terrified at the imminence of a publication that he was very near confessing himself the forger. But his father having taken such a stand, how would he ever credit his son's confession?

One day after dinner, "to procure some peace," William Henry exclaimed suddenly, "Well, sir, if you are determined on publishing the papers, I deliver this message from the gentleman —'You do it at your own risk' as he will have no concern in the business or ever give up his name to the world."

Ireland accepted the terms. In his own way he was as vain and as reckless as his son. Indeed, on March 4, the day after writing to Mr. H. about proposed publication of the papers, he issued his prospectus without waiting for a reply. It announced that the materials would "speedily be put to press," and gave an account of them. The descriptions were such as to arouse curiosity: Southampton was identified only as "a noble personage," and the Profession was spoken of as "the expression and feeling of his very soul upon a subject the most momentous that can occupy the thoughts of mortal man." The price to subscribers was to be four guineas. "Any gentleman, on sending his address in writing, or being introduced by a subscriber, may view the MSS. at No. 8 Norfolk Street on Mondays, Wednesdays, and Fridays, between the hours of twelve and three. . . . Mr. Ireland informs the public that with the above papers was discovered an historical play, founded on the story of Vortigern and Rowena, taken from Holingshed, and which is in the handwriting of Shakspeare. This play being intended for theatrical representation, will not be printed till the eve of its appearance on the stage."

Mr. H. not having answered the letter of March 3, Ireland began to plague his son anew. In order to postpone matters William

Henry tried to raise new excitement by telling his father that Mr. H. was busy preserving the manuscript of the unknown play, *Vortigern*, by having made for it an iron case to be covered with crimson velvet, studded with gold, and to be embroidered with Shakespeare's arms.

A month passed without an answer from Mr. H. Samuel wrote again. His tone was one of complaint. He had had every reason to believe that he "should one day have the favor of becoming acquainted with a Gent." to whom he owed so much. This favor, it now appears, he is to be denied. He is consequently "deprived of laying before the public any authority as to the originality of the Papers." William Henry must have informed Mr. H. that there was a way of satisfying the public without mentioning Mr. H.'s name. The Ireland family is now "so involved and implicated in the business [Mr. H., if he existed, might have coolly responded that he had not asked them to be!], that something is absolutely necessary to be done, and that immediately, or the consequences may be fatal." If Mr. H. would only agree now to send along some of the pictures, drawings, and new papers which had been promised, they would constitute "a new specimen of evidence" and tend "to give authenticity to the Papers, and thereby give relief to the mind of an oppressed family." Ireland also hinted that another work (i.e., the *Picturesque Views* of the Avon), which he had prepared at considerable expense and which was now ready to be issued, would have to be withheld until the question of the Shakespeare manuscripts had been cleared for the public.

The last was no doubt an exaggeration. But there were a few grumblings beginning to be heard. A few weeks previous, in the March issue of the *Gentleman's Magazine* there had appeared a letter from K. S. He had seen Ireland's Prospectus, and was taken aback that such a publication "should be ushered forth with as little diffidence or preliminary apology." The manuscripts will not be accepted on the endorsement of the undiscriminating. "The public would certainly have been gratified to know that these extraordinary Mss. have been deemed genuine by Dr. Farmer, Messrs. Steevens or Malone." That alone could give the papers some standing. It is also strange that "an actual deposit of two guineas should be required before a scubscriber can obtain the privilege of admission to examine" the Papers. No objection could be made if the usual admission charge of a shilling were asked. A reasonable fee would enable everyone to judge for himself whether the papers are what they are claimed to be. No information has been given as to where these documents have been. All Mr. Ireland tells us is that they have "fallen into his hands" like the golden shower into Danaë's favored lap. Nor does K. S. like Ireland's calling Shakespeare "the mighty Father." That is "a denomination at which the very shade of our moral and modest poet would recoil."

K. S. was answered in the next issue of the same periodical. The anonymous writer accuses him of dishonesty, for his tone seems to seek no reply. As for Dr. Farmer and Messrs. Steevens and Malone, do they have a monopoly of authority on matters Shakespearean? Has this triumverate applied to see the Papers? They have not. Is not that their fault, rather than Mr. Ireland's? And why should Mr. Ireland ask only a shilling as admission to his priceless relics, so that the public may "view, tear, and steal" whatever it chooses?

In June K. S. published his rebuttal. Why need Farmer, Steevens, and Malone have applied for permission to see the Papers? Why should they risk applying when they have been given to understand "that the company of Shakespeare's editors was not wished?" There may be others who are as competent to judge as these three, but surely there are none who are more so. If they are not acceptable, why not ask scholars like Bishop Percy, Dr. Porson, Ritson, Chalmers, or Douce?

As a matter of fact, Dr. Parr had written Farmer a long letter in Ireland's house in his host's presence, urging that respected scholar to come to London for the express purpose of viewing the

Papers, as a duty to himself and the world. Richard Farmer, D.D., was a leading Shakespearean scholar of his day, and neither Johnson nor Steevens hesitated to avail themselves of his knowledge for their own editorial labors. His *Essay on the Learning of Shakspeare* is a classic in its field. He was a man of wide scholarship in English letters, and during his lifetime he amassed a large library of rare books. (It is an interesting comment on the availability of rare editions that though his library cost him under £500, when it was disposed of at his death it brought £2,210.) Though he was often in London, Farmer preferred not to leave the comforts of Cambridge to examine the Ireland papers, whatever his duties to the world.

As for his colleague Richard Porson, a truly great scholar, professor of Greek at Cambridge, he had been asked to sign the Certificate of Belief drawn up by Parr, but refused to do so; signing Professions of Faith, he said, was against his principles. The next year he wrote a letter to the *Morning Herald,* giving as his name "S. England," in complement to S. Ireland, and in it said that a learned friend had found "some of the lost tragedies of Sophocles" in an old trunk. As a specimen he gave twelve Greek iambic verses, which when translated turned out to be his version of a familiar rhyme, "Three Children Sliding on the Ice":

> Three children sliding on the ice
> Upon a summer's day,
> As it fell out, they all fell in,
> The rest they ran away.
> Now had these children been at home
> Or sliding on dry ground,
> Ten thousand to one penny
> They had not all been drowned.

Of course, the two men whose disapprobation was most to be dreaded were Steevens and Malone, the giants of Shakespearean scholarship.

George Steevens was a man of the most unfortunate inconsistencies of temperament. His importance to the development of

Shakespearean learning is beyond question. A lover of patient scholarship, he was the first to understand the significance of the quartos of Shakespeare's plays, most of them published during the dramatist's lifetime, though without authorization. Garrick generously loaned him his sizable library of quartos, and in 1766 Steevens issued a four-volume work containing twenty quarto plays as well as the quarto edition of the sonnets. Capable of the most painstaking study, and ever ready to aid the serious projects of other students, he was nevertheless subject to lapses of taste which are shocking. Thus, although he pleaded in vain with Garrick to restore the original *King Lear* to the stage, he also advised him to give *Hamlet* "with all the rubbish of the fifth act omitted," unless Garrick wished to present it after the tragedy as a farce. Garrick took his advice about the revisions, and was promptly attacked by Steevens in the periodicals in a manner fairly outrageous. Steevens was given to anonymous onslaughts against friend and foe alike. For example, it was he who, behind the scenes, more or less engineered the involvement of Garrick in the Shakespeare Jubilee. Yet, before and after the three-day fiasco at Stratford, he kept supplying the press with epigrams, verses, and letters ridiculing Garrick anonymously. As Garrick put it, "When I was busying myself about that foolish hobby-horse of mine, the Jubilee, my good friend Master Steevens was busying himself, every other day, in abusing me and the design." Steevens later boasted that he had published at least forty attacks on Garrick, because "it was fun to vex" him. It is not surprising that Garrick decided thereupon to put an end to their intimacy.

Boswell tells us that Steevens was known for his philanthropy to those in need, that he had a fine mind and was an excellent talker, but that he had the reputation of being malignant. Johnson corrected that: "He is not malignant. He is mischievous. He only means to vex them." Boswell argued that there was some evil in being mischievous. Though Steevens had declared he would "rather be a sodomite than an infidel," he did not scruple to carry off another man's wife, and Boswell concludes that Steevens was a man "of good principles but bad practice." Later, Boswell himself had cause for pique, for after publicly praising *The Life of Samuel Johnson* Steevens was going about privately disparaging the work. Perhaps the best estimate of Steevens was that of his friend Dr. Parr, who described him as "one of the wisest, most learned, but spiteful of men." Parr himself was always in the middle of some controversy, but there the similarity ends. For Parr enjoyed the direct attack and the open battle, whereas Steevens' methods were by preference subterranean.

Under the guise of perpetrating a practical joke Steevens himself indulged in a little bit of forgery. In 1763 he fabricated a letter, published in the *Theatrical Review,* which pretended to be from the hand of the Elizabethan playwright George Peele, describing a meeting at the Globe Theatre with Shakespeare and other dramatists. Taken seriously, this document was later reprinted, and for a time was a source of much confusion to scholars. At another time, as a piece of personal spite against Gough, the director of the Society of Antiquaries, Steevens by means of acid engraved some Anglo-Saxon letters on a chunk of marble, placed it in a shopwindow at Southwark, and called it to the attention of the Society as a piece of the tombstone of Hardecanute, dug up in Kennington Lane. A drawing of it was made and reproduced in the *Gentleman's Magazine* for 1790, and a learned paper was written upon it by Samuel Pegge.

Steevens eventually managed a quarrel even with his great contemporary Malone. Because Malone had differed in a few matters with Steevens' *Shakespeare,* Steevens embarked upon issuing another edition of his own after Malone's appeared in 1790. In order to make Malone, an extremely careful and cautious editor, seem inept, Steevens in his 1793 edition deliberately altered the text quite foolishly in a number of places. He also avenged himself on two clergymen by footnoting certain ribald passages with quite obscene comments, and attributing the notes to the innocent and respectable men of the church.

Yet this same man during his last years, when he was a frequent visitor at the home of Sir Joseph Banks, used to carry daily for Banks a nosegay attached to his cane, on his long walk from Hampstead, where he lived, to Soho Square.

As a rival collector of Hogarth prints, Samuel Ireland had been the object of Steevens' animosity. And when the Shakespeare Papers became a matter for public discussion, Steevens attacked them with particular acrimony, though always anonymously. William Henry says of him that though his "memory will be handed down to posterity as long as Shakespeare exists," Steevens followed his usual methods and "like a mole worked in secret, and when occasion served, stung with the subtlety of a viper." Steevens, in fact, continued his fury even after most people had lost interest in the Ireland affair.

Edmond Malone, a great friend of Boswell and a leading authority on Shakespeare, was an adversary of a different complexion. Tiring of the law, Malone came to London in 1777 to devote himself to literature. Soon after their first meeting, he became an intimate of Boswell's, who dedicated the *Tour to the Hebrides* to him. Malone worked with his friend on the revision of *The Life of Samuel Johnson* so earnestly that Boswell gratefully declared that he could not sufficiently acknowledge his obligation, so valuable had been Malone's suggestions. There are few names which reappear as often and with as much pleasure in the Boswell papers as Malone's.

Shortly after his arrival in London from Ireland, Malone was encouraged by Lord Charlemont and also, for a while, by Steevens to contribute to Shakespearean criticism. Steevens gave him his collection of old plays, and pretended to have given up the field of Shakespearean research to Malone as his heir apparent. In 1778 Malone published a very shrewd and essentially sound suggestion for the chronological arrangement of the plays. He busied himself next with editing the poems, some of Shakespeare's sources, several of the Shakespearean Apocrypha, and supplements to Johnson and Steevens' edition of the plays. He then embarked upon a seven-years' task of preparing his own edition of Shakespeare; it was this undertaking which caused Steevens to break with him. His most significant contribution was to Shakespeare's biography and to our knowledge of the history of the Elizabethan and Stuart theatre. For these he was an assiduous student of old records and documents, a careful sorter of fact from legend, though sometimes the victim of his own stubborn nature. The fruits of his investigation appeared in 1790 in his edition of Shakespeare, into which he introduced 1,654 emendations. Burke admired the accomplishment so much that he dedicated his *Reflections on the French Revolution* to him.

Scrupulously honest in his studies, Malone was a perfect literary antiquary rather than a critic. Both Kemble and Mrs. Siddons expressed their admiration of his elegant manners. And the young Boswell has described him as a "cordial and steady friend, combining the utmost mildness with the simplest sincerity and the most manly independence. Tenacious, perhaps, of his own opinions, which he had seldom hastily formed, he was always ready to listen with candor and good humor to those of others."

Only twice did Malone turn from his Shakespearean labors to engage in literary squabbles. The first time was in 1782 when he refuted Bryant's attempts to prove Chatterton's forgeries genuinely medieval. Malone's efforts at humor here, as in his later sally, were never successful, for like that of many excellent scholars his prose was rather heavy-handed. But Walpole, while deploring the attempts at wit, agreed that Malone had destroyed the enemy with his "own artillery." The other occasion when he participated in public warfare was his exposure of the Shakespeare Papers. He was one of the Irelands' earliest foes; he was assuredly their most formidable one.

Malone made it his business to avoid examining the Shakespeare Papers in any way that could be construed as a public act.

He was aware of the authority that would attach to his verdict. It was not his method to pronounce judgment after a mere cursory look at the documents, as Boswell and the other enthusiasts had been ready to do. If he did not at once give weighty reasons for discrediting Ireland's papers, he would be interpreted as having endorsed them. Then if upon fuller study he later could document his objections, his pronouncements would be interpreted as emanations of spite.

He therefore hit upon the expedient of trying to see the Papers elsewhere than at Norfolk Street, which was now the recourse of great numbers of outsiders. Through a common friend he suggested to Caldecott, an amateur and ungifted Shakespearean scholar who knew Ireland, that he would be happy to inspect the documents at Caldecott's home if they were left there. The opportunity for Caldecott to avenge himself on Malone for his own inferiority as a scholar was too good to miss, and he icily informed the great editor through his mediator that Ireland's papers would not be removed from their Norfolk Street archives "for any person whatever, with the exception of His Majesty the King," and that so far as he knew Ireland had no intention "to show them to any Commentator or Shakespeare-monger whatever."

Next Malone attempted another such plan through Ireland's friend the Honorable John Byng. If Byng could persuade Ireland to bring the Southampton correspondence and the Heminge and Condell pieces to Byng's house, Malone would come there and have with him "a facsimile of Lord Southampton's handwriting which will at once ascertain the matter." He stipulated, however, that his name was not to be mentioned—that he was to be identified only as a "gentleman." Ireland absolutely refused anything but an open visit to his house, which Malone declined. From that moment it was war.

Sometime in February, 1795, William Henry began to present his father with the work which was to be the focal point of the contention, the heretofore unknown tragedy by Shakespeare, *Vortigern*. With this invention he raised himself far beyond the reach of even the genius Chatterton!

Without an idea in the world as to where the play was to come from, William Henry had announced the existence of an unknown tragedy written out in the Bard's own hand. Then, as usual, the inspiration for the new forgery came from the Norfolk Street house itself. His father had made a large drawing after Mortimer's painting of Rowena offering wine to Vortigern, and this drawing hung over the mantel in Ireland's study. Learning that the story was to be found in Holinshed, he took down a copy of the *Chronicles* from his father's shelves, read the Vortigern passages, and decided that the subject was perfect for his purposes. As usual, too, he impetuously announced the title before he had written a single line. Naturally Ireland soon was tormenting him for the manuscript, which he tendered in small sections, as he found time to write them, in his own handwriting, saying he had copied the pages from the original. "The play, though procrastinated in the delivery, did not actually occupy more than two months' time in the composing, notwithstanding the inconveniences I had to surmount from Mr. Ireland's unceasing applications, from the questionings of numerous persons who inspected the papers, and the difficulty I found in snatching opportunities to proceed with the manuscript."

When Samuel Ireland let it be known to his visitors that an unknown play of the Bard's on the subject of Vortigern and Rowena had been unearthed (actually Rowena makes but a brief appearance in the play William Henry was writing), it was a topic of enthusiastic comment that by enchanting coincidence Ireland should so long have owned a drawing on the same subject.

In the meantime, William Henry's friend Montague Talbot had decided to give up the hated profession of law and surrender himself to his love, the stage. To try his luck in a more undemanding location, he set out for Dublin. Before his departure both friends agreed to correspond, William Henry promising to omit no detail in what was happening to the fabricated documents. Talbot did not wish to miss the fun. After he had written two such letters to Dublin, William Henry was urged by his friend to correspond in code. That would be safer. Their "talisman" was a sheet of paper in which several holes had been cut out; this sheet placed over a received letter would reveal the secret message—the rest of the message having been filled out so as to be wholly unintelligible. Each lad had a sheet with the holes identically placed. It added to the thrill of forgery.

William Henry was so busy these days that he had written the earlier portions of *Vortigern* before having the time to inform Talbot of his newest venture. But the news of such an important discovery had reached Dublin, and Talbot wrote to William Henry complaining that he had not taken him into his confidence. Ten days after the receipt of this letter, Talbot was suddenly back in London for a brief visit. His friend apologized for his recent silence, assuring him that he had been so much harassed by his new forgeries that he had no mind for anything else. And, in truth, when Talbot saw how the collection had swelled at Norfolk Street, he was astounded by the numbers as well as the variety. "As Mr. Talbot was a friend of the Muses, he became anxious to add a portion of his own composition in the course of the production of Vortigern; and as his continuance in London was but for a few days, I promised that I would send to him when at Dublin, the plan of some of the scenes of Vortigern, leaving the language to himself, which, when remitted to me, I was to copy." So William Henry agreed. But after Talbot's return to Dublin he reflected that the arrangement would result in two styles totally different from each other. Moreover, Talbot had had no experience in imitating the Elizabethans. So the collaboration never took place. As *Vortigern* was written William Henry continued to give portions of it to his father. Considering the fashion of creating it, we can only marvel that it did not become far worse than it is. Once he had surrendered the part completed, he had no way of improving or revising what he had written the day before.

Summer was approaching, and still the recalcitrant Mr. H. had not responded to Ireland's plea for either a meeting or some substantial evidence as to the authenticity required by the forthcoming publication. William Henry's quasi-hysterical promises of more wonders to come had the effect of aggravating Ireland's impatience and his own persecutions.

Suddenly one of the visitors to Norfolk Street said something which precipitated William Henry into the maddest of his ventures. *Suppose,* the visitor said, *someone should find a descendant of Shakespeare: would not that descendant lay claim rightfully to all these documents which your friend Mr. H. has been giving you?* William Henry decided to produce papers which would establish beyond all question his right to the documents he had so painfully and dangerously created himself. And while he was at it, he would take the opportunity to allay certain doubts which were beginning to arise.

It happened that there had been a man by the name of Ireland with whom Shakespeare had had some business dealings. On the basis of this, the boy invented one *William Henry Ireland,* a good Elizabethan, and stepped forth with a Deed of Gift to this same William Henry Ireland, written in Shakespeare's own hand:

I William Shakspeare of Stratford on Avon butt nowe livyng in London neare untoe a Yard calledd or knowne bye the name of Irelands yarde in the Blackfryars London nowe beyng att thys preasaunte tyme of sounde Mynde ande enjoyinge healthe of bodye doe make ande ordeyne thys as ande for mye deede of Gyfte for inn as muche as life is mouste precyouse toe alle menne soe shoulde bee thatte personne who att the peryle of hys owne shalle save thatte of a fellowe Createure Bearyng thys inn Mynde ande havyng beene soe savedde myeselfe I didd withe myne owne hande fyrste wryte on Papere the conntennts hereof butte for the moure securytye ande thatte noe dyspute whatever myghte happenne afterre mye deathe I have nowe causedd the same toe bee written onn Parchemente and have heretoe duly sett and affyxedd mye hande and Seale Whereas onne or abowte the thyrde daye of the laste monethe beyng the monethe of Auguste havynge withe mye goode freynde Masterre William Henry Irelande ande otherres taene boate neare untowe myne house afowresayde wee dydd purpose goynge upp Thames butt those thatte were soe toe conducte us beynge muche toe merrye throughe Lyquorre they didd upsette oure fowresayde bayrge alle butte myeselfe savedd themselves bye swimmyng for though the Waterre was deepe yette owre beynge close nygh toe shore made itte lyttel dyffyculte for themm knowinge the fowresayde Arte Masterre William henrye Irelande notte seeynge mee dydd aske for mee butte oune of the Companye dydd answerre thatte I was drownynge onn the whyche he pulledd off hys Jerrekynne and Jumpedd inn afterre mee withe muche paynes [!] he draggedd mee forthe I beynge then nearelye deade and soe he dydd save mye life and for the whyche Service I doe herebye give hym as folowithe!!! [sic] fyrste mye writtenn Playe of Henrye fowrthe Henrye fyfthe Kyng John Kyng Leare as allsoe mye written Playe neverr yett impryntedd whych I have named Kyng henry thyrde of Englande alle the profytts of the whych are whollye toe be for sayde Ireland ande atte hys deathe thenne toe hys fyrste Sonne namedd alsoe William henrye ande atte hys deathe toe hys brother ande soe onne butte inn case of faylure of Issue thenne toe the nexte of kynn ande soe on for everre inn hys lyne Ande I doe alsoe give untoe sayde Ireland the Sum of ten Pounds as a preesaunte oute of the

whyche I doe require hym toe buye oune Rynge as a Remembraunce In Witnesse whereof I have toe thys mye
deede of Guyfte sette mye hand and Seale in the
preasaunce of the twoe Witnesses whose Names are alsoe
affyxedd toe the backe hereof thys fyve ande twentyethe
daye of Octoberre beynge in the Yeare of oure Lorde one
thousande six hundrethe ande foure ande in the seconde
Yeare of oure Soveraygne Lorde Kynge James 1604

William Shakspeare

(L.S.)

Sealed and delyveredd in the presaunce of us

Jo: Edwards

Jos: Byggett

Deede of guyftte from Shakspeare toe Irelaunde

2 James

What a pity that Garrick was not alive to read this! He would
have deeply appreciated that Will of all Wills who had been part
of a company too merry through liquor! And what a wonderful
authentication of the unusual *King Lear* script already unearthed,
to find it here bequeathed to William Henry's ancestor—one
might almost say, his namesake—who had thoughtfully saved the
life of the Matchless Bard.

It is too bad, of course, that in 1604, the year of the Deed of
Gift, *King Lear* had not yet been written. But that is a mere detail. It is also odd that Shakespeare should be disposing of plays
which, once written, were not his to bestow, since they belonged
to his acting company. That is but another detail. It is a little
stingy of the Bard to grant but ten pounds to the man who saved
his life; it sounds much more like what would have been handsome pocket money for a boy of the same name. Again, only detail. What is, perhaps, most impressive is that William Henry,
fairly well convinced of his own illegitimacy, is here giving himself an imposing genealogy, by linking himself with the preserver

147

of Shakespeare's life—a hero equal to England's greatest.

Accompanying the formal Deed of Gift, William Henry had also found a paper of heart-warming feeling:

Givenne toe mye mouste worthye and excellaunte Freynde Masterre William Henrye Irelande inne Remembraunce of hys havynge Savedde mye life whenne onne Thames

WILLIAM SHAKSPEARE

Inne life wee wille live togetherre Deathe shalle forre a lytelle parte usse butte Shakspeares Soule restelesse inne the Grave shalle uppe Agayne ande meete hys freynde hys IRELAND Inne the Bleste Courte of Heavenne O Modelle of Virretue Charytyes sweeteste Chylde thye Shakspeare thanks thee Norre Verse norre Sygh norre Teare canne paynte mye Soule norre saye bye halfe howe muche I love thee Thyne

WM. SHAKSPEARE

Keepe thys forre mee ande shoude the Worlde prove sowerre rememberre oune lives thatte loves the stylle.

On one side of this marvelous document was a pen-and-ink drawing of Shakespeare's arms, on the other a drawing of the Ireland family's. These two were joined together by a chain. Sir Isaac Heard, Garter King-of-Arms and a signer of the Certificate of Belief, suggested to Ireland that because of the apparent connection between the families of the Bard and of Ireland, a junction of the two coats of arms should take place, and that Ireland ought to couple on his own shield the bearings of Shakespeare.

There was still one more piece accompanying these priceless papers: a sketch of that ancient William Henry Ireland's most unusual house. If Mr. Samuel Ireland had made himself into something of an artist with his pencil, and if one daughter of the

Young Samuel Ireland in a care-
free mood, before the time of
his son's meteoric career.

Left: In his twenties William Henry Ireland
cultivated the air of melancholy considered
appropriate for young men of a poetic nature.

A miniature portrait of William
Henry Ireland, painted on ivory
by Samuel Drummond (c. 1825).
At this time William Henry was
about fifty.

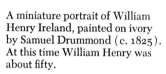

Above, an engraving by Samuel Ireland of the octagonal wooden amphitheatre erected for the Shakespeare Jubilee at Stratford in 1769.

Below, Shakespeare's Monument, from an engraving made by Samuel Ireland for his *Picturesque Views.* The door was the entrance to the charnel house.

According to John Jordan,
wheelwright turned poet,
Shakespeare and his friends
after a drinking contest "took
their repose" under the Crab Tree.

Samuel Ireland heard of the
existence at Ann Hathaway's Cottage
of the Shakespeare Courting Chair,
in which "our bard used to sit . . .
with his Ann upon his knee." Both
drawings were made by Ireland Senior
for his *Picturesque Views* of the Avon.

The forged receipt of John
Heminge as written by William
Henry and copied by Malone from
the facsimile; *right*, a facsimile
of John Heminge's actual signature.

The superscription (*Forre Mastr William Shakspeare*)
and parts of the forged Southampton letter
(*Deare William*, etc.), copied from
the facsimile by Malone.

Below, portions of authentic letters by Southampton.

Part of
William Henry's
forged letter from
Queen Elizabeth
to Shakespeare.

Below, samples of actual letters written by Queen Elizabeth,
as published by Malone in his *Inquiry.*

Below, William Henry's forged alphabet (printed by Malone) and,
below that, Elizabeth's "genuine alphabet."

"The Oaken Chest or the Gold Mines of Ireland a Farce."
Here the entire Ireland family is involved in falsification. William Henry, at
the left, exults over an ancient book.

"The Spirit of Shakspere Appearing to his Detractors." In the cowering
group Samuel Ireland, with arms raised, is depicted as the main villain.

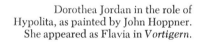

A goblet now in the possession of the author. A document accompanying the goblet stated that it was "Made from Mulberry Wood from a tree at Stratford-upon-Avon under which Shakespeare used to act."

John P. Kemble, actor-manager at the Drury Lane Theatre, from a portrait by Sir Thomas Lawrence.

Dorothea Jordan in the role of Hypolita, as painted by John Hoppner. She appeared as Flavia in *Vortigern*.

Edmund Malone, in the portrait painted by Joshua Reynolds. Malone, an assiduous student of old records and documents, was fully equipped to act as William Henry's chief adversary.

EVER ACTED.

...tre Royal, Drury-Lane

This prefent SATURDAY APRIL 2 1796.

Their Majefties Servants will act a new Play in 5 acts called

VORTIGERN.

With new Scenes Dreffes and Decorations,
The CHARACTERS by

Mr. BENSLEY, Mr. BARRYMORE,
Mr. CAULFIELD, Mr. KEMBLE,
Mr. WHITFIELD, Mr. TRUEMAN, Mr. C. KEMBLE,
Mr. BENSON, Mr. PHILLIMORE,
Mr. KING, Mr. DIGNUM,
Mr. PACKER, Mr. COOKE,
Mr. BANKS, Mr. EVANS, Mr. RUSSEL,
Mr. WENTWORTH, Mr. MADDOCKS, Mr. WEBB,
Mafter GREGSON, Mafter DE CAMP.

Mrs. POWELL,
Mrs. JORDAN,
Mifs MILLER, Mifs TIDSWELL,
Mifs HEARD, Mifs LEAK.

The Prologue to be fpoken by Mr. WHITFIELD.
And the Epilogue by Mrs. JORDAN.

The Scenes defigned and executed by
Mr. GREENWOOD, and Mr. CAPON.
The Dreffes by Mr. JOHNSTON, Mr. GAY, and Mifs REIN.

To which will be added a Mufical Entertainment called

MY GRANDMOTHER.

Sir Matthew Medley, Mr. Maddocks, Vapour, Mr. Bannifter, jun.
Woodly, Mr. Sedgwick. Goffip, Mr. Suett, Soufrance, Mr. Wewitzer.

Charlotte, Mifs De Camp, Florella, Signora Storace.

☞ The Publick are moft refpectfully informed, that this Evening, and during the reft of the Seafon, the Doors of this Theatre, will be Opened at Half paft Five, and the Play to begin at Half paft Six.

Printed by C. LOWNDES, Next the Stage-Door. *Vivant Rex et Regina.*

The 36th. night, and laft time this Seafon, of HARLEQUIN CAPTIVE. Will be on Monday.

On Wednefday, (3rd time The Comedy of The PLAIN DEALER: COMICK OPERA, in which Mr. BRAHAM will make his Appearance, will be produced as fpeedily as poffible.

...ce will be given of the next reprefentation of The IRON...

Playbill for the opening — and only — performance of *Vortigern* at the Drury Lane Theatre.

house could make engravings and the other paint miniatures, the illegitimate and still insufficiently prized son could wield a pen in the way of drawing too! Beneath the picture was an utterly charming subtitle:

Viewe o mye Masterre Irelands house bye the whyche I
doe showe thatte hee hath falselye sayde inne tellynge mee
I knewe notte howe toe showe itte hymme onne Paperre
ande bye the whyche I ha wonne fromme * the Summe o 5
shyllynges

W. SHAKSPEARE

William Henry took some care in preparing these documents, and in physical appearance they are the most convincing in the collection. So far as the handwriting went, practice was surely making perfect. Or it may be that he felt the amazing coincidence of a Georgian William Henry Ireland's coming into possession by mere chance of papers belonging to an Elizabethan William Henry Ireland would be the hardest of his tales to swallow, and that special attention was called for. In any case, swallow it almost everyone did. The visitors to Norfolk Street were well habituated to the tendency of the Papers toward delightful coincidence—coincidence with one another, or with fragments of Shakespearean lore, or with the visitors' own cherished illusions, or with the *décor* of the Ireland house. This new coincidence was merely the most wonderful and gratifying of all—except to the *Morning Herald*, which wryly remarked: "The *swimming* reasons given in a paper of yesterday in favor of the authenticity of certain *musty manuscripts*, shew to what Dangers we may expose ourselves by *wading* too far in pursuit of an *object*."

But William Henry was not long in coming up with substantiation for his most recent forgeries. In mid-June he informed his father that Mr. H. had discovered documents "tending to prove that I was the direct descendant of the William Henry Ireland to

---

* William Henry carelessly ommitted "hymme."

149

whom the bequest was made in the deed of gift, and that consequently he no longer regarded my possession of the manuscripts as a favor but looked upon them as my own right by descent." William Henry himself had seen an illuminated manuscript, found in an old chest in Mr. H.'s country house, which depicted Henry V in the act of bestowing a banner to a knight kneeling before him. This picture bore the inscription, "Ireland, thou hast deserved well for thy valor, and shalt have a part of our Arms of England for thy bravery." Most marvelous of all, this manuscript afforded a genealogy of the Irelands, each of whom had signed the document as having been received into his hands, beginning with the Arthur Ireland (good name for a knight!) thus signally honored by Henry V at Agincourt, through Montgomery Ireland, down to William Henry Ireland, Shakespeare's rescuer, who had come into possession of this historic monument in 1567 upon the death of his father.

Naturally our own William Henry was prepared to create this manuscript. He called on Mr. Thane, collector of autographs and a leading authority on them, who informed him that no signature of Henry V had been unearthed. William Henry made several attempts, despite this news, to fabricate the Ireland genealogical table, but feared that this was indeed too difficult a manuscript to forge. And so he abandoned that project. Of course, he had given his father a new topic with which to plague him.

In his efforts to cleanse the festering conviction of his illegitimacy William Henry was doing magnificently well. Since his father would not put an end to his mystifying dubieties when approached on the question, he rose above circumstance and royally bestowed upon his sire and himself an illustrious line. With such eminent forebears one's legitimacy or illegitimacy became a trifling matter, hardly worth considering.

And what a forebear was the sixteenth-century William Henry Ireland turning out to be! It must have made the young man dizzy to consider the marvelous ways of such genius as his own. For in addition to ennobling the Ireland name, and settling forever young William Henry's title to the forgeries, this invented Ireland might turn out to answer the most teasing of all Shakespearean mysteries, the identity of the "Mr. W. H." to whom the sonnets had been dedicated. What an unthought-of coincidence! Who was more entitled to that dedication than the William Henry who had saved the Bard's life, and for whom he nurtured the most passionate kind of friendship?

As for Samuel Ireland, his middle-class snobbery was sufficiently great to induce him to remain silent about his obscure beginnings; he was also sufficiently middle-class to revel in the radiance of his newly found origins. His own secret convictions and his extraordinary gullibility now cooperated to confirm his noble lineage. He at once set his friend Sir Isaac Heard the task of searching through the records of the Heralds for the grant of the Ireland coat of arms.

Ireland was now torn between his concern over the mysterious conduct of Mr. H. in withholding so many promised treasures and his pride and self-importance as possessor of the most-to-be-envied hoard of rare Shakespeareana. The subscriptions for the projected publication of the Papers were pouring in. Among the subscribers were many important persons: Boswell (who died in May of this year), George Chalmers, Dr. Parr, the actor Macklin (verging on his hundredth year), the celebrated actress Mrs. Jordan (very, very close to the Royal Family), Viscount Torrington, Warren Hastings, the Poet Laureate Pye, the Duke of Leeds, the famous author Sotheby, New College, Glasgow College, and Richard Brinsley Sheridan. Burke and Pitt had both accepted the Papers as authentic, and before the year was out the Prince of Wales became equally convinced.

Naturally Ireland was anxious to see the grant to his family by Henry V at Agincourt. If the other documents had been donated freely, surely this one, which so dearly concerned himself and his family, ought to join the others. It was a logical excuse for breaking Mr. H.'s long silence. So he wrote to him, tactfully, urging his burning desire "to view the grant of Arms"—surely Mr. H. could understand that—but at the same time making it clear that Mr. H. was not to part with it until convenient. He did not omit his former request for a meeting, and asked that Mr. H. do him the favor "of taking a family drive with us."

As usual, Mr. H. sent his thanks through William Henry, and promised a personal gift to Ireland himself in the form of a handsome escritoire. This intended liberality warmed Ireland's heart; and soon he was in receipt of an even more remarkable letter from the gentleman:

> For some time back it has been my wish to give you a letter unknown to your son. In doing this I assure you I break my promise, and therefore must beg, nay insist, on the strictest secrecy from you. As his father, I think it but right that you should know by what he often tells me is in general thought of him. . . . He tells me he is in general look'd upon as a young man that scarce knows how to write a good letter. . . . I have now before me part of a *Play* written by *your son* which for style and greatness of thought is equal to any one of Shakspeare's. Let me intreat you, Dr. sir, not to smile, for on my honor it is most true.

It is hard for the modern reader to smile at this. One is suddenly aware of the hunger in the boy's heart for recognition from his father which even now, with all the gifts of the counterfeited manuscripts, must obviously have been granted but grudgingly. How intolerable it must have been to his adolescent mind to hear all the encomia lavished on his creations while his own abilities were brushed aside! At least through his friend Mr. H., who had a due appreciation of his genius, he could call them to the attention of that father for whose respect he was starving. Mr. H.'s letter continues:

He has chosen the subject of Wm. the Conqueror, and tells me he intends writing a series of plays to make up with Shakspeare's a complete history of the Kings of England. He wishes it to remain unknown, therefore I again rely on your honor in this affair. It must appear strange why I should have taken so particular a liking to him. His extraordinary talents would make anyone partial—I often talk with him and never before found one even of twice his age that knew so much of human nature. . . . *No man* but your *son* ever wrote like *Shakspeare.* This is bold, I confess, but it is true. . . . I have read what he has written of the Play and got him to give me the enclosed speech. . . . I promised him I never would show it . . . it is not a chosen one I assure you, but *you* may judge of the . . . grandeur of thought and then ask if it is not close on the heels of Shakspeare. It was originally composed in my room. . . . He never comes in to me but instantly notes down everything that has struck him in his walk. I have frequently asked where he can get such thoughts, all the answer he makes is this "I borrow them from nature." I also enquired why he wishes to be secret, to which he says "I desire to be thought to know but little." Let me beg you to examine him closely; you will find what I advance is but the truth. He likewise often says his mind *loathes* the confined *dingdong* study of the law, and yet he says he will remain quiet till a proper opportunity. . . . He told me he took the enclosed from walking alone in Westminster Abbey.

Mr. I—upon my honor and soul I would not scruple giving £2,000 a year to have a son with such extraordinary faculties. If at *twenty* he can write so what will he do hereafter. The more I see of him the more I am amazed. If your *son* is not a second Shakspeare I am not a *man.* Keep this to yourself, do not even mention it to any soul living . . . I . . . will make him the bearer as usual. . . .

I remain, Dr. sir,

H.

Put a seal upon your lips to all that has passed, but Remember these words. Your *son* is brother in genius to Shakspeare. He is the only man that ever walked with him hand in hand.

The excerpt from *William the Conqueror* shows at least one trait held in common with the author of the Shakespeare Papers, an unwillingness to punctuate. Earl Edwyn is meditating outside the Abbey:

> O my good Lord how lingering passed the time
> Whilse in yon porch I did wait your coming
> Yet as this Cloistral Arch this bright heaven
> Doth shine upon the Emerald tipt wave
> And paints upon the deep each passing cloud
> E'eene so the smallest and most gentle Plant
> That waves fore the breath of thee sweet heaven
> To man gives food for contemplation. . . .

So much accustomed to antique spelling, William Henry's pen now and then betrayed him when he was writing in his own person.

Samuel Ireland noticed none of this, nor were his suspicions at all raised by the letter, as it is not unreasonable to suppose they should have been. He at once thanked Mr. H., whose letter had given him "infinite pleasure": he has read his son's lines "and that with a degree of astonishment I cannot express, as I assure you it is the first specimen of my son's poetical talents I have ever seen." (Little did he know!) If Ireland has seemed to complain of William Henry's lack of knowledge, it was only a result of his desire to get the boy to read the right authors. "Your good opinion of him weighs strongly on my mind, and I am happy that he has fallen into the hands of such a friend." No matter how delighted, however, Ireland did not forget his own concerns: "There is indeed, Sir, but one circumstance attending your friendship towards him that gives me pain, and that is my being so total a stranger to one to whom I owe so much. If it is your wish to remain unknown to the Public, may I without intrusion on your friendship request to have an interview on the most private ground imaginable. . . . It certainly appears strange to the world that my son at his age is entrusted to the knowledge of such a friendship, while I am kept totally in a state of suspense. I here pledge my honor that no one person in the world shall know more than they know at present—but it is for my own gratification that I say so much, and I flatter myself that for a moment placing yourself in the situation in which I now stand—you would think much as I do on the subject. . . . I thank you for the Deed of Gift, and for your intention of sending me the schedule of all the Documents that are to come forth—amongst which permit me again to mention the grant of Arms, which if it should come before the Court in Doctors Commons will be a material object to proceed on, and without which I cannot, as I am informed, take any steps to a property in the Papers, and consequently cannot prepare the preface nor the work for the public eye. . . ."

When there was no immediate answer to this, Ireland renewed his importunities with his son, second Shakespeare though he was. Before the week was out there was another letter from Mr. H. Surely, the gentleman observed sadly, Mr. Ireland must have incautiously betrayed the letter written to him as a secret, for William Henry has asked about it, though without being satisfied. The lad is still writing copiously, "and even cried like a child because the pains in his head would not permit him to apply as he wished. . . . He has told me you talk a great deal to him now, and he tells me he hopes I have not blab'd." Not that Mr. H. wishes to advise Mr. Ireland on how to deal with his own son! (A reference, no doubt, to the repercussions in the Ireland house because of an impertinence in the matter of using powder for the hair.) After all, when it comes to knowledge of the world it is to Mr. Ireland that Mr. H. would "look for *Information*" rather than be so bold as to attempt to dispense it. For indeed, as for William Henry, "he never utters a syllable unbecoming a dutiful and loving son. O Mr. I.—pray look upon yourself, happy in having a son *who if he lives* must make futurity amazed." Young Ireland was showing an infallible symptom of genius, according to the sentimentalists, the expectation of an early death.

But Mr. H. had not been manoeuvred into a declaration concerning a meeting. Since Ireland was not interested in writing him letters the replies to which contained no reference to his requests or suggestions, and instead treated him to hymns on his son's genius, he decided it was a waste of time to correspond further.

There was no reason to feel desperate. His *Picturesque Views* of the Avon was warmly received. It paved the way splendidly for the forthcoming publication of the Papers. The volume was studded with glowing remarks on the Matchless Bard, which were universally gratifying, while at the same time heralding praise for the new discoveries. In the Preface Ireland modestly remarked that if he had succeeded "in the smallest degree to have elucidated any circumstance of Shakspeare's life, or any passage in the noble effusions of his more than human mind," his utmost wish was gratified. This was an undertaking for which Ireland was ill equipped, but doubtless his readers overlooked the fact that there were no such passages in the book itself. The total lack of imagination in the neat plates is well accounted for; his drawings are faithful to the facts, for he is sure the artist must be content to reproduce what Nature has accomplished. Shakespeare was the only poet who "had to him alone that mysterious veil withdrawn by nature," though, it must be granted, "that a partial view has sometimes been opened to Milton." In the enthusiasm over Stratford, Ireland pauses to hope that it is something better than mere curiosity that directs Shakespeare's admirers toward "that spot which gave birth to the most extraordinary genius this or any other country has ever produced." It is his particular pleasure to be able to lay before the public anything nearly connected with the Bard's life. In relating the various Stratfordian myths, he recounts that of the Crab Tree and gives rather flimsy evidence to substantiate it: "Of the truth of this story I have very little doubt: it is certain that the Crab Tree is known all around the country by the name of Shakspeare's Crab."

In the later pages of the book occurs an interesting passage in which Ireland inveighs against those who have done violence to the Bard's records by fabrications: "They rob the age of the testimony it gives of itself, they pollute the source from which only the scholar can draw his materials to deduce the history of his native tongue. . . . Such must be the consequences of the wretched systems of some modern critics of at least no small pretensions; and such and no less are the sacrifices they expect to be made to their petty studies and frivolous acquirements." A man who stood in his own dubious position at that moment must have been an innocent indeed to pen such words! Another Oedipus, he was inviting the wrath of the gods when he felt secure enough to attack, as everyone knew he was doing, Steevens and Malone.

AS FOR MALONE, who had heard of the contents of the Deed of Gift to William Henry Ireland, he was savagely amused. But his disquieting public comment had been that of a scholar. How many Elizabethans, he wished to know, had been baptized with two Christian names? It was not the sort of query to impress the average citizen.

But great things were ahead for Samuel Ireland. Sheridan, as a subscriber to the forthcoming publications, claimed first rights to produce *Vortigern* at the Drury Lane. Ireland was by no means loath to grant him the permission, and allowed him to see the manuscript of the play as it was delivered sheet by sheet. Sheridan agreed to a production some time before the book of Shakespeare Papers appeared, which was to be in December.

In the fall of 1795 the *Morning Herald* began to publish Henry Bate Dudley's mock version of the much-talked-of, but still unread, *Vortigern.* The parody attracted so much attention that Ireland was compelled to make a public announcement that Dudley's *Vortigern* had nothing in common with the new Shakespearean play. Dudley, known as "the Fighting Parson" because his clever articles had often precipitated him into fights and duels, prefaced his parody with a slighting paragraph in the *Herald:* "The SHAKESPEARE *discoveries,* said to have been made by the son of MR. IRELAND of Norfolk Street, are the Tragedy of LEAR, and another entitled VORTIGERN, now first brought to light, both in the Bard's own handwriting. In the same chest are said to have been also found an antique MELANGE of *love-letters! professions of faith! billets-doux! locks of hair!* and *family receipts!*—The only danger as to *faith in the discovery* seems to be from *protesting too much."*

The parody itself was entitled "Passages by Distinguished Personages on the Great Literary Trial of VORTIGERN AND ROWENA, a Comedy Tragedy, whether it be or be not from the Immortal Pen of Shakespeare?" It was later issued as a book. The only difficulty, says our satirist, in lending faith to the Papers "seems to be from the indiscretion of *finding too much!"* Sheridan has declared that *Vortigern* "is the finest play Shakespeare ever wrote!—not that he has had leisure to read it!—but he had . . . the solemn assurance of the great Lord Salisbury himself." As for the lock of hair, "Mr. Justice Collick, the first *Hair Merchant* in the universe, has critically inspected it, and, regardless of the *sacred head of fiction* from whence it was shorn," says that a whole head of it would be "worth no more than 3*s.* 9*d.* an ounce." Among the "receipts" which the public may not have heard about, Dudley speaks of "A Recipie howe to make a Goodlie Plumbe Pudinge." This document must be genuine because the Bard "could not endure the *stones* of plumbs. As Shakespeare says, 'dearest chuck, I prithee make me *geldings* of the PLUMBES!'"

Despite these boisterous beginnings, when the installments of the parody proper began to appear—and a long series it was—it turns out to have nothing to do with the Irelands or their papers. Dudley was simply using the much-discussed collection as a mask for volumes of attacks on contemporary men and women of the nobility and leaders in national politics. However, when these satires were issued months later in book form, each volume bore on its title page a motto which it was pretended came from *Vortigern:* "Open me a huge Wardrobe aboundinge in motlie habittes, and marke howe fantasticallie poore mortals will arraie themselves. VORT. & ROW." Dudley had no access to the manuscript, and of course no such passage exists in William Henry's play.

This harmless, if extended, sally can have done little hurt to the Irelands directly. What it did succeed in doing, however, was to swell the chorus of laughter which was beginning to be heard from several quarters.

As for Sheridan, the more he read of *Vortigern,* the less he admired it. It must have been, he decided, an extremely early work of Shakespeare (for whose plays he did not himself especially care), and he began to hedge at committing himself to a contract for its production. At last he signed the agreement in September. Samuel Ireland was to receive £250, plus one-half of all profits exceeding £350 per performance. The terms were anything but generous, but Ireland anticipated a long run for the play.

In November, Montague Talbot was again in London for a visit. The atmosphere was becoming sufficiently tense to suggest to William Henry that he prevail upon Talbot to stand ready to support him if support should be needed. Before Talbot's arrival, William Henry, to quiet his father's growing uneasiness over Mr. H.'s mysterious conduct, had unexpectedly announced that, to be honest, Montague Talbot was acquainted with Mr. H. too. Talbot would be in town if Ireland senior wished to put any questions to him.

As soon as Talbot reached London, William Henry coached him on what to say. Ireland understandably insisted that Talbot appear for dinner. Their guest proved almost tongue-tied, and to open the sluices of speech Ireland showed him one of Mr. H.'s letters. Did Talbot recognize the hand? Yes, he thought he did. Would one not say it was a *feminine* hand? (What was Ireland trying to cook up?) Talbot stumbled, but managed not to commit himself. When his host continued to hammer away at the unaccountability of Mr. H.'s reluctance to be seen or to answer direct questions, Talbot blurted out that because of something he had heard Mr. H. say in passing he gathered that the gentleman was discomfited because an ancestor of his, a contemporary of Shakespeare's, had been a player. Himself a man of position, Mr. H. did not wish the public ever to learn of his having such a lineage. Talbot added that Mr. H. had only recently come upon a Deed which would explain a great deal; once he had erased a certain name that was on it, it should be given, like the rest, to William Henry. After that Talbot took refuge in silence.

Dinner over, he retired to his lodgings, where that same night Ireland senior called upon him. The best the old man could accomplish was to wring a promise from the young actor that he would write him a full account as soon as he had reached his new destination, Wales. Before Talbot left town, it was agreed between him and William Henry that the former write to Ireland, "acquainting him that he was likewise present with me on the discovery of the papers."

Ireland had a new excuse for writing to Mr. H., which he did two days later. He pleaded the urgency for documenting the Preface to the Shakespeare Papers, since he now had "a host of unbelievers to combat with." He asked for but a few lines "relative to the nature of the discovery of the papers," as well as what should be said to explain withholding Mr. H.'s name. Then his greed intruded: "After the sacred treasures you have given to my son, I fear, my Dear Sir, you will think me obtrusive in reverting to the schedule of what yet remains behind, of the pictures, books, Grant of Arms to Ireland. . . . And for the first, particularly the whole length portrait of Shakspeare of which the World has heard much talk, that being brought forth at this instant would certainly add much to the validity of the whole, and, most prob-ably, slacken the public wish to knowing the name of the Donor —a name that I do not think they have any right to know. . . . Mr. Talbot a few days ago mentioned to me you had a Deed you intended to favor me with when you had erased a name in it." Ireland would, of course, be in a heaven of delight to see the new document. The volume of the Papers is now out of the hands of the printer, he concluded, and but awaits the requested prefatory word from Mr. H.

But Mr. H. would not respond by pen. He was offended, Wil-liam Henry reported, that his handwriting had been compared to that of a woman.

All other things failing, Ireland now asked his son to write out a formal statement of how the Papers first came into his hands. William Henry was pleased to oblige:

November 10th, 1795

I was at chambers, when Talbot came in, and shewed me a deed, signed Shakspere. I was much astonished, and mentioned the pleasure my father would receive could he but see it. Talbot then said I might shew it. I did not for 2 days; at the end of that term he gave it me. I then pressed hard to know where it was found. After 2 or 3 days had elapsed, he introduced me to the party. He was with me in the room, but took little trouble [!] in searching. I found a second deed, and a third, and two or three loose papers. We also discovered a deed, which ascertained to the party landed property, of which he had then no knowledge. In consequence of having found this, he told us we might keep every deed, every scrap of paper relative to Shakspeare. Little was discovered in town, but the rest came from the country; owing to the papers having been removed from London, many years ago.

S. W. H. Ireland

William Henry, it would seem, was tired of standing alone among all the ghosts of his own creation, and was trying to fortify his position by converting Talbot openly into an ally. But the story told here differs radically from his earlier accounts. Talbot is now described as having been a friend of Mr. H.'s in advance of himself, and in possession of the Mortgage Deed before he himself had seen it; according to his first versions he had met the noble gentleman by accident at the house of a friend of the Irelands' (as he had sometimes said) or at a coffee-house (as he had said at other times). The property belonging to Mr. H. is here supposed to have been unknown to the gentleman, whereas the previous tale concerning the document in question was that its discovery happily settled a legal matter long the subject of lawsuits. A new emphasis, moreover, is placed upon the contents of Mr. H.'s country house rather than upon his London lodgings, where so much was supposed to have been unearthed.

Now it was more important than ever for Ireland to hear from Talbot. And hear from him he did, as William Henry had arranged he should. It was a remarkable letter which came from Wales:

Carmarthen, November 25, 1795

Dear Sir: If since I left London I have had a leisure moment to keep my word and write you an Account of the Papers of Shakspeare, I have not had spirits sufficiently collected, owing to hard study and hurry of business, to give you that precise account of them I wish you to have from my hand. I have now the pleasure to communicate all you will in Honor require from me, and all I can reveal to you and the world.

The gentleman, in whose possession these things were found, was a friend of mine, and by me your son Samuel was introduced to his acquaintance. One morning in rummaging from mere curiosity some old lumber, consisting of deeds, books, & c., in a closet of my friend's house, I discovered a deed with the signature of William Shakspeare, which induced me to read part of it, and on reading the words "Stratford on Avon" I was convinced it was the famous English Bard: with permission of my friend (whom I will in future call Mr. H——) I carried the deed to Samuel knowing with what enthusiasm he and yourself regarded the works of that author, or any trifling article he was possessed of; though I was prepared to see my friend Samuel a little pleased with what I presented to him, yet I did not expect that great joy he felt on the occasion. He told me there was nothing known of the handwriting of Shakspeare, but his signature to some deed or will in Doctors Commons, and pressed me to carry him to H——'s house, that he might see if there was amongst the lumber I had spoken of, any other such relique. I immediately complied with his request. This was Samuel's first introduction. For several successive mornings, we passed some hours in examining different papers and deeds, most of which were useless or uninteresting. But our labor was rewarded by finding a few more relating to Shakspeare. These we took away, but never without H's permission. At last we were so fortunate as to discover a deed in which our friend was materially concerned. Some landed property which had been long the subject of litigation was here ascertained, and H's title to it clearly proved. H now said in return for this, whatever you and Mr. Ireland find among the lumber, be it what it may, shall be your own (meaning those things which we should prize for being Shakspeare's). Mr.

H just before my departure from London strictly enjoined us never to mention him as the possessor of these papers. Tho' I wished until Sam should have completed his researches, that little should have been said on the subject, yet I was ignorant why H. when the search was finished, should still wish his name concealed. I thought it absurd and could not prevail on him to mention his reasons; tho' from some trifling unguarded expressions, I was at last induced to believe that one of his ancestors was a cotemporary of Shakspeare in the dramatic profession; that as he H. was a man somewhat known in the world, and in the walk of high life, he did not wish such a circumstance should be made public; this suspicion was, as it will presently appear, well founded. Whilst I was in Dublin, I heard to my great joy and astonishment that Sam had discovered the play of Vortigern & Rowena, the Ms of Lear &c. &c. I was impatient to hear every particular, and principally for that purpose made my late visit to London. I found H. what I always thought him, a man of strict honor, and willing to abide by the promise he made, in consequence of our finding the deed by which he benefitted so much. He left us to adjust the division of the profits, and the following resolution made between Sam and myself met with his compliance; that in consequence of Samuel's diligence and my negligence in searching for the valuable articles, and some other agreements between ourselves (which is immaterial to mention) that had been made before my Departure from London, I should *not* receive, as we had agreed, an equal share, but that Sam should receive two-thirds of the profits arising from the performing and publishing the play of Vortigern and Rowena, and I only one.

I will now explain the reason of H's secrecy. On account of your desire to give the world some explanation of the business, and your telling me that such explanation was necessary, I renewed my entreaties to him, to suffer us to discover his name, place of abode, and every circumstance of the discovery of the papers, but in vain. I proceeded to prove as well as I could the folly of its concealment, when he produced a deed of gift, which he himself had just found in the closet, just before my departure from London, in January last, but which I had never seen before. By this deed William Shakspeare assigned to John ———— who it seems was really an ancestor of our friend H. every article contained in an upper room, in consequence of their having passed together many evenings in mild discourse, and in smoaking their pipes together in that very apartment. The articles, as furniture, cups, miniature picture, and many other things, are specified in the deed, but excepting the miniature (which has lately been found among the lumber, and which is a likeness of Shakspeare himself), very few of them remain in H's hands, and the rest unfortunately cannot be traced. It is supposed that many valuable papers have been lost or destroyed, as the whole lumber is never remembered as being at all valued, or guarded from the destructive hands of the lowest domestics. When I parted from you a few weeks since H. promised me that the deed of gift above mentioned should be sent you, first erasing and cutting out the name of the grantee.* I hope, my dear Sir, I have omitted nothing in relating these circumstances, and though this account may not enable you perfectly to satisfy many, who from idle curiosity would know more, yet the liberal-minded, I am sure will allow that you have just reasons for withholding

* When Ireland published this letter in his *Vindication* (1796), he subjoined a footnote here: "Within a few days after the receipt of the above, the deed of trust alluded to, was brought to me by my Son, without any erasure, as mentioned in the above letter, and was the deed of trust to John Heminge, inserted in the folio volume of the Shakspeare." For this deed of trust see below.

what is, and is to be concealed. I most earnestly beg
you will send me a copy of Vortigern and Rowena, as soon
as it can conveniently be written, with the margin marked,
according to the curtailment for Stage representation.

M. Talbot

Ireland was evidently not at all pleased that suddenly Talbot
should come in for a share of the money to be earned by *Vorti-*
gern—who knew whether he would not also demand a share in
the profits from the sale of the volume of Shakespeare Papers?—
and the old man therefore made no response of any kind to his
correspondent in Wales. As for the new Deed of Gift, he had had
enough of mystery, and informed William Henry that he would
have nothing to do with the document if any name were erased
or cut out.

Hastily William Henry brought his father the last of the imposing documents. It is certainly the most fascinating.

It had not been until 1747 that the true Last Will and Testament of Shakespeare, dated March 25, 1616, had come to light, in
the Registry of the Prerogative Court of Canterbury in Somerset
House, London. A document consisting of three sheets of paper,
each sheet of different size and origin, its body is in the handwriting of a clerk or scrivener. In this order the will leaves the following legacies: to his daughter Judith a sum of money; to his
daughter Susanna certain Stratford property; to Susanna's
daughter a sum of money; to his sister Joan money, wearing apparel, the house in which she lives, and its furnishings; to Joan's
children money; to his niece Elizabeth all his plate, with the exception of a gilt bowl; to the poor of Stratford money; to Thomas
Combe his sword; to Thomas Russell and Francis Collins money;
to Hamlet Sadler, William Reynolds, Anthony Nashe, John
Nashe, John Heminge, Richard Burbage, and Henry Condell
money with which to buy rings; to his godson William Walker
money; to his daughter Susanna, New Place as well as all other

properties in Stratford and its environs and in London; "I gyve vnto my wief my second best bed with the furniture [i.e., the furnishings of the bed]" (this is an interlineation, which was plainly an afterthought); to his daughter Judith the gilt bowl; to Susanna and her husband Dr. John Hall, all the rest of his goods, jewels, and household possessions.

This will was at once considered unsatisfactory by many and is apparently still held so. Since its authenticity is beyond cavil, some modern commentators have been put to the necessity of explaining away the "second best bed." There have been several who, to their own satisfaction, have demonstrated that the second best bed in those days was a better bed than the first best bed. Those scholars who are content to murder one of the greatest and most grimly eloquent jokes in the annals of biography are welcome to do so, if it makes them more comfortable. But Shakespeare's intent will always be, to the unsentimental, clear enough.

The eighteenth century was also perturbed (as are still our twentieth-century devotees to the idea that Bacon, Oxford, Ralegh, Essex, Queen Elizabeth, Derby, etc. etc., in combination or singly, were the true authors of Shakespeare's works) that the Bard had left no direction for the future of his works. Only a very few scholars then understood that the plays were not the dramatist's to dispose of. Moreover, they had been composed to be acted, not to be read. But these facts are as generally unknown to the public today as they were to William Henry's contemporaries. Several imaginative pieces have been written in our own time to account for Shakespeare's failure to mention the plays in his will. Somebody wrote a one-act play in which Shakespeare, during his last hours, is seen tearing up all his manuscripts and consigning them to the flames, one by one.

Young Ireland's final imposing document undertakes to remedy the shortcomings of the last will, and at the same time to take care of the problems he was now faced with. On the other hand, though it is rather more interesting to read in itself than the authentic will, this Deed of Gift does not seem in any way to correspond to the description Talbot had given of it in his letter to Ireland. No doubt young Ireland, who was telling himself so many lies these days, rapidly forgot what he had instructed his friend to say. However, as usual, his father made no comment on the discrepancy between the advance notice and the document as it actually read:

I William Shakspeare being of Stratforde on Avon . . . Having founde muche wickedness amongste those of the lawe and not liking to leave matterrs at theyre wills I have herein named a trusty and tried friende who shall afterr mye dethe execute withe care myne orderrs herein given But in case I shoulde att any tyme hereafterr make a Will. . . . I have lefte some things nott herein given or disposedd of thatt maye serve toe fylle upp said Will and therebye cause no hyndraunce in the Executyonn of thys mye deede of gifte But shod. I nott chaunce make a will thenn I doe give all such thyngs afsd. nott herein mentd. unto mye lovynge Daughterr and herr heyres for everr— Firste untoe mye deare Wife I doe orderr as folowithe thatt she bee payde withinne oune monthe afterre mye dethe the somme of oune hondrythe and fowre score Pounds from the moneys whyche be nowe laynge onn Accompte of the Globe Theatre inn the hands of Master John Hemynge Alsoe I doe give herr mye suyte of greye Vellvett edged withe Silverr togr. withe mye lyttelle Cedarr Trunke in wyche there bee three Ryngs oune lyttell payntyng of myselfe in a silverr Case & sevenn letterrs wrottenn to her before oure Marryage these I doe beg herr toe keepe safe if everr she dydd love me—Toe mye deare Daughterr who hathe alwaye demeaned herrselfe well I doe give as folowithe the somme of twentye Pounds and sevenne shyllyngs . . . & for raysyng sd. summe of 20 l. &

168

sevenne shyllyngs I doe herebye orderr Masterr hemynge
toe sell mye share of the two houses neare the Globe butt
shod. that nott bee enough thenne I doe orderr him toe
make itt upp oute of the Moneys inn hys hands onne
Accompte of the Theatre—I doe allso give herr mye suyte
of blacke silke & the Rynge whyche I doe alwaye weare
givenne toe mee bye hys Grace of Southampton thys I doe
bet herr as she dothe love mee neverr toe parte fromm Toe
mye good Cowleye whom I muche esteeme & who hathe
always loved mee I doe orderr as folowithe thatt Masterr
Hemynge doe paye toe hymm fromm the Oakenn Cheste
att oure Globe Theatre mye Playes hereafterr mentd. Mye
Tempese Mye Mydsomerrs dreme. Mackbethe. Henry viii
& mye altered Playe of Titus Andronicus all written bye
myselfe & placed inn sd. Cheste as of usuage att oure
Theatre & shod. they bee everr agayne Impryntedd I doe
orderr thatt theye bee soe donn from these mye true writtenn Playes & nott from those nowe prynted. . . . To Masterr Lowinne oure beste Actorr I doe orderr as folowithe
ye. lyke somm of 5 l. to be pd. bye Hemynge & thatt hee
delyverr toe hymm the Playes thatt doe followe Mye
moche ado aboute noethynge The Wives of Windsore.
Rycharde ye 3d as allso mye Coryolanus. . . . Toe Master
Conndell who hathe done me manye services I doe orderr
as folowithe thatt hee bee allso pd. ye somm of 5 l. & thatt
hee . . . Rememberr mee afterr mye dethe I doe herebye
orderr hymm a plaine Golde Rynge of ye worthe of 20
shyllyngs Toe my good Kempe I doe give 3 l. & a gold
Rynge itt muste bee lyke Value 20 s. Toe Masterr Burbage
I give as folowithe from the Cheste afsd. mye 2 Playes of
Cymbelyne & Othello together withe mye chose Interrlude
neverr yette Impryntedd & wrottenn for & bye desyre of
oure late gracyowse & belovedd Quene Elisabethe called
ye Virginn Quene & playde 3 tymes before herreselfe. . . .

There follow gifts to Master Armynne, Master Shancke, Master Ryce, Master Greggs, to Greggs' little son for the "trouble he hathe hadd" in delivering letters to the Globe, and finally—the most important part of this Deed—the bequests to Heminge himself:

as a Recompence forr ye troble [!] hee will have in seeynge thys mye deede ryghtlye executedd I doe herebye orderr thatt hee doe take for hymself ye somm of 10 l. & 20 shyllyngs toe buye hymm a Golde Rynge I allsoe give hymm out of sd. Chestt ye Playes folowg. Mye Gentlemenn of Verona alterrd mye Measure for Measure Comedye of Errorrs Merrchaunte of Venice Togetherr withe mye newe Playe neverr yette imprynted called Kynge Hy. vii these toe bee whollye for sd. J. Hemynge. And as there wille stille remayne in hys hands 287 l. & 14 shyllyngs I furtherr orderr hym toe brynge upp that Chylde of whome wee have spokenn butt who muste nott be named here & to doe same I desyre hym toe place owte sd. Moneye in ye beste waye he cann doe tylle sd. Child shall be of Age fyttenn toe receyve sd. Moneye & withe whatte shall comm uppon sd. Moneye soe toe Instructe hym as aforesayde I allsoe orderr Masterr Hemynge toe selle mye three howses inn ye Borowghe & toe putte oute ye. Moneye comynge from same forr sd. Childe I allsoe give toe sd. Chylde ye eyghte Playes thatt be stylle inne sd. Cheste as allso mye otherr Playe neverr yett Impryntedd called Kyng Vorrtygerne thys as allso ye otherr eyghte toe bee whollye forr ye benyfytte of sd. Chylde as welle ye pryntynge as playinge same and shoulde I chaunce write more as bye Gods helpe & grace I hope toe doe I herebye give ye Profytts of evry Kynde comynge fromm anye suche newe playes orr otherr Wrytyngs untoe sd. Chylde & hys heires forr everr trustynge toe mye

freynde John Hemynges honorr and allso onn hys promys
of beyng clouse of speeche inn thys laste Matterr. . . .

The Deed is dated February 23, 1611, over five years before the
date of Shakespeare's death.

Had Ireland senior known enough about Shakespeare, he
could have found reasons aplenty to withhold this document from
publication. The opening paragraph is apparently calculated to
cast doubts upon the true will: we are free, as a result of William
Henry's inventions, to suspect either the evil machinations of lawyers or else (since Shakespeare's Last Will and Testament was
drawn up in March, 1616, a month before his death) a weakening
of the Bard's faculties. Not having that will to work from, and
perhaps having only a vague recollection of its contents, William
Henry was at the same time opening the door to whatever provi-
sions it actually contains.

It is astonishing that neither he nor his father should have
been concerned at the reference to but one daughter in this Deed
of Gift. It seems impossible that Samuel Ireland, Shakespearola-
tor, should not have known with the rest of the world that there
were two daughters. Were the names of Judith and Susanna unknown to the forger, since he mentions neither? Quite possibly,
for the gaps in his knowledge were formidable for one of his daring. Or was it simply that he was in such haste, as usual, that he
could not wait the opportunity to refresh his memory?

Was the reader of this Deed to envisage Mrs. Shakespeare
hugging her husband's suit of grey velvet, according to approved
eighteenth-century notions of inflated passion, in transports of
sorrowing love after his demise? It is, however, gratifying to see
that William Henry's Bard has not lost his obsession with the dis-
pensing of rings. The reference to seven letters written to Miss
Hathaway before marriage is a deft way of substantiating the letter and poem to her already unearthed—and also evidence in advance of more to come, perhaps. It is, however, difficult to under-

stand why the recipient of these letters should not have treasured them in a chest herself, rather than allowing her husband to do so. Again, it is odd that the Bard needs to sell his share in two houses near the Globe to raise £20 7s. when he is able to leave his wife £180, and knows that £287 will be in Heminge's hands. There is, too, more evidence on the Southampton matter, together with the giving away of more rings. Once more, plays, which having been written for the Bard's company were no longer his property, are bequeathed. However, William Henry explains for those who knew no more than himself why the plays, already taken care of in this Deed of Gift, did not need to be mentioned later in the true will. As for *Henry VIII*, that was written (in collaboration with Fletcher) at a date later than the date on this deed. William Henry seems to have had a continuing prejudice against Condell, for here we see him less highly esteemed than others.

The next passage, the most astonishing, the most matchless in brazen invention, yet contains something touching in it. The reference to "that child of whom we have spoken but who must not be named here" was perhaps dictated by the rankling conviction in William Henry's heart of his own illegitimacy. He was placing himself in distinguished company. Moreover, if the adored Shakespeare could father a bastard, who would blame Ireland senior for a similar lapse?

This was in truth a "revelation" startlingly dramatic. No wonder that after making it William Henry began to weary of his document. Was his lethargy too powerful for him to bother remembering names for the eight other plays that are to be given Shakespeare's bastard?

But there is the significant detail of the old chest. One was induced to assume that this was the same chest which was now in Mr. H.'s possession. If so, is not the implication that Mr. H. is actually a descendant of the Bard's illegitimate son? And would not this explain his reluctance to be known by the general public as connected with the Shakespeare Papers?

Other implications might be read too. Mr. H.'s designation probably originated, as I have suggested, in William Henry's devotion to *Love and Madness,* but it now opened new avenues of speculation. Could not "H" stand for Heminge? Had the trusted Heminge after the Bard's death betrayed his trust, abandoned the child, and withheld from him his inheritance? Or had he given the child his own name? Or had that preserver of life William Henry Ireland come again to the rescue, adopted the boy, and given him *his* own name?

At any rate, the innuendos were sufficient, it was to be expected, to allay Samuel Ireland's impatience to have Mr. H. reveal himself. Whether Mr. H. were a descendant of the Bard's bastard or a descendant of a treacherous Heminge—in either case his reluctance to be thereby known to the world was fully comprehensible in a man of rank.

And, miracle of miracles, suddenly *Vortigern* is identified by the Bard as his own, a "play never yet imprinted." Its profits too are to go to Shakespeare's son—and now, by extension, to William Henry, and through William Henry's generosity to his beloved father. In all this there emerges an apparent confusion. Are we to think of the illegtimate son of the Bard as the antecedent of Mr. H. or of William Henry? But the confusion itself makes sense. Mr. H. actually lived nowhere but in William Henry's brain, and it is understandable that he might have thought of the "said Child" as an ancestor to both of them.

SEVEN

Storm Clouds

ACCORDING TO the original agreement between Sheridan and Ireland, *Vortigern* should have already been produced at the Drury Lane. But Sheridan had been less and less enthusiastic about his impulsive commitment as William Henry produced the successive pages of the play. He confessed dissatisfaction with the drama as a whole, and was of the opinion that it was an early inferior work of Shakespeare's. By haggling over the terms he was able to procrastinate, and thereby to eliminate Covent Garden as a contender for the privilege of producing the "lost" work. It was not until September 9 that Sheridan signed a contract with Ireland, and then, as we have seen, on miserly terms. The first performance was to be held not later than December 15 of that year.

But time passed and no effort was made to construct the new scenery which had been promised. Ireland began to suspect, quite accurately, that the magnificent costumes and sets which had been assured would not be forthcoming. Though neither of these were being made, the Drury Lane management suddenly demanded Ireland's manuscript of the play for making a copy with modernized spelling. Alarmed, Ireland wrote to Sheridan, voicing his fears that "it is intended to substitute old Scenery for the new ones which you have always promised."

To placate him Sheridan arranged a meeting between Ireland

174

and the Drury Lane's actor-manager, John Kemble, for November 17. When Samuel Ireland appeared with his son at the theatre at the appointed hour, they were told that Kemble had already left the premises. Ireland returned home and at once sent a note expressing his belief that Kemble was "a luke-warm friend to the play"—a declaration which was in fact a vast understatement.

John Philip Kemble, son of an actor, and brother to the celebrated Mrs. Siddons, had had two decades of varied experience outside London before appearing at the Drury Lane in 1783, where he was first seen in a much-admired *Hamlet*. During his nineteen years of association with the company he was to enact nearly every leading male role Shakespeare had created, frequently opposite his sister. A man of noble and expressive face and voice, of easy grace and natural elegance, he was nevertheless subject to adverse criticism because of his mannerisms and affectations on the boards. By choice he pronounced "insidious," "hideous," "cheerful," "fierce," and "merchant," as *insijous, hijeous, churful, furse,* and *marchant.* In his acting ("the Kemble school") he was given to a declamatory style. The judgments of his contemporaries are pretty much at variance with one another. Leigh Hunt said that he was grand rather than passionate, and incapable of communicating the idea of love, but added that he was without equal in his soliloquies. Hazlitt, who much preferred Kean, praised Kemble for achieving a sense of the grandeur and beauty of the antique. Scott lauded him for his gentlemanlike feeling. Lamb confessed that he would always see Hamlet as Kemble. And Byron called him "the most supernatural of actors."

In the year of the *Vortigern* transactions Kemble was having his own emotional difficulties, which resulted, at the close of 1795, in his publishing rather amazingly an apology for having made amorous, violent, but unencouraged attacks upon Miss De Camp, a member of the company who later married his brother Charles. It is just possible that these disturbances may have been somewhat responsible for his ungracious conduct to the Irelands, for though a vain man and overly fond of the bottle, he was generally commended for his tact and kindness.

The only response Ireland had for his letter of complaint on Kemble's ill-treatment was a cold request that he either return his advance royalties or submit the manuscript of the play at once. Ireland did neither, for he had found a valuable friend in one of the darlings of the stage, Mrs. Jordan.

Dorothea Jordan, Irish by birth, was especially admired for her performances at the Drury Lane in comedies. Hazlitt was mad over her voice, which he declared to be "a cordial to the heart. . . . To hear her laugh was to drink of nectar." She was a large woman, "soft and generous, like her soul." After bearing a daughter to her first manager, and four children to Richard Ford, she became the mistress of the Duke of Clarence, the future William IV. To him she bore ten children, all of whom took the name of Fitzclarence. An amusing story is told of a retort she made to His Majesty George III. Hearing that his son, the Duke of Clarence, was giving her an allowance of a thousand pounds a year, the King wrote her a letter reducing the amount to five hundred pounds. On the bottom of a playbill she sent this reply to George: "No money returned after the rising of the curtain."

This kindhearted woman had taken a liking to young William Henry, and with the gathering of hostile criticism she became a loyal partisan of the Shakespeare Papers. On November 18, the very day after Kemble snubbed the Irelands at the theatre, Mrs. Jordan arranged a meeting between them and her princely lover at St. James's Palace. They brought with them the manuscript of *Vortigern* to show Clarence, who naturally felt that his regal station lent him authority on all matters. He was satisfied that the play was authentically Shakespeare's, and encouraged Ireland to refuse surrendering a copy of it to Drury Lane until work on the scenery should have at least begun. He added some words of spirited disparagement on Sheridan and Kemble, and subscribed on the spot to seven copies of Ireland's imminent publication of the Papers.

Such august attention could not but have borne fruits. In a matter of days William Henry was able to tell his father that he had discovered another Shakespearean play, also hitherto unknown, *Henry II*. He thought he could profit from the opinions he had heard concerning *Vortigern*, and was the more inspired when he remembered how the Bard's genius "had been so amply displayed in dramatising the histories of our Henries." He spent ten weeks in composing *Henry II*, and never troubled to copy it in the disguised hand on old paper—for a good reason. Before he could get around to write it in an antique hand his time of glory was over.

The month of December, 1795, was anticipated as a month of joy. Anna Maria Ireland would marry her young man of India House, *Vortigern* was to be produced at the Drury Lane, and Ireland's volume of the Papers would appear. Anna Maria was married, but December 15 came and went and *Vortigern* remained unproduced.

On December 24, 1795, the *London Times* carried an advertisement apprising Mr. Ireland's subscribers that his volume of the Shakespeare papers: "will be ready for delivery THIS DAY at his house in Norfolk Street." It was impressively entitled *Miscellaneous Papers and Legal Instruments under the Hand and Seal of William Shakespeare, including the Tragedy of King Lear and a Small Fragment of Hamlet, from the Original Manuscripts in the Possession of Samuel Ireland*. The large folio also contained facsimiles of the drawings and of the lock of Shakespeare's hair. *Vortigern* and *Henry II* were not included—the discovery of the latter, in any case, having occurred too late for the press.

Ireland's Preface would indicate that, despite all his worries over Mr. H. and the adverse comments in the air, he himself entertained not the slightest doubt of the genuineness of his possessions. Ever since the Papers began to be delivered to him he has spared, he declares, no labor to certify their validity. There has not been one impartial literary critic to whom he has been unwilling to submit these documents. "He has courted, he has even challenged, the critical judgment of those, who are best skilled in the Poetry and Phraseology of the times in which Shakspeare lived; as well as those, whose profession or course of study has made them conversant with ancient deeds, writings, seals and autographs. Wide and extensive as this range may appear, and it includes the Scholar, the Man of Taste, the Antiquarian, and the Herald, his enquiries have not rested in the Closet of the Specialist." He has also consulted the "paper-maker" and professional writers. The unanimous verdict has been that these Papers are authentic and that "where there was such a mass of evidence, internal and external, it was impossible . . . for the art of imitation to have hazarded so much without betraying itself, and consequently that *these Papers can be no other than the production of Shakspeare himself.*" Something is naturally owing to the public in way of explanation as to how the editor came by these documents. "He received them from his son, Samuel-William-Henry Ireland, a young man then under nineteen years of age, by whom the discovery was accidentally made at the house of a gentleman of considerable property." Ireland then tells the story of his son's finding "some deeds very material to the interests of this gentleman. . . . In return for this service, added to the consideration that the young man bore the same name and arms with the person who saved the life of Shakspeare, this gentleman promised him everything relative to the present subject, that had been or should be found either in town or at his house in the country." The editor himself is confident of the authenticity of these Papers. Because of his indebtedness to the gentleman, to whom he is not known personally, he does not feel justified in asking him "to subject himself to the impertinence and licentiousness of literary curiosity and cavil unless he should himself voluntarily come forward." When the editor applied to him for permission to publish, "this was not obtained but under the strongest injunction that his name should not appear." It has been hinted that the disclosure of the gentleman's name would settle all doubts. But who suggests this? Not "the real Critic or Antiquarian," who have their science to fortify their conclusions.

There follows a rhapsody on the "Genius of Shakspeare." After which Samuel Ireland permitted himself the folly of expressing his literary judgment: "The alterations made in the printed copies of Lear are manifestly introduced by the players, and are deviations from that spontaneous flow of soul and simple diction, which so eminently distinguish this great Author, this Child of Nature; and . . . the additions and alterations interspersed . . . have not unfrequently been introduced at the expence of the natural course of the narrative . . . and uniformity of the author's style. . . . The MS. here presented to the Public must have been the original and, probably, the only one by the author."

The attempt to impose on others, the editor reflects, is a grave crime. But just as serious is accusing someone else of trying to impose on others. This charge has been made against the editor. He can only say that had he even the ghost of a suspicion that these Papers, every one of them, were not authentic, he would never have published them. The Preface concludes with an announcement that besides *Vortigern*, now being prepared for staging at the Drury Lane, "another and more interesting historical Play has been discovered amongst the other papers, in the handwriting of Shakspeare: this will in due time be laid before the public." The editor is also in possession "of a great part of Shakspeare's Library . . . with Notes in his own hand," exhibiting the Bard in a new light as "the Critic and the Moralist," of "acute and penetrating judgment, with a disposition amiable and gentle as his Genius was transcendant." Every sincere admirer of the Bard will agree with the editor that nothing should be lost, "scarce even 'One drop which fell from Shakspeare's pen.' "

The publication of the Papers was for Ireland a happy event

with which to usher in the Christmas season. It gave him an importance before the world such as he could never have dreamed of attaining. But it may have seemed merely the cause of and prologue to a higher joy—the maximum of privilege to a true middle-class Briton: an invitation to Carlton House for an audience with the Prince of Wales! The generosity of Mrs. Jordan, who not in vain was raising a large family for the Prince's brother, had opened even those exclusive portals for him. The appointment was for December 28.

On the morning of that day, when Mr. Jermingham came to Norfolk Street to escort Samuel Ireland to felicity, it must have seemed inconceivable that anything could sophisticate the perfection of the occasion. He offered a private inspection of the sacred papers to his escort, but found him not particularly eager for the experience. Well, it did not matter; His Royal Highness was!

But just as they were ready to leave in a coach a thunderbolt was hurled at Ireland. The wielder was, of all people, his good friend and neighbor, the attorney Mr. Albany Wallis. Marching in with aggressive steps, and indicating his pocket, Wallis declared, "I have here something to show you that will do your business for you, and knock up your Shakespeare papers." These dreadful words were, of course, also heard by Mr. Jermingham, who was standing by the fire.

Wallis was himself something of an antiquarian. It was he who had unearthed among the papers of the Featherstonehaugh family the mortgage deed which had served as the model for William Henry's first Shakespearean forgery. That deed Wallis had presented to Garrick, who in turn had bequeathed it to the British Museum. Wallis had just discovered a deed authentically signed by John Heminge!

On such a day to have this happen! Ireland was now shown Heminge's signature on the new-found document. It was, naturally, totally dissimilar to the one inscribed by William Henry's left hand on his Shakespeare-Heminge paper, already broadcast to the public in his father's volume. There was nothing that Ireland could counter, in the face of such evidence, nothing he could do until William Henry came home. It is easy to imagine the tumult of his thoughts as he left for the coveted audience.

When William Henry published his *Confessions* a decade later he was careful to imply that this shaking challenge had presented itself at an earlier date. Perhaps he did not wish to appear to have poisoned his father's pleasure on such a unique occasion. Whatever anguish Ireland experienced during his audience with the Prince of Wales remains undocumented; the account in the *Confessions* contains no hint of the old man's perturbation. We are merely told that William Henry asked his father for a full account of the visit to Carlton House, which he later amply reports. The Prince was most informal, and questioned Ireland on every point connected with the Papers with a sagacity Ireland had never before witnessed among scholars. Having examined the documents carefully and listened to Ireland's reading aloud of the Profession of Faith, the Prince declared that the external appearance of the Papers certainly testified to their validity, but that to come to a final decision would require more reflection than this cursory inspection. But he complimented Ireland upon the discovery, since Shakespeare belongs not only to the literary world but to the English nation.

It is possible that the Prince was too good a diplomatist to commit himself finally to an acceptance of the Papers. It is equally possible that Ireland, with Wallis' visit at the back of his mind, helped the Prince avoid such a commitment. Or again, since the account was written long after William Henry's bubble had burst, perhaps he was altering the facts so that the Prince might appear less gullible than he had been. This last view is supported by the consideration that in his narrative of the earlier audience with the Duke of Clarence, William Henry pictures the Duke as having held out against belief until his doubts about the fantastic spelling had been satisfactorily answered by Ireland. After all, the Prince of Wales was due to become king of England, and Clarence too might succeed to the throne, as indeed he eventually did.

We may well imagine that the time spent in the Prince's presence must have been for Ireland more pain than pleasure, though it is fair to assume that he gave no voice to the suspicions which were crowding in upon him. But on his return home, he did not spare his son when William Henry put in an appearance at three o'clock. Horrified, William Henry hurried up Norfolk Street to see Wallis. It took but a glance at the attorney's valid Heminge paper to see that he was apparently about to be undone. Mumbling some excuse, he dashed home, where his family noted his agitation and the perspiration on his brow. He ran out again, saying that he must see Mr. H. at once for an explanation.

From Norfolk Street he ran to his employer's offices, with the memory of Heminge's valid signature pounding in his brain. As soon as he got there he committed to paper a signature as much like the document's as he could recollect, and then penned a receipt with the antique ink upon an old paper: it recorded some theatrical disbursements. With this document he ran back to Wallis' house.

Wallis compared this new paper with his own and was struck with the similarity. William Henry now told him that he had run to Mr. H., who was luckily at home, and expressed his alarm at the disparity between the signatures of Heminge on the Wallis deed and the Shakespeare document. Amused at the boy's concern, the magnanimous Mr. H. had smiled, gone to his writing table, opened a drawer, and extracted from it this second Heminge document, saying, "Take that to Mr. Wallis's, and see if it does not correspond with the handwriting to his deed."

Seeing William Henry still puzzled, his benefactor had explained: there were *two* John Heminges in Shakespeare's day—one connected with the Globe Theatre and the other with the Curtain Theatre. The John Heminge of Mr. Wallis' deed and this second receipt was the man well known to be Shakespeare's friend; the John Heminge who had gone down to Stratford for Shakespeare was of the Curtain, but also had some slight connection with the Globe. To avoid confusion between these two of the same name, Mr. H. had concluded, they were "distinguished by the appellations of the *tall* John Heminges of the Globe, and the *short* John Heminges of the Curtain."

Wallis was perfectly convinced by this interesting story, and apparently did not feel it odd that the unknown Mr. H. should have had an authentic Heminge signature so ready at hand, particularly after Mr. H.'s firm asseveration of indifference to his vast pile of old documents—an asseveration which had initially been the cause of his opening his hoard to young William Henry's curiosity.

It was a narrow escape for the boy, and a fairly amazing exploit. It took him, from the time he first saw Wallis' paper, ran home, then to his employer's chambers to write the new paper, returned to Wallis' with his fresh discovery and the tale of a short and tall Heminge, and finally went back to the office to re-execute the receipt (which he did to make it more convincing), only seventy-five minutes. Wallis' house was at the bottom of Norfolk Street in the Strand and the conveyancer's chambers were in the New Inn. No wonder he was not suspected of forging this new paper.

The rewriting of the Heminge receipt was owing to a sudden emergence of artistic conscience. When William Henry appeared for the second time at Wallis' and was comparing his new forgery with the true paper, it occurred to him that he could have done better with Tall Heminge's autograph. A second study of it enabled him to manufacture a closer resemblance. To fortify the authority of the signatures of both Short and Tall Heminge, William Henry in the next few days discovered several more receipts.

His father's mind was at peace again, though doubtless he would have given much to have that audience with the Prince all over again. As for Wallis, it was, for a while at least, well that he too was reassured. Before long he would be called upon to step forth to affirm anew his faith as a Believer.

This tumultuous day, it turned out, ended with joy, as it had begun. Mr. Pye, Poet Laureate, visited the Irelands to read *Vortigern* in modern spelling. Encouraged, unquestionably, by the interest of the Prince of Wales, he offered to write the Prologue for the play's production at the Drury Lane. He was moved by *Vortigern*, being a man of no taste, declared it a fine play, and wished with a sigh that he could have composed it himself. The work was plainly a creation of the Matchless Bard—there were "so many passages in his style and of so much excellence" that it was absurd to doubt the authorship for a moment. Pye shed some tears appropriate to the occasion, and averred that he had not been so deeply affected by any play for a long time. He would get busy on the Prologue at once.

By the beginning of the new year Ireland was having to cope with difficulties enough over the production of *Vortigern*. But with the publication of the Papers public contention began in earnest and his difficulties multiplied. The first shots of malice came from James Boaden, who, as we have seen, was one of the earliest and most fervent of Believers. But he was a friend of George Steevens, a man who doted on the opportunity to be malevolent in a good cause, and it was probably pressure from that venerated scholar which urged upon Boaden a change of heart. At first, Boaden contented himself with publishing in the *Oracle* extracts of his own composition which purported to be from the Irelands' *Vortigern*, the text of which he had never seen. His inventions, though harmless, had the effect of subjecting the play to mockery in advance of its presentation, and of confusing his readers as to whether or not the passages in the *Oracle* were truly from the newly discovered play of Shakespeare.

Boaden had not subscribed to the papers. When they were printed at last, he asked Ireland for a copy, promising dubiously in his note that the *Oracle* would "exert every means to keep the work in the public eye." By now Ireland had reason enough to give that promise the worst of interpretations, and naturally refused. To this refusal Boaden at once countered with a message in print from "Maister William Shakspeare in the Shades to Samuel Ireland Esq.":

> CONUNDRUMS! LOVE LETTERS! PROFESSIONS *de foi,*
> And straggling INDENTURES in form *de la loi,*
> A copy corrected of Britain's old LEAR
> (Where with pleasure I see nothing ribald appear).
> And to these many sports of the sons of the STAGE
> Add the favorite works in retirement of AGE
> On which my weak brain you affirm set more store
> Than all it had ever imagined before. . . .

But Boaden was planning a heavier blast than this. To prepare for it he did not refrain from a piece of trickery. On December 24, the day the book appeared, he had sent to Ireland for a copy; refused, Boaden asked White's of Fleet Street for the loan of the volume. When Ireland saw the extract in the following day's *Oracle,* he complained to White, who demanded the return of the book. On sending it back, Boaden wrote his thanks for a view of "the most splendid imposition" he had ever beheld. On January 11, 1796, Boaden issued his *Letter to George Steevens Esq.,* a critique of the Papers.

Naturally he had to account for his earlier support of them. When he became aware of them, he says, he went to Norfolk Street and there heard Samuel Ireland "read them at leisure." Boaden was too anxious to think them authentic, he admits, and for some time believed them so because of the antique writing, the old paper, the old watermarks. "To a mind filled with the most ardent love and the most eager zeal, disarmed of caution by the character too of the gentleman who displayed them, it will not be a subject of severe reproof that the wished impression was made. I remember that I beheld the papers with the tremor of purest delight—touched the valuable relics with reverential respect, and

deemed even existence dearer, as it gave me so refined a satisfaction." But later, in the privacy of his study, doubts began to
accumulate. There was too much about the Papers at war with
known fact. He therefore gave up going to Norfolk Street.

Now that the Papers are published, he agrees that it is of no
importance from whom they came. But Ireland's Preface to the
volume is amazing: he asserts that *King Lear* as we have known
it is to a great extent the work of players, and deviates from the
Bard's own spontaneous flow of simple diction. Having read the
new *Lear*, Boaden can only say of Ireland's remarks that they are
incredible. The players are converted to polished masters of versi-
fication and Shakespeare into a writer without ear for rhythm or
even the capacity "to number ten syllables upon his fingers,"
Boaden then points out the "glaring" absurdities and the "nonsen-
sical, disjointed, inconclusive and mutilated form" of this so-called
original version, as well as its Chattertonian spelling. His objections to the other Papers are just as sane and moderate. The one
document that irritates him is the Deed of Gift to Ireland, and he
summons undeniable facts to demolish it. The greatest mystery to
him is how Ireland can have believed in these forgeries. After all,
he draws and engraves, has a taste for the black letter, has a fine
collection of books, and the patience of a true antiquary. Why does
he think the antiquity of the paper proof of the validity of the
contents? Anyone can procure more Elizabethan paper in a week
than Shakespeare could have written upon.

Boaden appended to the pamphlet the "Extracts from Vortigern" which he had printed in the *Oracle*. His genial parodies indicate that had he been tempted to forgery, he would have made a
more convincing impostor than William Henry. On the other hand,
since he was writing in burlesque he was freer to ape Shakespeare's lines, which he does, while William Henry, composing a
new play, could not take that easier way.

(A few decades later, when the business of the Ireland forgeries was already forgotten history, William Henry met Boaden

in London. By that time Boaden had achieved some literary fame because of his biographies of Kemble and Mrs. Siddons. The two men walked together for a little and inevitably their talk drifted to the subject of the Papers. Boaden was not of a mind to soften his old censure of the forgeries: "You must be aware, sir, of the enormous crime you committed against the divinity of Shakspeare. Why, the act, sir, was nothing short of sacrilege; it was precisely the same as taking the holy Chalice from the altar and ******* therein!!!")

Boaden's shot was quickly followed up. In its issue of January, 1796, the *Monthly Mirror* commented on the Ireland volume in capital letters: "THE WHOLE IS A GROSS AND IMPUDENT IMPOSITION, AN INSULT TO THE CHARACTER OF OUR IMMORTAL BARD, AND A LIBEL ON THE TASTE AND UNDERSTANDING OF THE NATION!!"

Such outspoken ill will seemed the prelude to more dangerous attacks, for it was well known that at any time adverse criticism would be forthcoming from the two giants of Shakespearean scholarship, Malone and Steevens. Each was said to be engaged on a mighty sally against the Papers. With things becoming so crucial, Ireland thought it wise to push the *Vortigern* production to a fulfillment. Since Pye had promised his Prologue immediately, and since a prologue in those days was as necessary to the success of a play as a good *hors d'oeuvre* is to a good dinner, he reminded the Laureate of his promise. The Laureate mumbled his apologies for not having written a line: he had seen Kemble, who had insisted that the Prologue must not take a strong position with regard to Shakespeare's authorship of the play. Ireland lectured Pye on having the courage of his own convictions, and the poet agreed to embark on the composition immediately.

Nevertheless, it was not until the end of January that Pye had a Prologue to submit. It was considerably less than satisfactory. It flattered the audience:

> No fraud your penetrating eye can cheat
> None *here* can Shakspeare's writing counterfeit . . .

As well might a taper pretend to be "the orb of day" as "modern Bards" to catch any of Shakespeare's "celestial fire." If, therefore, the audience finds marks of the master, if its "tears of pity flow," its breast "with horror" fills and "with rapture" glows, that will be the proof that this work is indeed Shakespeare's. But if such proof is lacking, despite the stamp of approval given by "critics, antiquarians, Heralds," such authorities are not to be believed. The discerning eye can at once differentiate the counterfeit from true coin of the realm, so too the audience will judge by reading "the laws of Nature in the heart."

This was not even noncommittal. The jibe at Sir Isaac Heard ("Heralds") and the Ireland circle was obvious. The reference to counterfeiting intolerable. It is understandable that Heard's assistant, and Ireland's good friend, Francis Webb, should agree with a lady who had been shown Pye's Prologue, that "one would think that one of the *other* party" had written it.

It was almost impossible to get Pye to alter it since Kemble already had approved it. Pye said that he did not wish to alienate Kemble since he himself was then working on a play which he hoped to see produced at the Drury Lane. A gentle man, Pye at length yielded to Ireland's indignant protests, and softened the offending passages. Instead, he urged the audience not to trouble itself too much about the Shakespearean authorship of the play. Why worry about its being an illegitimate child, if the child itself be "strong and hearty?" But even the revised Prologue was bound to give more comfort to the enemies of the Papers than to the Believers.

In anticipation of the onslaughts of Malone and Steevens, Ireland had asked Francis Webb to issue a pamphlet stating the firm faith of a True Believer. Webb tried to beg off, not because his heart was not in it, but because he felt unequal to the responsibility, and proposed Dr. Parr as a more authoritative and imposing advocate. Finally Webb agreed. At the time his apologia was issued, Boaden's attack had just appeared. Webb did not therefore undertake to answer it.

It is touching to see the man's decency displayed in a cause unworthy of it. In *Shakspeare's Manuscripts in the Possession of Mr. Ireland* by "Philalethes," Webb vows that he never knew Ireland until introduced to him "by a gentleman of the first character and reputation"—Isaac Heard, no doubt. Knowing Ireland very well now, he can testify that he has always been open and candid. Webb observes that all the Papers must be either authentic or forged. Men of authority have certified the antiquity of the writing materials; moreover, all the papers "reciprocally illustrate and confirm each other. This is remarkably the case respecting the Deed of Gift to IRELAND, on the extraordinary circumstance of saving Shakspeare's life when nearly drowned in the river Thames, and also in that very important Deed of Trust to John Hemynge." Now, since the age of the documents is beyond question, if these are forgeries, they must have been fabricated in Shakespeare's own day. What could have been the point of such falsifications at that time? The Papers have not been put to any use since they were written, and have been lying all the while in obscurity. What reason could anyone have had for forging them? On the other hand, "they are so numerous and yet consistent, so various and yet so minute and particular" as to indicate their validity. Considered individually, they are so unconnected in time and circumstance as to render the idea of forgery impossible. Why should anyone forge a legal document when he cannot possibly profit from it? Would not a forger have contented himself with "less minute and circumstantial evidence than that of a lock of the Poet's own hair?" The verses accompanying that lock are such "as a simple swain, as he then was, would have transmitted to his fair. . . . Nature and Nature alone produces documents like these."

What a superstructure to erect upon a false premise! Had Webb but entertained the contingency that the Papers could have been written *after* Shakespeare's day, he would have had no argument.

William Henry must have felt his heart expand at this public evaluation of him as the equal in genius of the Bard. For but a couple of months more would he be allowed to exult in his deceptions. But he must have been in a delirium of pleasure when, in approved eighteenth-century rapture, Webb wrote that the variety and interest of these Papers are all unified "by the exalted genius and unbounded imagination of him to whom they relate." Some authors could be imitated, but not Shakespeare. "To imitate him, so as to pass deceit on the world, appears to me next to impossibility. Who can soar with his sublime genius? Who could soar with his boundless imagination? Who could rival his pregnant wit? Who with intuitive inspection discover the workings of the human mind, and by the natural evolutions of the passions interest us so deeply, as this matchless poet?" If these Papers are not Shakespeare's, "to whom do they belong?" For his own part, even without the certainty of the antiquity of the papers and parchments, he would have said at once that there never was but *one* man who could have produced such works, that he, and *he only,* has produced him." Had not the Bard's name appeared on the Papers, Webb would "not have hesitated to have ascribed them to him."

Poor Webb! What did he later do when forced to face the fact that his "Matchless Poet" was only a sentimental adolescent? We do not know. It is safe to assume that he found it wise to abstain from all literary judgments for the rest of his life. His brave support of the Irelands was based upon inadequacy of taste, but in this regard he was not inferior to most of his contemporaries. Adaptations, additions, and rewritings of Shakespeare's masterpieces had so much vitiated his century's appreciation that there were very few lovers of the Bard who had more than a distant understanding of what his plays actually are like. This, I believe, was a chief source of Ireland's gullibility too.

Sheridan was long past his promised time for the production

of *Vortigern,* but he was at last beginning to prepare for it. It was generally felt, quite correctly, that the performance at the Drury Lane would provide a verdict on all the Papers. Meanwhile, despite Boaden's attack, support for Ireland and detraction of his collection were fairly evenly balanced. Most people were suspending opinion until Malone should be heard from and *Vortigern* seen. But the picture gave token of shifting rapidly, almost from day to day, as the newspapers evidence. That had its real dangers. With public backing there was nothing to prevent postponing the production so long that desire to see the play would be wearied. Worse yet, with enough encouragement the performance itself could be managed to ridicule *Vortigern* into universal mockery. No play in the world is safe from the destructive hands of burlesque.

On November 4, for instance, the *Tomahawk* had paid Ireland a graceful compliment on the "newly discovered play." But the very day after his tumultuous experiences with Mr. Jermingham, Albany Wallis, and the Prince of Wales, the same newspaper was saying that Ireland appeared too much "*afraid* of the critic *eye,*" when one remembered that "EVERY GENTLEMAN and EVERY SCHOLAR, and every ANTIQUARIAN, naturally suppose that he would be eager to *invite* CRITICISM, instead of being *eager* to shun it." And the very next day after that, December 30, the paper printed verses indited to him:

> Ireland, Ireland, tell to me,
> "Who wrote Shakespeare's writings?"—THEE! . . .

Henceforth it would be Ireland senior who would be charged with the forgery, not his son; and even among those who believed William Henry the culprit, the majority would be satisfied that the father was the real instigator. Despite William Henry's later admissions, nothing would avail to alter the injustice to Samuel Ireland.

Of course, much of the scoffing was no more than good-natured banter. On January 25, 1796, for example, "An Antiquary" reports in the *Tomahawk* the finding of a copy of Ben Jonson's work in an old trunk, not to be wondered at in "this day of *trunk-finding*": in a "neat old hand" Shakespeare's name is inscribed in the book with this notation: "Theis was thee celebratted authore offe that naimme who wrotte comoedies and tragoedies." But there is something more ominous in the warning of the February issue of the *English Review:* "Literary men consider an attack on their taste and understanding as a more heinous crime than the attempt upon their purse."

On February 16, Walley Chamberlain Oulton came to the rescue of Ireland with his *Vortigern under Consideration,* issued anonymously. A Dubliner by birth, Oulton while quite young wrote many farces and musical extravaganzas, all of them popular. Scholars have been particularly indebted to him for a series of compilations of contemporary theatrical history; in 1804 he published *Shakespeare's Poems.* In his pamphlet Oulton does not declare that *Vortigern* is by Shakespeare; he merely insists that it could be. Certainly he hopes that it is, largely because of the "present dearth of Dramatic Entertainments." There is nothing disturbing to him in Ireland's claims for the *Lear* manuscript: Shakespeare was indifferent to future fame and "the performers *did* take liberties with his pieces." Here Oulton has a crushing argument: "Do they not take liberties *now?*" *Vortigern* may very well be a play which Shakespeare had laid aside. As for the other Papers, "There is an uniformity in the handwriting which I think beyond the power of the most ingenious *forger.*" If any forger could have written *Vortigern* in a style similar to the Bard's, why should he ascribe it to the latter "when he might attain the honorable appellation of a SECOND SHAKESPEARE?" No doubt some of the "mean paragraphs" which have been appearing are owing to the fact that "*some* are afraid" that *Vortigern* "may probably correct the present vitiated state of the Drama," that current flimsy productions "will not be able to withstand so formidable an opposition." Why should the play be judged by an individual or by

"SECRET tribunal" (Boaden was the author of *The Secret Tribunal*, a tragedy) instead of by the public at the theatre? The quaint spelling of the Papers is no objection to them, for "had the spelling been similar to the first printed edition of Shakespeare, there had been greater cause for suspicion." Moreover, the uniformity of the Papers makes their fabrication improbable; no one forger could have written them all.

Oulton's justification of a reference to the Globe before the Globe Theatre had been built is a curious piece of rationalization: "A *Globe* I understand to be a round body, having every part of its surface equally distant from the centre." Now, there was at the time of the manuscript letter a theater in Southwark, and its shape was roughly hexagonal—near enough to a globe to be thought of as one. Why then could the Bard not have been referring metaphorically to *any* theatre as a globe? Moreover, "the stage is an epitome of the 'Great GLOBE itself:' it is not at all unlikely that Shakespeare should make it the general appellation of whatever Theatre he was concerned in:—whether on the BANKSIDE or BLACKFRIARS. He himself said—'All the World's a Stage' and would consequently represent the Stage a *World* in miniature." Oulton's good intentions have surely driven him to the limits of speciousness.

Oulton reflects on the other Papers. The Love Letter, if genuine—no matter how ridiculed by Boaden—"is a precious relic." Boaden has deliberately overlooked the confirming circumstance of the accompanying lock of hair. The Profession of Faith is not to be dismissed, as Boaden does, as containing only pious acquiescence; Oulton reads in it a powerful conviction of "the resurrection and immortality of the soul." No one, further, need make capital of Mr. H.'s unwillingness to reveal himself to the public. Why should that gentleman subject himself "to all the paltry sarcasms and insinuations of every miserable paragraph writer?" As for the Elizabethan William Henry Ireland, he is rendered the more credible just because the drawings on that document are so rudely executed. Their very crudity rules out forgery; what forger would bother inventing such trifles? And the volumes of the Shakespeare Library are so numerous that no man could possibly have ever "completed so laborious an undertaking" except the Bard himself; yet Boaden has made no reference to it. Oulton concludes: "Let Vortigern be tried by a JURY OF *Boxes, Pitt* [*sic*], and *Galleries;* their verdict of 'Genuine' or 'Not Genuine' belongs to THEM only; and it is impossible to judge of a Play before representation. . . . JOHN BULL is no *Calf* to be led by every Ass. He would rather . . . that VORTIGERN and the Play Succeeding may be the genuine Works of Shakespeare; that the Stage, too long disgraced with pantomimes in prose and metre, may resume its wonted dignity."

Except for the exegesis on the Globe, Oulton's pamphlet made a brave showing for the Ireland case. But in the same month of February, 1796, there appeared a sprightly little volume, issued anonymously but written by G. M. Woodward, the caricaturist, *Familiar Verses from the Ghost of Willy Shakespeare to Sammy Ireland,* which must have unsettled Ireland senior with its ridicule. Willy Shakespeare's ghost castigates him for daring to disturb his repose. But for Samuel Ireland he might be taking his rest in "Stratford's hallowed fane." Having in the past conjured spirits from the deep, is he now patiently to hear that he himself has been brought forth from locked trunks?

> . . . in *auncient dirtie* scrolls,
> Long shreds of parchment, deeds and *mustie* rolls.
> .   .   .   .
> Samples of hair, love songs, and sonnets *meete,*
> Together met by *chaunce* in *Norfolk street;*
> Where, fruitful as the vine, the tiny elves
> Produce *young manuscripts* for SAMMY's shelves.
> Dramas in embrio leave their lurking holes,
> And little VORTIGERNS start forth in shoals.
> .   .   .   .
> Freely the cash comes down—lead boldly on,
> The book complete:—Four guineas!—*Presto!*—gone!

> More papers found!!! a neighbor [i.e., Albany Wallis]
>   here hard by—
> . . . .
> Has found some writings in an hand the same,
> The very dots, the stops—the self-same *Shak*,
> That soon must lay each quibbler on his back. . . .

There follows some merriment at the expense of Ireland for his trip to Stratford and his hunt for Shakespeareana. The scene changes to Norfolk Street, where Kemble "with academic grace" pronounces the Papers to be genuine—our versifier plainly was not in touch with matters at the Drury Lane. Malone, "a trusty blade," comes in and "states the whole a sham." Steevens supports Malone's accusations; Burke and Sheridan back Sammy Ireland. But Sheridan is not deeply affected; he does not care whether the play is Shakespeare's or not since "VORTIGERN can't fail the house to fill," and that is all that matters to him. Boydell looks grave but holds his tongue. In the end, despite his wrath, Shakespeare's ghost promises not to show Ireland up. Why should he feel any vengeance due to Ireland in particular, when the plays are dealt with so outrageously by everyone connected with the theatre?

> To speak the truth, I give it on my word,
> For years long past, my Muse has felt the sword—
> Such hacking, slashing, cutting here and there,
> Some parts press'd down, and others puff'd to air,
> That I make oath, and swear it on the spot,
> I know not what is mine and what is not.
> . . . .
> But hold!—Methinks I scent the morning air.
> . . . .
> Sammy, adieu!—*Farewell!* remember me!

The author of this witty satire, though coarse in his drawings, shows himself here as a man of rarely balanced sense. To be just, there was not much excuse for the violence of abuse which was to be the share of the Irelands on the grounds of their distortions of the Bard, in view of the violations sanctioned every week on the London stage. It was a point that few else had the taste to make.

In March judgment was still generally unbiased. The *Analytical Review* compares the discovery of another play by the Bard to the discovery of another gold mine; after copious quotations from the Papers, the editors conclude that Ireland's claims will "undergo an impartial examination at the bar of an intelligent and candid public." (The British public was as traditionally "candid" as the Bard was matchless.)

At the Drury Lane *Vortigern* was being rehearsed. The Believers were at least as vocal as the non-Believers, but who could say that one lightning-bolt from Malone would not ruin the cause of the faithful? Why had Malone not been heard from? What was he planning?

Following Webb's suggestion, Ireland begged Dr. Parr for his public support. If the athletic scholar still believed in the Papers, a pamphlet by him would be better than an army. Alas! Parr cautiously reminded Ireland that he had inspected but the earliest of the documents; he had never seen Queen Elizabeth's letter or any of the plays. The objections of the learned at Oxford to the punctuation and spelling had raised doubts in his own mind, so that he too now was tempted to suspect the authenticity of the dramas, though he assured Ireland that he freed him of any intention of imposing on the world. For the present Parr preferred to keep his judgment suspended.

At this juncture it was at least a relief that Ireland's friend J. Wyatt continued the assault on Boaden by issuing his *Comparative Review of the Opinions of Mr. James Boaden*. His procedure was to discredit the *Letter to George Steevens* by juxtaposing Boaden's earlier and later pronouncements on the Papers. Wyatt begins with a statement of the fullest belief in the Papers, and he does not doubt they will "derive additional lustre and more permanent credit" when placed before a fitting tribunal. That has not been possible "because the host of *erudite* commentators *will not see them* lest they should be convinced." Boaden has been actuated by personal pique or unaccountable caprice: he never explains what caused him to fluctuate from his first enthusiasm. After an exhibition of the inconsistency of Boaden's first and recent criticisms, Wyatt devotes himself to a specific defense. Forgers prefer to elude investigation; Ireland has encouraged "the most rigorous scrutiny" of the Papers, and has shut his door to no man. The result has been "an almost unanimous" affirmation of their validity. How Ireland came into possession of the manuscripts is a matter of no consequence. "They need no pedigree . . . the stamp of their author is to be found in their style, diction, and sentiment." Wyatt thus sums up the case against Boaden: "With *no knowledge* of his subject . . . he was originally *profuse* in his commendation, and *officiously* desirous of defending what *needed not* his feeble support. With *equal rashness* he then veered to the *opposite side,* and commenced an attack on what is far *superior* to his hostility. . . . If a sensation of envious jealousy, or malignant animosity should have dictated this *outrage* upon the *character* of Mr. Ireland, and upon the *productions* of *Shakspeare,* it would merit not contempt, but the most perfect abhorrence!" It is reported that a party is now forming to obstruct the just exercise of public judgment "by means of tumult and violence." If such an attempt be made at the theatre, "it will no doubt be repelled by a generous indignation" on the part of a British audience, "and will recoil with a tenfold shame upon the heads of its instigators." The chief point is not even justice to Mr. Ireland. "It is the cause of English literature, the cause of genius and of truth, that is at stake!"

It would perhaps have been strange if no opportunist had appeared in the midst of the dissension to capitalize upon it for his own advantage. The Ireland controversy had its Francis Godolphin Waldron (1744–1818). A man of the most inferior talents, he had been a member of Garrick's troupe, became a prompter at the Haymarket, wrote a number of plays, made a number of adaptations, did some acting, and in all these endeavors it is a kindness to say he exhibited mediocrity. His motives for thrusting himself into the Ireland business are not difficult to find. Every once in a while the strangest of all madnesses seizes writers: attempting to rival Shakespeare on his own ground by writing a sequel to one of his masterpieces. In the twentieth century there have been at least two plays written with the descriptive title of *The Merchant of Venice Act VI;* Mr. St. John Ervine wrote *The Lady of Belmont* to show the later collapse of the marriages of Portia and Jessica; and Ludwig Lewisohn wrote a once-popular novel, *The Last Days of Shylock.** Voltaire himself attempted a sequel to *The Tempest,* and twenty years before the to-do over William Henry's forgeries so had Waldron. The play had, understandably, remained unproduced. Now, seizing upon a phrase in the Shakespeare Papers, he renamed it *The Virgin Queen,* and issued a pamphlet in which everything else, hastily put together, was but an excuse for presenting sections of his masterwork to the public. It is impossible to read his *Free Reflections on Miscellaneous Papers* without contempt.

Boaden, he says, has anticipated him in most of what he had wished to state. Waldron thinks "the ingenious impostor may be ranked with Chatterton in fame," but hopes he will "find better fortune than did that ill-fated and ever-to-be lamented youth!" Waldron wastes no time coming to his objective. In the Deed of Gift there is mention of another hitherto-unknown play "called ye Virginn Quene." In a faint pretense at satire, Waldron suggests that this must be a sequel to *The Tempest,* and that Claribel, Ferdinand's sister, must be the Virgin Queen of the title. He then presents his own version of that play. All the preceding remarks would have led his readers to expect some sort of burlesque. Instead, what follows was obviously written in dead earnest, in a manner equally deadly. It is some mitigation of the bad taste of the time that Waldron's publication of his extracts incited no one

* See the present writer's *The Truth about Shylock* (New York, Random House, 1962), pp. 345–48.

with a wish to see more. *The Virgin Queen,* it is pleasant to report, remained unproduced.

No similar strictures can be made on the anonymous *Precious Relics, or The Tragedy of Vortigern Rehears'd,* a dramatic piece in two acts. The model for this lively piece is a good one, Sheridan's *The Critic.* The persons involved in the Ireland controversy are more than hinted at in the loose plot. Henry in love with Harriot, knows the weakness of her guardian, Mr. Wisepate, for antiquities. While visiting at the old man's country house he has pretended to discover various manuscripts, including "The Play of Vortigern," the work of the Bard, which is now being rehearsed in London. Wisepate presses Henry: has he found any more deeds of gift? Mrs. Wisepate, a simple soul, distrusts the precious relics which have been discovered, but Wisepate ridicules his wife's fears. He has Shakespeare at his fingertips and once played Hamlet at a private performance. He reminds her that the papers were found in an iron box in their country house; but she reminds him that the house then existing on their grounds was a new one, the older one having been completely demolished by fire twelve years ago. But Henry remarks that an iron box would have been safe from the ravages of the flames. Wisepate hands his wife a manuscript love letter: "Oh Cupidde. I've not an hole to putte my headde in," which she reads as, "Oh Cupiddy. I've not any holy to putty my poor heddy in."

Henry's friend Craft (William Henry) has helped him with the deception by stealing some valuable documents from Sir Mark Ludicrous (Sir Isaac Heard), and has imitated those papers (but Sir Mark's rarities are forgeries too!). Craft has composed the *Vortigern,* and demands Harriot as compensation, if he is not to expose the facts and ruin Henry. Mr. Dupe (Samuel Ireland) has been entrusted with bringing out the precious relics in print. Sir Mark arrives to examine the papers, and pronounces everything authentic. Dupe shows him a ring containing a lock of the Bard's hair; this Sir Mark wishes at once to purchase, but

Dupe will not part with it. There is also a paper with Hamlet's famous soliloquy in a first version. Sir Mark thinks that strange: "I had the first copy of it too, but lost it when Mr. Craft visited me." There are also portions of *Lear*. Sir Mark is impressed, and declares his desire to own all the manuscripts. Just then they are summoned to the theatre to witness a rehearsal of *Vortigern*.

The second act takes place in the theatre. There is trouble over the Prologue. Moreover, a wicked scribbler has just published a pamphlet against the play, *Oracle versus Dupe*. The rehearsal begins. The play opens with "a great noise."

> VORTIMER. Why this loud clamor? Are the people
> mad? . . . .
> Go stop their voices.
> (MRS. WISEPATE. Oh do, for heaven's sake.
> WISEPATE. Damn it!—Hold your tongue—Must not
> they make a noise if Shakspeare
> bid them? . . .)
> VORTIMER. Go stop their voices.

The Fool observes that the commotion is due to the arrival of the Saxons.

> VORTIMER. More Saxons! Has my father then invited
> Another, and another, and another
> To make us a new race?—Oh shame upon
> him. . . .
> Oh hear, great Jove.—Now, of your winged
> lightning
> An humble handful lend, to blast the eyes
> Of all those comers-in and livers-on!

The lines continue this spoofing amiably. On the subject of love Vortimer makes it clear that he knows his *Macbeth:*

> VORTIMER. Out—out—vain folly!
> Love is an idle fancy—a mere toy
> To win and please an hour before the marriage
> And then to charm no more! A theme fit for a
> novel,
> Full of darts and Cupids, swelling out the volume!
> (SIR MARK. Egad! That is Shakspeare's style!)

It is obvious from the fact that in what follows Kemble, enacting Vortigern, gets into such a fit of laughing as prevents his continuing, that the anonymous author, though unfamiliar with William Henry's play, knew fairly well what was going on at the Drury Lane. This is evident too from his reference to trouble over the Prologue.

Indeed, as the time for presenting the real *Vortigern* approached, the transactions at the theatre were becoming more and more alarming. Kemble had made it abundantly plain that he was no friend, and that the fate of *Vortigern* was in unsympathetic hands. He had already caused the Poet Laureate to write a Prologue unfavorable to the play.

Suddenly Kemble's sister, Mrs. Siddons, announced that the delicate condition of her health required her withdrawal from the cast: "Mrs. Siddons compliments to Mr. Ireland; she finds that 'Vortigern' is intended to be performed next Saturday and begs to assure him that she is very sorry the weak state of her health after six weeks of indisposition renders her incapable of even going to the necessary rehearsals of the play, much less to act. Had she been fortunately well she would have done all in her power to justify Mr. Ireland's polite sentiments on the subject when she had the honor of seeing him on Saturday." This was a serious blow, and the Irelands naturally never ceased to believe her dropping out of the cast was due to her brother's machinations. It is true that earlier in the month, in a letter to Mrs. Piozzi, Mrs. Siddons had made it clear that she held no more faith in the play than did Kemble: "All sensible persons are convinced that 'Vortigern' is a most audacious imposter [*sic*]. If he be not I can only say that Shakespeare's writings are more unequal than those of any other man." Nevertheless, this same letter makes it equally clear that she was at the time ill. In fact, her ill-health required her absenting herself from the boards so long that Sheridan "deprived her of her emoluments during that season."

Kemble's malice, however, was manifest enough in his determination to present on the same bill with *Vortigern* a musical farce, *My Grandmother,* the plot of which had to do with the gullibility of an art collector. Further, Ireland was unable to get Sheridan to advertise the play as Shakespeare's. Even his compromise suggestion that it be described as a tragedy "discovered among the Shakespearean manuscripts in the possession of Mr. Ireland" was rejected. The announcement merely introduced "a play called Vortigern."

But truly dastardly was Kemble's expressed intention of presenting the play for the first time on April 1, April Fools' Day. That was indication of what he purposed doing in his enactment of the title role. With the exception of kindhearted Mrs. Jordan, *Vortigern* had not a friend at Drury Lane. The author of *Precious Relics* was well informed when he spoke, as he did, of the actors wishing to draw and quarter the play.

With every reason to expect that actors and management alike would do all in their power to ruin *Vortigern's* fortunes—and what could they not do?—Ireland made a brave attempt to circumvent their villainy by appealing to the Prince of Wales that His Highness himself appear at the opening, and thus make public his patronage of a work in which he had already expressed interest. The expedient failed. The Prince responded that unfortunately he would not be in London at the time, and therefore could be of no help. But the Duke of Clarence, unquestionably at the suit of the mother of his children, did make it his business to attend, and leave no doubt that he was a partisan of the Believers.

On one subject Ireland now decided to remain firm. Even if Pye was the Poet Laureate, he was simply not going to chance having that Prologue spoken in the theatre. Pye, a timid man, must have been only relieved at the decision; he was no more anxious to anger Ireland than to alienate the Drury Lane. To the rescue came Sir James Bland Burgess (1752–1824), "the type of the old English gentleman," a prominent politician active in the antislavery movement, and an intimate of the royal family. He was the author of a number of plays himself, and possessed some modest skill in composing verses. Touched by the spectacle of Ireland's being harassed on so many sides, he expressed the willingness to write a Prologue which would leave no doubt as to his open-mindedness on the matter of authorship. Ireland gratefully accepted.

Another opportunity offered to strengthen Ireland's position before the opening of *Vortigern*. Albany Wallis had discovered some new deeds relative to Shakespeare and a real Elizabethan Ireland, and Samuel Ireland therefore drew up another testimonial for the signing of such Believers as now remained. It stated that the undersigned, having examined Mr. Wallis' new discoveries and having compared the signatures with those on Mr. Ireland's Papers, "declare our firm belief in the authenticity of the autographs of Shakespeare and Hemynge in the hands of Mr. Ireland: Isaac Heard, Gr. K. at Arms; Francis Webb; Albany Wallis; Richard Troward; Jonn. Hewlett, Translator of Old Records, Common Pleas Office, Temple; John Byng; Francis Townsend, Windsor Herald; Gilbert Franklin, Wimpole Street; Matthew Wyatt, New Inn; Richard Valpy, Reading; Joseph Skinner; Frank Newton, Wimpole Street." Ireland later declared that he could have got many more signers, had time permitted. Nevertheless, this roll of Believers, though richer by the addition of another Herald, lacked some of the important names which had given prestige to the first certificate of credulity. Boswell had been granted the bliss of dying in the joyful conviction that he had seen the invaluable relics of the Bard. Parr's name was absent, as were those of the archaeologist Tweddell, Lauderdale, Croft, Pye, Kinnaird, and Somerset. Heard, Webb, Wallis, Hewlett, Byng, Valpy and Wyatt had remained faithful. The new Believers were men of no great consequence. It is not odd that this second testimonial carried no great weight with the public.

There was still Malone to fear. That he was nearly ready with his thunderbolt was only too sure now. He had made a public announcement:

SPURIOUS SHAKESPERIAN MANUSCRIPTS

Mr. Malone's detection of this Forgery has been unavoidably delayed by the Engraving having taken more time than was expected, and by some other unforeseen circumstances, but it is hoped it will be ready for publication by the end of this month.

The question was, would the charges actually appear in time to create untold mischief before *Vortigern* was presented at the beginning of next month? If Fortune would but delay Malone's onslaught until after the performance, the play might pass on its own (in Ireland's eyes, indisputable) merits, despite the ill will of Kemble and company. On the other hand, Malone's advertisement was an open accusation of forgery—his first to be made in the press in plain English. That called, even at this late hour, for counter-action.

William Henry at once made out a statement, ready to be sworn to before a magistrate; it attested that since Malone had publicly advertised the assertion that he had discovered the manuscripts to be forgeries, he, the deponent, Samuel William Henry Ireland "maketh oath that he this deponent's father, the said Samuel Ireland, hath not, nor hath any of the said Samuel Ireland's family, other than save and except this deponent, any knowledge of the manner in which he the said deponent became possessed of the said deeds or Mss. papers, S.W.H. Ireland." Obviously, William Henry was anxious to spare his father any involvement in disaster in case he were indeed exposed by the age's leading Shakespearean authority. But the statement itself is just as obviously evasive of swearing to the truth concerning the Papers. It is not surprising that Ireland was in no haste to have it sworn to before a legal authority.

(Years later William Henry stated that two months before this time he had asked Wallis to draw up an affidavit with the purpose of publishing it in the papers, and that Wallis had drawn up under the date of January 17, 1796, the following: "In justice to my father, and to remove the odium under which he labors respecting the papers published by him as the manuscripts of Shakspeare, I do hereby solemnly declare that they were given to him by me as the manuscripts of Shakspeare, and that he was totally ignorant and unacquainted with the source from whence they came, or with any matter relating to the same, or to anything save what was told him by myself, and that he published them without any knowledge, or even the smallest intention of fraud or imposition, but under a firm belief and persuasion of their authenticity, as I had given him to understand they were so." The existence of such an intended affidavit is more than open to question. It reads as though after his father's death William Henry was attempting to recompose the statement we have already quoted. This later one everywhere implies forgery, and therefore his father's knowledge of it, for he adds that Ireland was dissatisfied with it, and that it was in consequence never made legal. Certainly in mid-January, 1796, William Henry was making no admission of deception, and Ireland was as staunchly convinced as ever of the reliability of his papers. Besides, the opposition to the Papers had not then yet really begun with any force.)

As March arrived at its final week, Samuel Ireland began to breathe a little easier: Malone's book had not appeared. In lieu of an unsworn statement, and probably on the advice of Wallis, William Henry addressed a letter to the public to set at rest the mind of the audience which, it was hoped, would be crowding Drury Lane in a few days. In order to "remove every Degree of Suspicion" concerning the Papers, the letter said, Mr. Ireland is authorized to state that the documents "are by lineal descent the property of a Gentleman whose *Great-Great* Grandfather was a Man of Eminence in the Law into whose possession they fell . . . on the Demise of John Heminge's son who died about the year 1650. He is also authorized to state that had it not been for Mr. S. Ireland Junr. they would have been inevitably lost to the World, the Proprietor himself being totally ignorant of his possessing such a treasure." This was March 30, 1796.

On the next day, March 31, Malone's *Inquiry into the Authenticity of Certain Miscellaneous Papers* appeared. The time, the very eve of the production of *Vortigern,* was in one way far worse than if the book had appeared a month earlier. There was no way to reply to it before the performance.

Malone's book is portentous: it runs to four hundred pages, and is dedicated to the Earl of Charlemont, one of Ireland's subscribers. A footnote states that Malone is authorized to say that Charlemont "would not have given either his name or his money to the publication" of the Papers if he "had known as much of it as he now does." When he first heard of Ireland's manuscripts, Malone states, he was at the same time assured by various persons who had examined them "that every date affixed to these papers and almost every fact mentioned in them were alike inconsistent with the history of the time and with the ancient documents of which I was possessed." In the account of how these papers were discovered, nothing has been said of *where* the first three deeds were found. "What led the discoverer to examine the deeds and papers of the unknown gentleman?" At first it was said that the discoverer met the owner, a gentleman of large fortune, in a coffee-house, that the latter learned the other was interested in autographs and invited him to "rummage" among old deeds at the gentleman's lodgings. The discoverer went there and "in a very few minutes lighted on the name of Shakespeare." (Malone's training as a lawyer in viewing evidence microscopically was standing him in good stead!) The discovery of "a title to a considerable estate" would naturally cause the benefiter to desire to reward the discoverer. But in what country does that estate lie? Has there been any suit in consequence of the discovery? However, laying aside the gentleman's identity, Malone agrees that even if his name were known, "it would not substantiate the most insignificant paper that has been exhibited." Our author then proceeds to an exhaustive examination of the documents.

Queen Elizabeth's letter is obviously modeled on the letter James I is supposed to have written Shakespeare, as published in 1710 by Lintott. The spelling and the language, like those of Chatterton's forgeries, are not of "any particular period, but of various and different ages." But these Papers are worse than Chatterton's, for the orthography here is not that of any age whatsoever. Malone has never seen *and* spelled with a final *e* nor *for* written as *forre*. "The clumsy fabricator has seen *far* written in the old books *farre*" and so has made a false analogy. In the absurdest of manners "almost every word is over-laden with both consonants and vowels." Malone quotes Chaucer, a Paston letter, a poem of Surrey's, a document of Elizabeth's, the "dedication" to Sidney's *Arcadia*, and many other pieces to show that there exists no similarity between young Ireland's spelling and any known ancient work. He makes great point of the fact that *Master* was often spelled *Maister* but never, as in the Papers, *Masterre*. He also challenges anyone to produce an example of the word "excellence" being applied in Shakespeare's age, as it is in this letter, "to denote the purity or goodness of written composition, whether in prose or verse."

He reprints facsimiles of Ireland's example of Elizabeth's handwriting with examples of her actual writing; to simplify the examination, he extracts specimens of the Ireland alphabet and specimens of her true alphabet. From the Ireland facsimile of the (Short) Heminge's handwriting, Malone concludes "it was manifest from the unsteadiness and the unregularity of the strokes, that it could not have been the genuine handwriting of any one." Only a "drunkard or a madman" would write a script that inclines alternatively to the left and right. (William Henry, of course, had written it with his left hand.)

After quoting a few lines from the verses to Ann Hathaway,

Malone desists; "this namby-pamby stuff" is too sickening. Everything about the Southampton letters is mercilessly exposed as false. When he comes to the Profession of Faith, Malone remarks, "The kindness and pity of our merciful Creator are represented under the familiar image of a hen protecting her little brood under her wings. But whence the absurd introduction of a chicken?" There are many crudities in the Deed of Gift to Ireland; among them is the word "upset," which is so recent that it does not appear even in Johnson's *Dictionary.* "The Dutch Shylock with his blue night-cap, and his hands in his trowsers will, I am told, be recognized by anyone" who has visited Holland. As for the Deed of Gift to Heminge, Malone had not expected after Chatterton's exposure to hear again of "an OAKEN CHEST" at the Globe, which trunk, it seems, "contained not only our poet's theatrical but his domestick wardrobe, his love-letters to his wife . . . rings, pictures, caskets, and plays of all sorts, new and old." Shakespeare was perfectly aware, of course, that his plays, once written and performed, no longer belonged to him; yet in this deed "he very bountifully gives to individuals what already belonged to them all collectively" as members of the company.

When he comes to *Lear* Malone refuses to collate this version with the old: "Life is not long enough to be wasted in the examination of such trash." As for the imminent production, "I may perhaps be expected to say a word on the far-famed tragedy of KYNGE VORRTYGERNE, and all the KKYNGES and all the QQUEENES which have been announced from the same quarter." *Vortigern* can only prove to be as authentic as the *Lear.*

It has been said that a lifetime would have been insufficient in which to forge these documents. That is not true, says Malone. "Twelve short papers, four deeds, and two plays"—they all could have been produced in one year. Besides, "it is much more probable that the composition of all but the deeds was the work of one, and that of the Shakespearean rags . . . were sewn on by another"—male or female, he adds, who knows?

But Malone's dislike of the Ireland Papers goes beyond the sound objections of the scholar. The circle of Samuel Ireland's friends was unmistakably friendly to the principles of the French Revolution. As a detester of those principles Malone had an added incentive to demolish Ireland. He detected an overtone of republicanism in the Ireland versions of Shakespeare, and openly jeered at the suggestion that Shakespeare could have been guilty of such strictly modern expressions of treason. The influence was too plain—that of France, "which every friend to the welfare of mankind and peace and the true interest and happiness of England must wish blotted from the map of the world. . . . From the present contemptuous mention of KINGS, it is no very wild conjecture that the unknown writer is not extremely averse to those modern Republican zealots who have for some time past employed their feeble but unwearying endeavors to diminish that love and veneration which every true Briton feels, and I trust will ever feel, for ROYALTY." The blast is certainly unwarranted. William Henry, it is true, had allowed himself some easy platitudes about the "gilded bauble that environs the head of Majesty," but they were hardly the product of ardent republicanism or revolutionary zeal. Malone's prejudices had caused him to see what was scarcely there. These political allegations were bound, just the same, to have weight with the general public, only a few of whom had ever seen Ireland's publication of the Papers.

In the two days eventually intervening between the issuance of Malone's book and the presentation of *Vortigern* at the Drury Lane, five hundred copies were sold. Today his prose seems as heavy-handed in its satirical moments as it is ponderous in its scholarship. But then, as now, when an issue is as scandalous as the Ireland Papers, such considerations are not likely to be a deterrent to the general reader.

On April 2, 1796, the *London Times* carried an advertisement for the showing of *Vortigern* that night. The play was not ascribed to Shakespeare. The notice carries an addendum on

Malone's "malevolent and unmanly" attack, and appeals to the public to judge the tragedy impartially. The play itself is now in press "and will in a few days be laid before the public." It could hardly have been other than deliberate malice which caused the rival theatre at Covent Garden to announce for the same night a new play by John O'Keefe named, probably for the occasion, *Lie of a Day.**

---

* I had some difficulty in tracking down a copy of this play. When I had succeeded it turned out not to have been worth the search. There is small connection between the title and its plot, which deals with mistaken identity and the success of wily lovers in deceiving their guardian-dragons. There are but two short passages which could be construed as being connected with the Ireland affair, but since they have no connection with the plot either, they may very well have been inserted for the evening. One character says: "Zounds, it is two o'clock! but I can get to Drury Lane by the second act." A few lines further on he quotes from a play then being enacted there, "To atoms thus let me tear the wicked, lying evidence of shame." But these are too fragile to hang satirical intent upon. The title, however, was most probably mischievously purposed.

EIGHT

Point of No Return

KEMBLE'S WICKED ATTEMPT to present *Vortigern* on April Fools' Day having been frustrated, the play was given on the next night, April 2, 1796, at six-thirty. Because of raging public contention, the management of the Drury Lane was not disappointed in its expectation of a crowded house. More than three hours earlier there was already a long queue outside the theatre; two hours before curtain-time the neighboring streets were packed with the expectant audience. Presently numbers of noisy urchins were thrusting into their hands a bill composed by Samuel Ireland as an advance answer to Malone:

VORTIGERN

A *malevolent* and *impotent* attack on the Shakspeare MSS having appeared, on the *eve* of representation of the play of *VORTIGERN*, evidently intended to injure the interest of the proprietor of the MSS, Mr. Ireland feels it impossible, within the short space of time that intervenes between the publishing and the representation, to produce an answer to the most illiberal and unfounded assertions in Mr. Malone's *"Inquiry"*; he is, therefore, induced to request that the play of *Vortigern* may be heard with that *candor* that has ever distinguished a *British Audience*.

The precaution was not entirely necessary. Many were prepared to worship; those whose minds were already made up by the hostile criticism were not likely to have them changed by Ireland's handbill. Everyone was bound to have a good time, and the attendance was almost unprecedented. More than 2,500 people paid to get in; every place was taken, both pit and boxes having been sold out for days. This financial success was precisely what Sheridan had foreseen. He had assured Kemble that the play would enrich the theatre's treasury, and that "public curiosity, or rather the pride of having to decide whether a piece was actually written by Shakespeare or not, would fill the house for one night, even with advanced prices; 'for you know very well, Kemble,' said he, 'that an Englishman considers himself as good a judge of Shakespeare as of his pint of porter.'"

As Samuel Ireland entered a box in the center of the theatre, he was greeted with applause from the gallery (to which he had distributed some free tickets) and with a few jeers from the pit. Mrs. Freeman and Jane Ireland sat with him. The Duke of Clarence was present in a box too. As for the "discoverer" of the play, William Henry himself later said, "I did not enter the theatre till a very short period previous to the rising of the curtain; and the box being so very conspicuous, I soon retired from observation behind the scenes; where I continued the greater part of the time of representation, engaged in conversation with Mrs. Jordan." That generous woman, who for William Henry's sake firmly believed his story, did all she could to tranquilize and reassure the nervous young man.

Whitfield, who was to play the role of Wortimerus, delivered the Prologue which Burgess had written as a substitute for Pye's:

> No common cause your verdict now demands,
> Before the court immortal Shakespeare stands.

The verses went on to declare that some modern bards have attempted "with presumptuous wing" to "catch some portion of his sacred fire," but have always failed. This play, snatched from oblivion, claims respect and the right to a fair hearing since it bears

Shakespeare's name.

> We ask no more—with you the judgment lies;
> No forgeries escape your piercing eyes!
> Unbias'd then pronounce your dread decree,
> Alike from prejudice and favor free.
> If, the fierce ordeal pass'd, you chance to find
> Rich sterling ore, tho' rude and unrefin'd,
> Stamp it your own, assert your poet's fame,
> And add fresh wreaths to Shakespeare's honor'd name.

Burgess boldly took his stand among the Believers.

When Whitfield began the opening couplet he was shouted down by some of the rowdy, and his words were drowned by the noise. As he tried to continue he began to forget his lines. The volatile audience now overwhelmed him with its sympathy, and encouraged him to proceed. He assured them that it was nervousness which had made him stumble, and when he went on, it was without mishap. At the Prologue's conclusion he was rewarded with tumultuous applause—auspiciously for the tragedy itself, for the audience now gave the piece its polite attention.

ACT I, *Scene i.* The play opens in a large hall. Because of encroaching age Constantius gives half his power over the kingdom to Vortigern, whom he begs to accept it. Vortigern protests that these honors are so great and weighty that they might wear him down, and asks the King to choose someone else. But he consents at last and signs a paper which makes him king jointly with Constantius. Left alone, Vortigern (with echoes from *Macbeth* and *Henry IV, Part II*) reflects upon ambition and the burdens of the crown; he must be king alone. To accomplish that, he must kill Constantius and the two princes royal. "As the blow strikes one, all three shall fall!"

Scene ii. The action moves to a room in Vortigern's palace. His wife, Edmunda, is besought by their daughter Flavia to cease grieving. Edmunda cannot. Vortigern was once a loving husband: now he treats her with cold disdain. Her son Pascentius

enters to tell the news of Vortigern's elevation to partnership in
the crown; Edmunda sees that it is ambition which has lost her
Vortigern's love. The Fool comes in to recite lines similar to passages in *Lear*.

Scene iii. With passages from *Macbeth* in mind, Vortigern ex-
amines his new ambition. Two Murderers come in, and he ar-
ranges the murder of Constantius with them.

Scene iv. Constantius sends a ring to Vortigern (just as Duncan did to Lady Macbeth), and says a prayer which exhibits his
saintliness.

Scene v. The King has been murdered and Vortigern has seen
his corpse. As in *Macbeth,* the night has been disturbed by
strange, unnatural portents. Vortigern publicly blames the assas-
sination on the Scots, and he orders every Scot at court to be
seized.

Scene vi. Vortigern addresses the Barons and again accuses
the Scots of the murder. The Barons agree to declare them guilty;
they ask Vortigern to assume the kingship until the Princes return
from Rome. "The election lights" on the elder son, Aurelius.

Scene vii. Vortigern soliloquizes, "How stands it now?" He is
but Protector. He must have the crown. There is no word from
the Princes. Well, let them come, and "when come, there's room
enough i' th' ground for them." He intends to use Flavia as a lure
to win over the leader of the Barons, even though she is betrothed to Aurelius and in love with him.

Scene viii. Flavia tells her brother that their father has urged
her to break her troth with Aurelius; she asks Pascentius to save
her from such a fate by going into exile with her. Enter the Fool,
very Elizabethan—e.g., "Times must indeed be bad when fools
lack wit to battle wise men's ire." The Fool is to go along with
them. It is getting late and they must depart.

FLA. What hour is it?
PAS.   Near five o' th' clock.
     This brilliant mass o' fire, the golden sun,

> Hath just saluted with a blushing kiss,
> Yon partner of his bed, the vasty sea.

They leave, and so the first act ends.

Though no doubt restless the audience was still attentive enough. The Shakespeare they heard on the boards was so often watered down that they were not familiar enough with the true Shakespearean style. They could not be sure that the Bard had not written these lines. The brevity with which all the action was hurried over, often in a single short speech, the appearance of modern words like "joke," the total absence of all characterization, the emptiness of the verse—all this should have made it clear that *Vortigern* was not Shakespeare's. But the piece was certainly packed with vaguely Shakespearean echoes. The French quip, *Vous avez l'air mais pas le chanson,* was more than applicable to the play.

Act II of *Vortigern* was something of a hit with the audience.

ACT II, *Scene i.* At Rome, Constantius' two sons, Aurelius and Uter, who have been there for seven years, long for their native soil. Aurelius misses Flavia. A messenger arrives from Britain with news of Constantius: "Murder most foul hath ta'en him." Vortigern blames the Scots, "but under this pretence much lies conceal'd." Aurelius is advised not to return if he prizes life.

> AUR. Oh! horror! horror! my dear father murder'd!
> UTER. By whom, speak Messenger. Where, when, and how?

The Messenger is sure the culprit is Vortigern, and warns the Princes that assassins are on their way to Rome to murder *them.*

Scene ii. The same three characters are present. The Messenger reveals that every noble Scot in London has "suffer'd under this fell tiger's fangs," and urges the brothers to go to Scotland, where they will find friends. Their "Roman vestments" will disguise them. (William Henry's Romans were probably the only characters in Elizabethan drama who wore other than Elizabethan dress.)

Scene iii. Vortigern, Edmunda, their son Wortimerus, and attendants are at supper. Flavia and Pascentius are not there, though they have been summoned. Wortimerus is sent to find them. Edmunda speaks in their behalf, but is told to be quiet or leave the hall. She leaves. Wortimerus comes back: he cannot find his brother and sister. Vortigern sends for Edmunda again, and accuses her of knowing of the flight of the pair. She swears she knows nothing of it. Refusing to credit her, Vortigern tells her he hates her, and goes out. Edmunda is distracted.

Scene iv. Pascentius and Flavia (in disguise) and the Fool are escaping, and pause in a wood. Flavia is unhappy to have left their mother, and on her knees prays God's protection for her. The Fool is so moved he forgets to jest. Soon he sings a song to alleviate their weariness, "Then heigh-ho poor dobbins all. . . ." A Post enters bearing letters. Pascentius bribes him to tell their contents; the Post informs them that Vortigern is accused of Constantius' murder, and that the Princes are marching from Scotland.

The second act was accorded enthusiastic applause. Mrs. Jordan, who had been unfailingly kind to William Henry, congratulated him before the next act on the great success he was having. He, however, was still struggling with a presentiment that all would not end well, and answered that, despite the audience's approval, he was certain that the play "would not be a second time represented." His augury of failure began almost immediately to be substantiated.

ACT III, *Scene i.* Before the Barons, Vortigern accuses the Princes of returning to Britain to incite civil war. The Barons agree. The First Baron bids the trumpet sound to proclaim the Princes traitors. The trumpet sounds.

2ND BAR. Nay; stop not there, but let them bellow on,
Till with their clamorous noise they shame the
thunder . . .

This was the speech that opened the doors of mischief. The role of the Second Baron had been entrusted to Dignum, an inferior actor who was vain of his high tenor voice. William Henry had cause never to forget the moment, and has thus recorded what happened: "The idea of beholding that gentleman strut forth in tragedy is quite sufficient to excite risibility even in Melpomene herself. I have no doubt that that circumstance was justly appreciated by the acting manager of the day [Kemble], who in consequence suffered Mr. Dignum to *'bellow on';* which he did so effectually, by his guttural pronunciation, as to set the whole house in a convulsive peal of laughter—a circumstance highly conducive to the success of a tragedy!!"

It was the beginning of the end. The raucous laughter persisted unabated until at length Kemble himself, his objective achieved, had to step forward and ask the audience for silence. But the seeds of hilarity had been sown, and for the rest of the play, blossomed noxiously now and again. At one point, Charles Sturt, M.P., who had imbibed freely before the performance, "with the intonation of a bull," shouted from his stage box, "Give the thing a fair trial!" As Kemble later reminisced, "Such an appeal to the equity of the audience and from such brazen lungs, had some effect, and the storm was lulled." But not for long.

The scene continues. Vortigern sends to Saxony for aid against the Scots.

Scene ii. Against a quite un-Elizabethan "distant view of the sea," we find Aurelius and Uter now "habited as Britons." Aurelius is touched at being once more upon his native land, and bends his knees in prayer. (This is the third such prayer thus far in the play. Perhaps William Henry had been encouraged to work the pious vein to excess because of Dr. Parr's extravagant praise of the Profession of Faith.)

Scene iii. At the gates of London, Hengist, Horsus, and fellow Saxons arrive to aid Vortigern. (The scene has seven lines.)

Scene iv. The gates open. Vortigern greets them. (The scene

217

has eight lines.)

Scene v. In the open country, Flavia, Pascentius, and the Fool are still wandering. Flavia is fatigued. She sits and sings a melancholy song. Scottish troops enter, and urge the three to fight for Aurelius. They go with the Scots.

Scene vi. Edmunda has a mad scene. She has lost her mind and sings to her maids. Her scene ends with, "Farewell; good night, sweet! good night!"

ACT IV, *Scene i.* At Aurelius' camp there is a vapid love scene between him and Flavia. At the conclusion of its twenty-five lines she gives him a token to wear in battle.

Scene ii. Hengist and Horsus are ready for battle. Hengist hopes to entrap Vortigern with the beauty of his daughter Rowena. Then all Britain will be his. This scene has eleven lines.

Scene iii. A fight between the allies of Vortigern and the Scots takes place. The Scots are defeated. Three lines.

Scene iv. Horsus comes upon Flavia and Pascentius. He tries to buy her from her brother. The two men fight and Horsus falls. With his last breath Horsus, for no reason, tells Pascentius to go to Vortigern and warn him against Hengist.

At this moment bedlam broke loose in the theatre. The part of Horsus was enacted by the comedian Phillimore, whose nose was so enormous that today he would by nature have made the ideal Cyrano. Samuel Ireland never ceased to believe that Kemble cast him in the play out of pure malice. At any rate, Phillimore attempted to outdo himself in his death scene. Let William Henry recount what occurred: "The late facetious Mr. Phillimore, of *large-nosed* memory, was placed by the manager in a prominent point of view. . . . That gentleman, on receiving the deadly wound (which proved, indeed a *deadly blow* to my play), either from prior tuition or chance . . . so placed his unfortunate carcass that on the falling of the drop-curtain he was literally divided between the audience and his brethern of the sock and buskin; his legs & c., being towards the spectators, and his head, & c., inside the curtain. . . . This, however, was not the only calamity: for as the wooden roller at the bottom of the curtain was rather ponderous, Mr. Phillimore groaned beneath the unwelcome burden: and finding his brethern somewhat dilatory in extricating him, he adopted the more natural expedient of extricating himself; which for a *dead man* was something in the style of Mr. Bannister, jun. in the Critic, who tells Mr. Puff 'that he cannot stay there *dying* all day.' "

The audience responded to this prolonged buffoonery by hurricanes of laughter and loud applause. Sturt made matters worse in his indignation. A true Believer, he leaned over the stage and drunkenly made a series of tugs at Phillimore's cloak in a befogged and unsuccessful attempt to drag him into the stage box. After that there was small pretense of serious attention to the play. The audience waited gleefully for new signals for mirth, and some of the actors were not loath to supply them at regular intervals.

Scene v. The setting is a wood. Hengist fears that Horsus is lost. New troops have arrived, and with them have brought Hengist's daughter Rowena. He asks to be left alone with her. Hengist commands her to make Vortigern fall in love with her.

Scene vi. "A magnificent feast." In the middle of it Rowena enters. Vortigern is smitten with her beauty, and toasts her. When he asks her to sit next to him, his sons Catagrinus and Wortimerus object; Vortigern orders them to leave. He announces that since Edmunda is mad, his marriage to her is dissolved. With the consent of the court he proclaims his forthcoming marriage to Rowena. He gives Hengist all of Kent, though his nobles are resentful of that.

Scene vii. Wortimerus and Catagrinus discuss the turn of events. They will not allow their mother to be discarded. They decide to join the armies of Aurelius and are reinforced by the disaffected lords. They will take Edmunda with them.

Scene viii. Aurelius and Uter prepare for war. Wortimerus and Catagrinus come in, and joyfully greet Flavia and Pascentius.

Scene ix. There is a new fight, and this time the Saxons lose. Wortimerus is called a traitor by Hengist. They fight and Hengist is killed. Catagrinus comes in as Wortimerus speaks Hengist's obituary:

> He fought like one
> That begg'd a little time to save his soul.

Scene x. Vortigern learns that his sons have gone over to the enemy, and that Rowena has been taken prisoner. He bids his officer (like another Antony) kill him with his good sword. The officer refuses. Vortigern decides to fight after all.

During this scene Ireland came to the front of his box, leaned his head on his arm, then left the box to go behind the scenes.

ACT v, *Scene i.* On a couch in the palace Edmunda is still mad. Flavia and Pascentius are distressed at her condition.

PASC. O! dearest mother, say, dost thou not know me?
EDM. Aye, aye, right well, thou'rt one by name a man.

She recognizes a mark on her daughter's forehead, and thus begins to recover her wits. Word is brought that Rowena has poisoned herself.

Scene ii. The Tower is being besieged by the enemy, and Vortigern yearns for death. It is in the passage which follows that there occurs one line which brought down the house. The irony is that this speech, as a whole, is the best in the play; it rises very nearly to the tone of something poetic. There can be little doubt that Kemble deliberately grimaced and strutted and unfairly overemphasized Vortigern's lines to provoke the uproar which ensued:

> Time was, alas! I needed not this spur.
> But here's a secret and a stinging thorn,

> That wounds my troubl'd nerves. O! conscience! conscience!
> When thou didst cry, I strove to stop thy mouth.
> . . . .
> . . . O! sovereign death!
> Thou hast for thy domain this world immense:
> Church-yards and charnel-houses are thy haunts,
> And hospitals thy sumptuous palaces;
> And when thou wouldst be merry, thou dost choose
> The gaudy chamber of a dying King.
> O! then thou dost ope wide thy boney jaws,
> And with rude laughter and fantastic tricks,
> Thou clapp'st thy rattling fingers to thy sides:
> And when this solemn mockery is ended . . .

Somehow Kemble contrived to make this last line sound like a résumé of the whole evening. According to William Henry (who was convinced that this was the crux of a plot on the part of the "Malone faction"), Kemble "laid such a peculiar stress" on the line as made it "the *watchword* for the general howl." No sooner was the line uttered "in the most sepulchral tone of voice possible . . . than the most discordant howl echoed from the pit that ever assailed the organs of hearing." The uproar continued for ten minutes. Then "Mr. Kemble, having again obtained a hearing, instead of proceeding with the speech at the ensuing line, very politely, and in order to amuse the audience still more, redelivered the very line . . . with even more solemn grimace than he had in the first instance displayed." Apparently feeling, after a new and prolonged outburst, that he had been sufficiently destructive, Kemble advanced once more to ask the audience for quiet, and to remind them that the question of the play's "authenticity" depended on their "giving it a fair and full hearing." He had done his worst. He could now afford to appear the gentleman.

Unhappily, if the lines preceding this riotous laughter are among the best of the play, those following the fatal verse are among the silliest:

> And when this solemn mockery is ended,
> With icy hand thou tak'st him by the feet,

> And upward so, till thou dost reach the heart,
> And wrap him in the cloak of lasting night!

The borrowing from Mistress Quickly's account of Falstaff's death could not have been more luckless poetically; for that moment in Drury Lane it was purely catastrophic. There was no hope for anything but mirth for the rest of the performance.

The remainder of this unhappy scene relates that Vortigern has learned of Rowena's death by poison. He knows he can never win his fight. The enemy has broken into the Tower, but he will make a last stand.

Scene iii. "The Basse-Court of the Tower." Aurelius has told Vortigern's sons to stay with their mother: he does not wish them to have to battle their sire. Vortigern appears at the gate crying for another sword. The raven has croaked over the Tower and the crow has chattered over his head: evil omens. Aurelius enters and is recognized by Vortigern. They fight. Vortigern is thrown. He refuses to reveal who murdered Constantius. Aurelius is about to slay him when Flavia rushes to him: "He is still my father!" But Vortigern only curses her, and wishes to die. She gets to her knees to beg mercy for him. To force Aurelius' hand, Vortigern confesses that he is the murderer. But for Flavia's sake Aurelius spares his life. Vortigern is led out, and Aurelius is hailed as king. Vortigern sends a message that Flavia is free to marry her betrothed. She is hailed as queen. The curtain falls on a final speech by Aurelius.

When Mrs. Jordan came onstage to deliver the Epilogue, written by Robert Merry, she was treated with applause and respect, for she was a favorite:

> . . . do not frown, but give due share of praise,
> Nor rend from Shakespeare's tomb the sacred bays.
> The scatter'd flowers he left benignly save!
> Posthumous flowers! the garlands of the grave!

As a counteractive to its love of frivolity, the century was devoted to funerary urns; maidens applied themselves tenderly to working representations of them and of tombs in colored silks; minor poets ran over with references to graveyards and funeral wreaths—as somehow evocative of sublimity—and lines like those of the Epilogue were calculated to win approval. Moreover, Mrs. Jordan sensibly "skipped over some lines which claimed the play as Shakespeare's." She was granted an ovation—but it was only for herself.

For if the audience's sudden receptivity occasioned any false hopes, these were immediately allayed. When the actor Barrymore tried to announce *Vortigern*'s repetition for the next bill, violent yells of protest were heard all over the house, and there ensued a series of personal skirmishes which were not quieted for nearly twenty minutes. During this time the Duke of Clarence "made himself wonderfully and ridiculously conspicuous" among the Believers. At length Kemble appeared, to state that *The School for Scandal* would be given Monday night instead. Though generally acceptable, the substitution was not universally so. Sturt, who was furious, continued his riotous behavior. As Farington records, "When one of the stage attendants attempted to take up the green cloth, Sturt seized him roughly by the head. He was slightly pelted with oranges."

The story of April 2, 1796, at the Drury Lane became a gaudy patch of theatrical history. Though events quickly justified Kemble's distrust of the play, his own shameful conduct as manager and actor (for it was his duty, in any event, to do his best for the work) was so unpleasant a memory that he developed excuses and even rewrote the facts in his own mind. Boaden, his biographer, attempted to diminish Kemble's part in the fiasco by blaming Ireland for being in such haste to rush into print with his Papers. Had *Vortigern* and *Henry II* been presented before Ireland issued his volume, "discovery would have been averted or delayed. The plays under the notion of curtailment (always necessary to Shakspeare it seems) might have been purified sufficiently for success; our enthusiasm would soon have heightened to the *wonderful* any tolerable passages they might contain, and, at the PRESENT HOUR, some people might have thought it possible for Shakspeare to have written *Vortigern!*" There is more than a grain of truth in the last sentence, despite the play's inferiority.

The presentation of *Vortigern* became a ground for theatrical legendry too. The tale was inflated and distorted by frequent re-tellings. Years later Kemble related to Marsh, the chatty author of *The Clubs of London,* a version of the events of that night bespeaking a memory highly unreliable in most particulars, no doubt in consequence of embellishments added with new re-countings. Kemble, it is obvious, was only too willing to obliterate his own strokes of malice. He protests his innocence of "having pronounced with malicious emphasis, to assist the downfall of the piece," the fatal *solemn mockery* line and says, "The allusion was too obvious not to be caught in a moment by an audience wearied to death with what they had already gone through. . . . At this line, the most overwhelming sounds of mingled groan and laughter ran through the house; but Humphrey Sturt, whose ordinary tone of conversation reminded you of the noise of a frilling-mill, again obtained a few moments' silence. . . . The pause, however, was of short duration, for Phillimore, who played Vortigern [*sic!*] had to call out to the soldiers, as they were leading off Mrs. Jordan, who performed Rowena, 'Give her up! Give her up! oh, give her up!' This was too much. Humphrey Sturt threw himself back on the bench, and burst into a fit of horse-laughing, as deafening as the falls of Niagara, and the rest of the audience caught the infection. 'Give her up, give her up!' resounded from a thousand tongues; the hint was taken, and the curtain fell. . . . As for old Ireland, he never forgave either Phillimore or myself. He said that if I had *bona fide* intended to let the piece have a chance, I should not, as stage-manager, have given such a character as Vortigern to Phillimore; for that his nose was long enough to damn the finest play Shakespeare ever wrote. The younger Ireland, the fabricator of the fraud, was all this time sitting in one of the upper boxes, apparently unconcerned, by the side of Polly Thompson, or some such personage: the person from whose head, as he afterwards confessed, he had cut the identical lock of hair exhibited at the elder Ireland's as a lock from the head of Mrs. Anna Hatherewaye."

This highly amusing account may be true to the spirit of the occasion, but it is full of misstatements of fact. It is astonishing that Kemble should have forgotten that he himself enacted the role of Vortigern, not Phillimore, or that Mrs. Jordan enacted Flavia, not Rowena. Phillimore had been cast as Horsus and Miss Miller had been assigned Rowena. Sturt was a stout champion of the Irelands, and his name, moreover, was Charles, not Humphrey. William Henry was not in a box beside his Polly, but behind the scenes allowing Mrs. Jordan to assuage his misgivings. The curtain did not come down before the play was over. Worst of all, for the reliability of the account, there is no scene in the drama where Rowena is being led off; also there is no line which is even distantly like, "Give her up! Give her up! oh, give her up!" In a way, it is a pity that there was not, for it would certainly have been of a tone with others equally silly, and it is rather disappointing that Kemble's amusing bit was by nature of the facts untrue.

Also, it will be remembered, the lock of hair on exhibition at Norfolk Street was not that of "Dearesste Anna" but was her loving "Willys," "syncere and most trewe."

NINE

Disenchanting April

IT IS NOT DIFFICULT to imagine the turbulence in Samuel Ireland's mind as he left the Drury Lane that night. That William Henry should have been in a panic may also be supposed—but such indeed was not the case. He was hardly more than an adolescent. The strain must have been nerve-ravaging, but his chief emotion now was relief that the crisis, however ruinous to the Shakespeare "discoveries," was at least over.

Several of his father's friends soon gathered in the Norfolk Street house, and William Henry thought it likely they would be talking over the performance for hours. "I retired to bed, more easy in my mind than I had been for a great length of time, as the load was removed which oppressed me. I that night slept most profoundly, and even awoke in the morning much later than usual." He was upbraided at breakfast for his lack of feeling on so crucial an occasion. His family wondered how he could possibly have slept at all, his father laying stress on the money he had lost by the withdrawal of the play from the boards. But William Henry's conduct that night was not, after all, odd. He had embarked on his career as a forger only to please his father; as he was thrust unexpectedly into public prominence, he had learned to enjoy the respect people accorded him even though his father still withheld his; but William Henry's thoughts do not seem at any time to have dwelt upon the financial advantages he might reap. Ireland, on the other hand, was anew exhibiting what was, besides his ignorance, his besetting vice—greed.

Among the people who had called on Ireland after the play were the painters Westall and Farington, the latter of whom records in his diary for April 2: "Westall described *Young* Ireland to be a lad of no parts. Two years ago He was in some part of the country hunting with a party, & was invited by a gentleman to dinner, where the company got drunk. In this state Young Ireland, speaking of himself, said He was bred an Attorney: but that He did other things besides writing law deeds: that He had been employed in writing a Copy of all Shakespeares plays." This could not have been a dark reference to his forgeries, for William Henry had not been engaged upon them in 1794. William Henry's host was unimpressed by the boast; "the gentleman observed that must be a great waste of time, when he might purchase an edition for very little money."

The next morning father and son went to the Drury Lane to collect from Mr. Hammersly, the theatre's treasurer, the money due them. Ireland had already received £250 in advance, of which he had given his son £60. Their share for the preceding night was a little under £103, of which William Henry was granted £30 by his father. He was, therefore, richer for his efforts by £90 *in toto* —though just how much of this sum he had already spent on his writing materials and the Shakespeare Library it is impossible to state. He never made one additional farthing on his forgeries for the rest of his life. (His father had received the money, of course, because William Henry was a minor.) Kemble later told Boaden that the sum advanced had been a total loss to the management because of the cost of the scenery. At the time of that investment no one had imagined that the play could fail to achieve something of a run.

The reports in the press buried *Vortigern* under an avalanche of derision—safe enough now that Malone had published his cri-

tique. April 3 was a Sunday. The *London Times* of April 4 declared that "in the annals of the theatre there never was a crowd
as at Drury Lane"; the play it declared a copy of *Macbeth:*
"There is a *Duncan* murdered—a *Malcolm* flies—a *Seward* comes
to fight for him—let England and Scotland change places and the
likeness is complete." (This is an overstatement.) This paper concludes that of Ireland's manuscripts "the deeds are true and the
poetry forged." The *Monthly Mirror* for April asks to be excused
from delivering its sentiments "on this, 'Shakspeare's best play,'"
and praises the audience for its conduct: "There never was exhibited more candor and forbearance on the part of an audience on
the first night of any *Farce*"; when unable to restrain their conviction longer, they burst out in laughter and "King Vortigern and
the fabricator were dismissed to everlasting infamy and contempt. . . . So Master Samuel William Henry Ireland, you may
lock up your *Henry III* [*sic*], your King Edwards, and as Mr.
Malone says, 'all the other Kkynges and Qqueenes,' in the miraculous chest, and rest yourself assured that nobody will seek to de-
prive you of your just *inheritance*." (A reference, of course, to the
deed of gift to the Elizabethan Ireland.) Even the actors were
exonerated. Despite the outrages visited upon the lines by some
of the cast, the *European Magazine* for April had the dishonesty
to say that "the Performers did everything in their power to assist
the Piece, but without effect." It would have been fairer to say
that some of the actors had done everything in their power to assist the piece into disaster.

Not everyone was so disingenuous. The *Pocket Magazine* for
April declared that the failure at the Drury Lane, despite the
crowded audience's unwillingness to hear of a second performance, "does not entirely prove the fact of imposition, and still less
so against MR. IRELAND. It was the opinion of the late Dr. Johnson, as well as many other great men, that there are few of
Shakespeare's plays which would not be damned if produced before a modern audience." This is in consonance with the remarks

after the play by the Poet Laureate, who, despite his embarrassment over the Prologue and his mediocrity as a poet, was not an unjust man: "How many persons were there in the theatre that night who, without being led, could distinguish between the merits of King Lear and Tom Thumb? Not twenty."

The account in the *Annual Register* at least had the merits of rising into the realm of honest criticism. "The predominant sentiment in the audience was a wish to welcome with rapture the recovered offspring of their beloved Shakspeare. . . . [However, the historical events in the play] are warped into a resemblance to those of Macbeth, Richard III, & c. with the inadvertency of a copyist who is more intent on imitating the language than the genius of Shakspeare. . . . The play is destitute of all those gigantic metaphors and bold allusions which, approaching the limits of possibility, astonish, and alarm our imaginations into a sympathy with his sublime conceptions. The language, though evidently an imitation, is infinitely below the original. . . . The audience betrayed symptoms of impatience early in the representation; but finding its taste insulted by bloated terms, which heightened the general insipidity . . . and abortive efforts to elevate and astonish; pronounced its sentence of condemnation at the conclusion of the play; and we have no doubt that Vortigern, if it be published, will rank in character, though not in merit, with the perverted and surprising labors of the unfortunate Chatterton."

This is just. It also reveals how the rare man of taste and judgment, as the critic proves himself to be, had in 1796 to strain at the leash of eighteenth-century rationalism and neoclassic limitation when attempting to express his love of Shakespeare. This man obviously admired his Shakespeare for the right reasons, yet how oddly does his exposition of those reasons read today!

A versifier who was plainly enamored of the theatre, and more than a little familiar with its personnel, burst into song with a series of *Cantos on the Representation of Vortigern:*

> The iron chest,
>   I trust,
> Is laid to rest,
>   And rust. . . .

There are sketches of the performances: Phillimore, "Like a great boar rolling on earth, with his *huge snout*"; Benson [Hengist] showing "his arse"; Whitfield forgetting his lines of the Prologue; etc., etc. This long effusion was apparently penned in order to pay tribute to Miss Leak, who played the role of Attendant to Edmunda, and about whose loveliness the author rhapsodizes.

Whatever the public prints might say, Samuel Ireland himself maintained his faith in the authenticity of his Papers. He was to remain unshaken in his faith until his dying day. But after the fiasco at the Drury Lane his well-wishers urged that it was high time for the reluctant Mr. H. to come forth, declare himself, and confound the jeers of Malone and all the cohorts of Disbelievers. Even loyal Webb made it clear that unless the benevolent gentleman came out of hiding, he himself would now be forced to "entertain suspicions." Mr. H. must surely see that only he could save the situation. Until he was heard from, Webb must decline to offer another syllable in public support of the Papers.

Ireland's friends began to harass William Henry with a demand for the identity of Mr. H. Did not the boy realize that everyone was now saying that his father had *forged* the Papers himself? William Henry took refuge in a petulant reiteration of the avowed promise to protect Mr. H. from the public; it was a promise he had given on the gift of the first documents, and it was a promise which his father had renewed as the condition upon which the Papers might be published. Beyond this the boy refused to say anything.

In a spirit of genuine anguish, therefore, Samuel Ireland wrote on April 9 to Montague Talbot, who was again in Dublin. The subject of his letter, Ireland confesses, is "the most painful and oppressive that I have ever been engaged in in the Course of my Life, a matter of no less consequence than that of the happiness of myself and family, and may perhaps terminate in my ruin." He reminds Talbot that it was through him, according to Talbot's own admission, that William Henry came into possession of the manuscripts. Now the authenticity of the Papers is disputed by many, and the source of these doubts is the identity of the donor. The opinion of the experts was that the Papers were truly Elizabethan. Moreover, since they came into his hands from William Henry, he cannot believe that his son "would be so base as to involve me and his family in infamy and ruin by becoming an accessory with any person or persons in putting forth an imposition." With such a background for belief he published the Papers, and allowed *Vortigern* to be presented. But the play "has met with a fate that has involved me still further in inconvenience. I have been abused publicly and privately for such an attempt to impose on the Town, and I hear the public determination is to pursue me even to ruin. This I cannot but feel most acutely, as being totally ignorant of having done anything injurious. I feel it therefore incumbent on you, and indeed a duty that you owe to my injured family . . . to stand forward in some way or other to exculpate me from the Infamy that at present I inadvertently lay under." He assures Talbot that he does not hold him in any way responsible for what might ensue from the publication of the Papers, and declares it impossible that they could be forged. But he feels it only just that Talbot lend him support by declaring the truth of what he knows.

Talbot must have regretted enough his own insistence on having been the first to know Mr. H. He answered from Dublin on April 15. He tells Ireland that he deeply laments his predicament and will do what he can to extricate him from it, "consistent with my own honor and oath." He hopes his offer will be accepted as final, since any other proposal "must of necessity be declined by me, though my life were the forfeit for being secret. I will make an affidavit jointly with Sam, *That Mr. Ireland is innocent of any forgery imputed to him; that he is equally unacquainted with the discovery of the papers, as the world in general; that he has been only the publisher of them, and that the secret is known to no more than Sam, myself, and a third person, whom Mr. Ireland is not acquainted with. . . .* If I may venture an opinion, I still think that the papers are genuine, that Vortigern may have been one of Shakespeare's first essays at dramatic writing."

Talbot must have felt perfectly secure in proposing such an affidavit to be signed by him and William Henry: his friend would never perjure himself by swearing to the existence of Mr. H. At the same time he was proving his willingness to exonerate Ireland and yet remain a man of his word to the donor. He now undertook to extricate himself from some of William Henry's involvements in a way that was almost infantile.

The letter continues with a reminder to Ireland that he has never seen *Henry II*, and as for the manuscript of *Vortigern*, he never knew anything about that play until he was in London long after Sheridan had accepted it. "I must therefore depend on the veracity of others, as their coming from the same source as the few manuscripts I saw before I left London for the first time." It is odd that he should have anticipated less blame for being implicated only with the first "few" papers than for being connected with the whole collection. Ireland has suggested a plan of "making two gentlemen of respectability acquainted with every circumstance, who are to vouch to the world for the authenticity of the manuscripts." To this Talbot cannot agree; it "would not be consistent with our promise and oath."

Despite the nobility of Talbot's conclusion, such a plan was already afoot. The day before he wrote his letter, a preliminary committee of some dozen or more friends (including Byng, Burgess, Wallis, Wyatt, and the Chaplain to the Archbishop of Canterbury) convened at Norfolk Street. Whether or not William Henry was badgered into going along with the idea it is impossible to state, but he was present. The boy boldly proposed that "two respectable persons," not members of the committee there attending, be appointed "to receive the following information: The gentlemen are to be informed whence the papers came, the name of the gentleman to whom they belonged, by whom discovered, and in what place and manner."

The purpose of such a plan from his point of view is mystifying. Was it simply that he thought Talbot would have to be drawn in by two such men, and that he knew Talbot would refuse to break his supposed oath of silence to Mr. H., and that thus the matter would have to be dropped?

Unlike Talbot, however, William Henry would as soon have been hanged for robbing a bank as for stealing a loaf. Amazingly, he also presented this committee with a schedule of the further treasures which would be forthcoming from Mr. H. He marked with an asterisk the articles he himself had already seen, and which "would in a short time be put into his hands"; those without the asterisk were things which he had been told existed, but which in all honor he had to confess never having as yet seen: " *Play of Richard II in Shakespeare's manuscript; *Play of Henry II; *Play of Henry V; *62 leaves of K. John; *49 leaves of Othello; *37 leaves of Richard III; *37 leaves of Timon of Athens; *14 leaves of Henry IV; *7 leaves of Julius Caesar; *Catalogue of his books in his own manuscript; *Deed by which he became partner of the Curtain Theatre, with Benjamin Kele, and John Heminges; *Two drawings of the Globe Theatre on parchment; *Verses to Q. Elizabeth; *Verses to Sir Francis Drake; *Do. to Sir Walter Raleigh; *Miniature of Shakspeare set in silver; Chaucer with his manuscript notes; Book relative to Q. Elizabeth do.; Euphues with do.; Bible with do.; Bochas's Works with his Ms. notes; Barclay's Ship of Fools do.; Holinshed's Chronicles do.; Brief account of his life in his own hand; Whole length portrait, said to be of him in oil." This was *hubris* with a vengeance! Did the foolish youth imagine that by a renewed rapid turning-out of manuscripts and pictures he could outface

233

the world?

At any rate, the very boldness of the schedule had the effect of reducing the committee to at least suspended judgment. They indited a letter to Mr. H. asking his assistance in clearing the good name of Samuel Ireland. Mr. H. responded that he was prepared to cooperate! The committee met a second time and made out a list from which Mr. H. was to select two men of his choice; he was granted dukes, earls, bishops, and prominent political figures to choose from—though Byng prophesied, as it turned out quite accurately, that none of these illustrious persons was prepared to accept the dubious honor thrust upon him.

In the end the list had to be limited to Ireland's friends.

But the relief which William Henry felt following the failure at Drury Lane was spent under his father's new campaign to smoke out Mr. H., for the boy saw that the elder Ireland had taken on a belligerence that threatened to continue until the facts were known. William Henry became, to quote his own phrase, a "prey to the most agonizing disquietudes."

In hopes of putting an end to the suspense, he began tentatively to pave the way for an honest confession of his hoax. But how? He decided to employ his sisters as intermediaries. He managed to admit to them that he alone was the author of the Shakespeare Papers, that there was no Mr. H. They at once related this alarming confession to their father, but Ireland, to his son's stupefaction, dismissed the tale as a real fabrication, the product of "arrogance and vanity." Surely the girls must know that their backward brother did not have the ability even to manufacture the documents, much less to compose the verses or the variants to *Lear,* the poem to Ann Hathaway, and above all the finished works of *Vortigern* and *Henry II!* This was just a cock-and-bull story spun out because of Mr. H.'s unwillingness to make himself known, and had as its motive his son's self-aggrandizement. The boy, he wryly observed, had never had the effrontery to try palming off such a piece of nonsense directly on his father! Nor had he. William Henry was obviously too much in awe of him to attempt it after his confession had such a reception.

Like Macbeth, he found that he had become involved so far that returning were as tedious as go o'er. Yet that the day of reckoning was imminent he could not conceal from himself. He was well aware that his father was playing the spy. Since it was supposed that William Henry must be constantly meeting Mr. H., "it was imagined that by tracing my steps the residence of my mysterious friend must be discovered, which would have undoubtedly proved the case had there been any such being in existence. . . . By the picking of the lock of a window-seat [in his employer's chambers] the whole of my apparatus would have been displayed to view. I must here state that toward the termination of the business, when doubts ran high . . . I destroyed an infinite number of unfinished papers then in my possession, that no document might appear in evidence against me."

The committee was bent on having Mr. H. choose two men to whom he would reveal himself. Would it not be better, William Henry began to wonder, for him to relate the facts to two chosen friends of the family "and to consult with them as to the line of conduct it was most incumbent upon me to pursue, rather than longer remain in that state of dreadful anxiety?"

When he was given the list of names to submit to Mr. H., he decided to affix a mark next to two, Byng and George Chalmers, from whom he felt he "had the least cause to expect harsh conduct" on making a confession. The committee as a whole was well satisfied, but Chalmers obviously had little liking for the task. In the meantime Albany Wallis had offered an alternative plan. He would volunteer to hear Mr. H.'s secret alone; as an experienced lawyer he could set at rest any doubts in the mind of that generous man "as to any part of his property that might be endangered by such a disclosure" as he was now called upon to make. But Wallis had his conditions too. If he was to act as the recipient of Mr. H.'s confidence, he refused to share the honor with anyone else. Quite prepared to keep the secret about to be revealed to him, he could by no means undertake the responsibility of vouching that a partner would also keep his lips sealed.

Wallis' stand was more than welcome to William Henry. He informed the committee that Byng and Chalmers were not quite acceptable to Mr. H., but that he was certain that he could persuade him to accept Wallis. Everyone willingly agreed to this new arrangement.

A day was appointed for Mr. H.'s great revelation, to be made at Albany Wallis' house on Norfolk Street. The opportunity was too great for Ireland to resist doing some detective work. He stationed himself, unknown to his son, at the window of a friend who lived across the street from Wallis. Perhaps when Mr. H. appeared he would be instantly identifiable. If not, Samuel Ireland would at least know that mysterious gentleman if he ever saw him again.

William Henry arrived on time. After that there appeared only one other person. Excitedly Ireland asked his host's servant to follow the man, but the information was soon forthcoming that he was a fellow of no consequence. An hour later William Henry emerged from Wallis' house. Ireland at once got up, crossed the street, and demanded to know of his old friend what his son had had to say about Mr. H.'s failure to appear. Had the gentleman changed his mind? What had been William Henry's explanation? But Wallis remained obdurately uncommunicative. Ireland, in consequence, concluded that his son had been feeding Wallis with that absurdly farfetched tale of his being himself the author of the Papers.

After this William Henry was frequently in Wallis' company, but his father could never learn the matter of their talk, despite his endless queries. Impatiently Wallis reprimanded him: "Do not ask me any questions. It is not proper that you should know the secret; all will be well in time."

In point of fact, on that mid-May day while Samuel Ireland

played the spy across the road, his son was making a full confession to Wallis. Wallis was, as he well might be, astounded at the boy's revelations, and asked him a thousand questions. At length Wallis was convinced. A few days later William Henry even surrendered to the lawyer the remainder of the "antique" ink, as well as other fabricated documents and plans for projected plays. Naturally, he wanted the lawyer's advice as to what he must do next. Wallis recommended silence, and said that he himself would evade all questions "by stating that it was his opinion, as a professional man, that the supposed gentleman was not exactly safe in committing his name to the public." One understands that a lawyer has the obligation to hold sacred the confidences of a client. On the other hand, he is not expected to join a revealed conspiracy. Was Wallis acting out of pity for the boy? If so, why had he been prepared to expose him in December with his own Heminge document? Had he experienced a change of heart? Or was he indulging in the favorite exercise of lawyers, temporizing? Of all the ambiguous figures connected with the Ireland forgeries, Wallis is not the least inscrutable.

All these weeks the press had not ceased attacking Ireland. In its review of his publication of the Papers, for instance, the *British Critic* in its May issue, declares: "Suspicion, from the very beginning, has hung on every part of the transaction. The original story was most improbable, and it has strangely varied, without becoming probable. The papers themselves and the printed book offer in every part of their contents innumerable topics for objection, and little but objection; and the miraculous box or trunk, which, after having produced letters, drawings, printed books, Ms. plays, and such a farrago of things as never box contained before, still teems with discoveries. . . . Would you imagine, reader, that in a year and a half, or two years, the contents of one trunk could not be ascertained? . . . The publication of this volume proved fatal to the credit of the papers, and perhaps to the play of Vortigern." There follow passages of ridicule which assert that if these are the flowers of Shakespeare's garden planted by the Bard's own hands, then we must conclude that Shakespeare was "a downright blockhead." The Disbelievers, Malone, Boaden, and Waldron too, were being reviewed with approval even in June.

At the Ireland home Wallis' counsel to William Henry had resulted in a stalemate. It was for a short time as if the irresistible force of his father's demands to *know* had encountered the immovable object of his own silence. One of them had to yield. Naturally it was the boy. But when William Henry did yield, it was in his characteristic way, by the creation of new legends.

His father had twice or thrice rejected the assurances of the girls that their brother was the author of the Papers. William Henry himself twice or thrice attempted to broach a confession to his father, but Ireland, sensing an account he did not wish to hear, cut him short. If the rock of truth was to be treated as though surmounted by a six-headed Scylla, what was there for William Henry to do but fall into the Charybdis of further fabrications?

Early in May William Henry was seen riding a horse which he described as on loan from Mr. H., but which was soon shown to have been hired by himself. At Shepperton, whither the family repaired for a few days, he took Mrs. Freeman for a stroll in the garden, and there announced to her that he was about to be married to a lovely girl of seventeen who was madly in love with him, a young lady already rich in her own right, and the daughter of a wealthy family named Shaw who lived in Harley Street, great friends of Mr. H. William Henry and the girl had first seen each other at the Opera, where she had been immediately enchanted by his melancholy good looks, so much *à la mode*. Soon thereafter she contrived to meet him again, as if by accident, in the city. Her father had at first opposed the marriage, but the girl became so dangerously ill that her mother was able to persuade Mr. Shaw to allow William Henry to visit Miss Shaw as a suitor.

How much plate, linen, how many servants would the Shaws provide to set up the newlyweds? Ireland at once wished to know. He was delighted to hear that his slow-witted son had managed, and on his own, to arrange so splendid an alliance, and was at once for meeting Mr. Shaw himself. But as none of the Shaws was in evidence during the ensuing weeks, Ireland began to investigate and soon discovered that there were no Shaws on Harley Street, and so informed his son. The boy told him he had misheard the name: it was Shard. Again Ireland inquired, and found that the Shards did indeed live in Harley Street. But he also found that the said Shards had no daughter.

The Shaws were not William Henry's sole invention during this period. Mr. H., he told his father, anxious to compensate the actors who had seriously collaborated in the performance of *Vortigern,* had sent munificent gifts to Mrs. Powell, Caulfield, and others. He had, moreover, lent William Henry his own light two-wheeled carriage, equipped with two horses and grooms. William Henry appeared with the curricle and took his younger sister for a ride in it. It did not take long to learn that William Henry himself had paid fifty guineas for the horses, and still owed twenty more on account, and that he was having a curricle made for himself. To that Wallis put a stop as soon as he found out the facts.

William Henry also spoke of Mr. H.'s having promised him an estate of three hundred pounds a year, not very distant from his noble friend's, and quite near the sea. The estate included a magnificent and venerable house, its cellar stocked with vintage port. After a tour of the grounds with Mr. H., William Henry was introduced to an ancient steward who came with the premises. The boy and the older man were then treated to a superb dinner which included beefsteaks and an onion sauce served in a punch bowl. No other man living was ever privileged to see William Henry's castle.

Nor was his literary dreamworld atrophied. William Henry

had already permitted Covent Garden to read the discovered *Henry II*. Mr. Harris was said to have adored the love scenes, actually almost nonexistent, and to have assured the play a production next season. William Henry also told his sisters that he had shown Harris the complete play of *William the Conqueror* (of which at no time did he compose more than a few passages) and that the manager of Covent Garden was so much pleased with it that he agreed to pay him seven hundred pounds a year if William Henry would supply that theatre regularly with two plays a season. Harris and he were, in fact, now on such intimate terms that the manager had offered to keep William Henry's carriage horses in his own stable. Quickly following up this news, Ireland had an interview with Harris during which the Covent Garden official listened to him with vast astonishment, as though convinced that his visitor's "brain was affected."

Unenviable Samuel Ireland! To right and left he was being abused in the public prints. Most intolerable of all the many insults and the disparagement of his precious documents was the reiterated charge that he himself had fabricated them. The *Critical Review* for April accuses him of "a most suspicious propensity to prove that the forgery is too well planned to admit of possible detection, and at the same time to save himself from being regarded as the author, in case such a detection should arise." He must underestimate the British public if he imagines that it will swallow the tale of his having received the Papers from his nineteen-year-old son. "In a criminal court, he who has made use of a forged deed to his own advantage would be regarded as the author; and if he did not indicate how he came by it, he would be liable to every penalty of the law." Ireland promises to publish the rest of the documents in a two-volume supplement; but all the Papers deserve is "silent contempt."

Yet Ireland was unwilling, despite the chaos of his thoughts in the midst of all this abuse, to hear the truth either from his daughters or his son. Since such was the case, the boy made another attempt to shield his father. With his cooperation Wallis drew up an advertisement which was printed in the *True Briton,* the *Morning Herald,* and other papers.

SHAKSPEARE MSS.

In justice to my father, and to remove the reproach under which he has innocently fallen, respecting the papers published by him as the Mss. of Shakspeare, I do solemnly declare that they were given to him by me, as the genuine productions of Shakspeare, and that he was and is at this moment totally unacquainted with the source from whence they came, or with any circumstance concerning them, save what he was told by myself, and which he has declared in the preface to his publication. With this firm belief and conviction of their authenticity, founded on the credit he gave to me and my assurances, they were laid before the world. This will be further confirmed when at some future period it may be judged expedient to disclose the means by which they were affirmed.

S. W. H. Ireland, Esq.

Witness: Albany Wallis; Thomas Trowsdale, Clerk to Messrs. Wallis & Troward
Norfolk Street, May 24, 1796.

Obviously William Henry saw the handwriting on the wall. How to meet the inevitable?

Convinced that Ireland on the one hand would not accept the idea that he could be duped by his own son, and on the other hand too utterly despised his son's intellectual (not to say literary) talents to admit the possibility that the boy had forged documents which could successfully convince eminent men and himself (a seasoned collector!) of their validity, William Henry tried another ruse one day. What if, he asked his father, Mr. H., in order to end the discussion and remove himself from prying eyes—what if Mr. H. should now announce that he knew the Papers to be forgeries? That eventuality Ireland at once crushed. In that case, his father responded, Mr. H. would be revealed as a scoundrel who had deliberately set out to ruin the Ireland family —indeed, as also depraved and malignant, since he thus would have employed the son of that family as his "chief instrument. Such a wretch, surely, does not exist."

Ireland quickly confided this, like most other matters, to Mrs. Freeman, who, well indoctrinated, repeated that interpretation to William Henry. To her the boy countered: it might transpire that Mr. H. had not known the Papers to be forgeries *at first*, and that when he at length did discover that they were, he was unwilling to involve the Irelands any further. That would account for his ceasing to forward to Ireland articles which he had formerly promised, such as the much-discussed portrait, the miniature, and the coveted annotated volumes. Mrs. Freeman coolly observed, however, that when Mr. H. revealed himself, as he had agreed to do to the person chosen (whether Mr. Wallis or anyone else), that person would necessarily insist on seeing the promised articles too. If Mr. H. could not produce them, he must stand exposed as a complicated villain. She too concluded that such a villain "could not exist on the face of the earth."

Having begun, Mrs. Freeman soon decided to pursue the inquisition further. She remarked to William Henry that it was to be expected that Wallis would clear the Ireland family from the hideous allegations being made everywhere.—The boy reassured her: Mr. H. was "drawing up something" to be advertised in the newspapers.

Well, *had* Mr. Wallis met Mr. H. yet?—Oh yes indeed; he had met him two or three times.

Does *Wallis* now believe that the Papers are genuine?—He does, but Wallis is of the opinion that no new papers or articles "should be brought forward"—at least, for the present.

Do *you* believe the Papers genuine?—Most emphatically, yes.

Ireland had related to Mrs. Freeman, William Henry's ridiculous attempts to parade himself before his sisters as the author of the Bard's papers, and had been eloquent on how he viewed that fable. Mrs. Freeman now warned the boy indirectly that he had better abandon all notions of perpetuating *that* pose. She herself had just re-examined the Papers and was certain that they were not forgeries (though it is not clear why she should have considered herself competent to judge). If *any* person were to be so foolish as to pretend to be their fabricator, she cautioned him, he must expect to be branded only as "infamous." What could be more stupid than to try procuring a reputation for brilliance that way? Even if such a preposterous lie were believed, the result would be only to stamp that person as an impostor, not a man of talent, and an impostor he would be held until his dying day.— Yes, sighed William Henry, such indeed is the usual fate of genius.

And what, she demanded to know, of Talbot's role in the discovery of the documents?—Everyone, William Henry declared, was under a misapprehension about that. Talbot had had no more to do with them than Mrs. Freeman herself.

But had not Talbot himself announced that it was he who had given William Henry the first document?—About that subject, the boy mumbled, there was nothing he wished to say.

As May threaded its way toward its close William Henry knew that the day of reckoning must be soon, nor could he evade Mrs. Freeman's endless queries. He quit his post in the conveyancer's offices, and began to behave as though he himself were born into the same rank as Mr. H. His time was now spent lounging about town or driving on horseback or in the curricle, always with a groom attending, as befitted his delusions of social position. Some of this may very well have been done for the benefit of a certain person of whose very existence the Irelands seem to have had no inkling.

Mrs. Freeman did not learn of his new idleness without asking the pertinent questions. William Henry tried to make her understand that these days he was suddenly aware of the surge of great creative powers within himself. He felt himself possessed by such a daemon of Poetry as has been traditionally the familiar of great poets. He was moreover seriously thinking, he let her know, of seeking scope for himself by leaving England for parts unknown.

She was frankly alarmed at all this, and wrote to Talbot in Dublin to tell him how his old friend was conducting himself. She also took the opportunity of making some cogent reflections upon Talbot's letter of April 15 to Ireland. In it Talbot had said that though he was willing to sign the proposed affidavit with William Henry, nothing further in the way of a statement must ever be asked of him, since he would be compelled to decline. He felt obliged to keep the secret of Mr. H.'s identity, as he had vowed, even at the forfeit of his life. Why then, Mrs. Freeman wished to know, should the Ireland family (of which she considered herself an integral part) expect William Henry, "who is equally involved," to tell "the *real truth* either to Mr. Wallis or any other person?" William Henry had taken an oath too, and would insist upon respecting it quite as much as Talbot. What she feared most now was that all of William Henry's recent proposals were intended only to deepen the mystery. That, no doubt, is also, she added, why he intends quitting the country.

In the midst of what could have seemed to Ireland like a nightmare which refused to end, there occurred a piece of lunacy that must have convinced him that all these things were indeed occurring in a hideous world of dreams. One Saturday in May, as evening had begun to fall, a servant came up to announce that there was a woman waiting in a coach outside his door demanding to see him. He went down and found a fat, elderly female, who wished to know whether or not he was the present possessor of some Shakespeare papers that had been making such a stir in the world. Ireland asked why she wished to know. She replied that she had the best of reasons for asking: they belonged to her, all of them.

Rather dazed, he invited her into his house. He now observed that her hair was red, and as he asked her how she came to own the Papers, he had a distinct impression that he had seen her somewhere before. She declared that the documents had been stolen from her, that they were unquestionably hers for the simple cause that she "had written them all," and to establish her knowledge of them she added that there was "a great deal of religion in them."

He next asked her name and residence. Her name, she said, was Austin, and she lived at Chester. Suddenly Ireland remembered who she was and where he had seen her. Early in his acquaintance with Talbot the latter had invited him to go see "a curious character in Newman Street who had seen two moons—and had sworn to seeing men and horses galloping over them; this she saw going over London Bridge and called a boy to witness it." The affair had received more than its share of attention, and had been much talked of for a while. Out of curiosity Ireland had gone with Talbot and found her to be "an ignorant, uninformed woman" (there are, after all, degrees of intellectual unawareness!), but much addicted to "the wonderful." Disgusted, he had hurried Talbot out of the house as rapidly as possible. Talbot describes her as a tall, fat creature with red or auburn hair, in her mid-fifties, with a cast in one eye.

And here she was sitting in the Ireland home demanding the Papers as rightfully hers. Was it possible that she was somehow connected with Mr. H.? He decided that it was best to say as little to her as could be managed. If she had anything to discuss about the Shakespeare Papers, he told her, she must continue down Norfolk Street and see his solicitor, Mr. Albany Wallis, for everything was now in his hands. She left, but Wallis never saw her, nor did Ireland again. William Henry was unable to throw any light on the meaning of her visit.

Such an interview on the top of all the public ridicule now being amassed at his expense may very well have made poor Ireland feel that he was breaking under the strain. Certainly the invitation to come and stay with some old friends in Berkshire must have been a welcome one. He accepted gratefully, and extracting a promise from his son to let him hear from him regularly, he left London during the last week in May.

On Sunday, June 5, unable to keep his mind off what might be happening in London, he wrote his son this pathetic letter:

It is now more than a week, my dear Sam, since I left London; and not a word or a line from you!—In the situation, unsettled as you are, you cannot suppose but that my mind is much agitated, both on your account and that of the family. I expected, according to your promise, that you would certainly have written to me, and have pointed out what was your plan: and not only so, but your intentions with regard to the papers. I do assure you my state is truly wretched on both accounts. I have no rest, either night or day; which might be much alleviated by a more open and candid conduct on your side. Surely, if there is a person for whom you can for a moment feel, it must be for a parent who has never ceased to render you every comfort and attention, from your earliest moment of existence to the present.

I think you must sometimes reflect, and place yourself in imagination as at a future period of life,—having a son and being in such a predicament as I stand at present; and then judging what must be *your state of mind*, and what must be *mine at present*. I do not mean reproaches by this letter, but to assure you, that, if you cannot think me your friend, I fear you will be deceived in all friendships you may in future form. I do not recollect that any conduct of mine towards you has been other than that of a friend and companion—not that of a rigid or morose parent. It is therefore doubly unnatural that I should be forced to apply for information through any channel whatsoever, when I ought to hear it voluntarily from yourself. You seem to be estranging yourself, not only from me, but from all your family and all my acquaintances. Reflect well what you do and what determination you make; for this is the moment that may in all probability render you comfortable in your future establishment and future situation, or make you an alien to happiness for ever.

I have heard of my situation with the world, as to the papers at Reading, from many gentlemen there; who all agree that my state is truly a pitiable one; and all seem to dread the event. I know not the nature of your oaths and engagements, nor does the world; but it is universally allowed, that no obligation should lead a parent into ruin. . . .

Coming to the heart of the matter, he makes it plain that in his own mind there is no question about the authenticity of the Papers. The thing that must be done is to allay the false rumors, reports, and malign criticism which have blackened their fair fame:

If the papers are to be established as genuine, why delay to furnish me *with the documents so lately promised?*—But I will say no more on the subject at present.

By a paragraph in the Sun of Thursday last, it should appear that, though I am not in the secret, some persons are. The paragraph runs thus: "We are at length enabled to form a *decisive opinion* with regard to the manuscripts in the possession of Mr. Ireland, though motives of delicacy at present prevent us from rendering that opinion public!"

Pray give me a line by tomorrow's post, as I am impatient to hear from you: and believe me your very sincere friend and affectionate father,

Samuel Ireland

The "documents so lately promised" were, of course, those which had appeared on the list (asterisked and not asterisked) shown only weeks ago to the committee. Was Ireland in the very midst of his anguish indulging, despite himself, his besetting vice of greed for more and more antiquities? Or did he honestly believe that a greater accumulation would add the presumption of authenticity to those he already owned? If so, he should have known it was too late for that sort of reasoning. Most puzzling of all, how could he muster the stubborn perversity at this date to interpret the paragraph in the *Sun* as he did, instead of understanding it for what it plainly was, another rebuff?

About this affecting letter William Henry was to say that he received it "a short time" after his father's departure from London, and that its contents "struck deep" into his soul. "And I," he was to add, "from that period more bitterly cursed the fatal moment which involved me in a business fraught with misery to myself, and which had caused an incalculable degree of unhappiness to that being whom I had fondly hoped to gratify by the production of manuscripts."

That such were his emotions on reading the letter we may well believe. Indeed, it is likely that his regrets were even more bitter than he indicates. For he did not read the letter at the time he seems to imply. He was no longer at Norfolk Street when it arrived, and could have read it for the first time only at a later date.

The night before Ireland wrote that sad letter, that is, on Saturday, June 4, Jane Ireland left the Ireland house to stay for the weekend with her elder sister, Anna Maria, and her brother-in-law, Robert Maitland Barnard, at their house in Lambeth. On Sunday, the day of the letter, William Henry was alone with the servants at Norfolk Street. He confided to the maid the secret that he expected to receive fifty pounds the next morning, that he was going away soon, that he would make her a present as soon as he was able, and that she was not to put his linen among the things to be washed. "I shall take it away as it is," he informed her, "and pack it up at the Gentleman's I am going to, as there are new trunks for me there." He was going to use boxes temporarily, and these he would return.

It is always tempting to interpret everything William Henry says as an invention—that is, in fact, the injustice that his earlier biographers have uniformly done him. But the truth is that he did have reason to expect money the next morning. He had been seeing a great deal recently of his father's friend Gilbert Francklyn, of Wimpole Street, a retired West India planter, and had told him the truth about the forgeries. Francklyn apparently agreed with him that it would be better for him to leave his father's house, and promised to let the lad have some capital to start out with. But the money did not arrive on Monday morning.

All that morning William Henry was busy getting his clothes together. When they were packed he sent the boy for a coach. He put his things into the vehicle and, because the servants were listening, merely instructed the coachman to follow him as he set forth on foot. No one, therefore, had any idea of his destination. He assured the household, however, that he would return the same evening.

He did not return that night or on any other night to the house in Norfolk Street. When Jane returned from her visit on Tuesday, June 7, she was told the disturbing news, but waited all day in the hope that her brother would appear. By night it was obvious that she would not see him on Tuesday, and so with heavy heart she wrote a full account to her father.

TEN

Capers of a Scapegrace

MR. FRANCKLYN'S PROMISE of financial aid was not fulfilled for the simple reason that Mrs. Francklyn, a domineering woman, refused to allow her husband to subsidize William Henry. The boy, in consequence, went from his father's house to beggarly lodgings in an alley in Swallow Street, in a place described as a wretched hole. For the next ten days he lived on four pounds of potatoes.

Though his father's house saw him no more, he had many meetings with Wallis, who, as William Henry asked of him, remained secret about where the boy was living as well as about all he had confessed to the lawyer. At this period Ireland left a note with Wallis for his son: "I insist on having the affidavit drawn up by Sam, and signed and sworn to before a magistrate, in order to its being sent to Talbot, and then to be laid before the public: and I likewise insist on having the remainder of the papers so often promised me." Promised him, that is, by Mr. H.! There is something mad about Ireland's clamoring for the papers and articles Mr. H. was supposed to have assured him. One would think he had been caused enough trouble by those already in his possession. But it sounds as though he even suspected his son's claim of authorship as being a device to cheat him out of the promised forgeries.

William Henry had also developed an intimacy with his father's loyal friend and fellow-Bardolater, the Honorable John Byng, and with Mrs. Byng, both remarkably kind people. He was constantly at their house in Duke Street, and became a close friend of Byng's two sons, Frederick (afterward nicknamed "Poodle" Byng) and Henry John. Mrs. Byng was particularly magnanimous to him, touched, no doubt, by his being without resources, and moved to compassion by his having driven himself into a cul-de-sac. Her husband, when Francklyn failed to make good his promises, supplied William Henry with money to keep him in pocket for a while. Husband and wife were untiring in their efforts to reconcile Ireland and his son.

It was now more important for William Henry to convince his father that he had been capable of composing *Vortigern* and *Henry II* than it had once been to pass them off as the work of the Bard. He would never rest until he could win from his stubborn parent the admission that he was no longer the backward child whom his masters at school had given up as hopeless, but was now a genius, perhaps a genius of greater stature than even that of Chatterton, upon whom Ireland had sentimentally doted. To this end William Henry confessed the facts of the forgeries to Byng, and sat down before him to produce new forgeries as proof that he had written and composed the Papers. Byng, who had developed a liking for the boy, seemed to feel that William Henry had somehow given evidence of being "a prodigy one way or other," and showed the new testimony to Ireland—who refused to accept it as proving anything.

Ireland, with no idea of where his son was living, did not hear from William Henry until eight days after he had left home, June 14. William Henry first consulted Wallis on the wisdom of writing a letter describing himself as author of the Papers and referring to Wallis for complete details. Wallis thought this a good idea, and so William Henry penned "a very long epistle to Mr. Ireland stating the whole transaction, and craving his pardon in the most submissive terms." Wallis read the letter and approved of it before it was sent. It is true that William Henry in it begged his "dear father"—"for so I must still call you"—not to destroy the missive before reading it through, but the letter is certainly less than "submissive." He confessed at once to being the author of the Papers. By this time his father ought to be convinced that this was the plain truth, if only because of the new specimen forgeries made in the presence of Byng. But apparently Ireland was going to grant no more than the possibility that his son had *copied out* the documents; that the boy could have been their *author* he would continue stoutly to deny. This was intolerable to William Henry, and he exclaimed: "There it is I am wrong'd. Can you think so meanly of me as to be a *tool* of some person of genius? No sir I scorn the thought; were it not that I am *Author* as well as Writer I would have died rather than confess it." If he copied anyone, "it was the Bard himself." Though even here he in truth *plagiarized* nothing. "If there is Soul or Imagery" in the compositions, "it is *my own.*" As an inducement to forgiveness he added, "I beg your acceptance of the publication of Vortigern and the whole of the profits of Henry II." At the moment it seemed likely that the latter work would be presented at Covent Garden. "Should I live, my future labors shall equally be devoted to the good of my family. Do not wish to meet me, my dear father, I cannot yet bear it. I will instantly retire into Wales and give myself up to that study I so ardently wished for. If the writer of the Papers, I mean the mind that breathes through them, shows any sparks of Genius and deserves Honor, *I Sir, your son,* am that person, and if I live but for a little will prove it." (Here again we have the modish hint that a youthful death was sure sign of genius.)

William Henry also took the pains, in this letter, to swear some powerful oaths that neither Montague Talbot nor any man or woman living had had anything to do with composing the works of genius which he had fabricated.

"The effect produced by this letter was diametrically opposite to what Mr. Wallis had conjectured," William Henry reports, "although I was by no means astonished at the impression thereby made on Mr. Samuel Ireland's mind; who instantly attended on Mr. Wallis, stating it as his firm belief that there was not a word of truth in my statement; that he still believed the papers genuine; that no set of men could have produced the mass of evidence then in his possession; and that with respect to my assuming the title of author of the manuscripts, he was as fully convinced as that he then had existence I never could have produced them.—It was in vain that Mr. Wallis argued the point, and endeavored to convince Mr. Ireland that I had not deceived him by the confession in my letter: he would not be pacified, nor examine the similar handwriting of the documents then in Mr. Wallis's possession: and, still adhering to his own belief, he quitted Mr. Wallis, firmly maintaining that the manuscripts were indisputably the productions of William Shakspeare."

Despite Ireland's anger at the letter, he kept it very carefully. Later, he did not hesitate to cite from it William Henry's renunciation of all profits from the publication of *Vortigern* and *Henry II* as proof of his ownership of them—a title his son at no date ever disputed.

In the meantime William Henry eagerly anticipated a response from his father to his half-apologetic, half-boastful letter. His father was swift and intransigent in replying. Whatever William Henry's talent may or may not be, Ireland asks, whom does his son believe willing to associate with him or approve of him, if his "gross and deliberate impositions" are to be credited as such—particularly when he has used his own father as a medium for deceiving the world? For such impositions "the Law holds out certain death as a reward." The subject is too abhorrent to pursue further. There are, however, certain practical matters. Ireland has discovered that all the valuable books which William Henry had recently found are gone from Norfolk Street with his son. Yet but a few days before Ireland left for Berkshire his son had promised him that he would be free to purchase some of them. Worse than that, William Henry's debts are all unpaid. "I have not words to express the high indignation I feel at yr. unnatural conduct—words or reproaches are now all vain. You have left me with a load of misery and have, I fear, about you a load of infamy that you will find perhaps more difficulty than I shall in getting rid of."

Regretting the cold anger of this reply, Ireland sent his son the next day another letter of warning. If William Henry is indeed, as he insists, "the writer etc." (he would not say "author") of the documents, then he must realize the danger in which he stands. His character will be generally thought so depraved that no one will trust him, no one will be willing to receive him. Therefore, Ireland concludes, "do not suffer yourself from vanity or any other motive to adhere to any such confession."

William Henry's reaction to the admonition was a complete loss of patience with his father for refusing to admit his abilities and attempting to coerce him into keeping silent on acknowledging what was his own. So, far from heeding parental counsel, he promised only to engage at once upon writing a pamphlet to tell the world the whole truth. If the disastrous consequences which Ireland predicted should indeed follow, he concluded with his own threat: "I know what course to take." After all, had not Chatterton shown the way?

Samuel Ireland, who preferred to think William Henry's confessions a perverted vaingloriousness, in order to protect himself against what he considered an obsession, advertised his own innocence in the *True Briton* that June. The world, however, chose to brand him as the culprit. Stories about him, fed by the public's malicious love of gossip, were circulating about town. Some of them, completely unsubstantiated, survived another half century, as for example this one. Sheridan's unconcern and Kemble's hostility toward *Vortigern* before the performance were swelled by report into a "quarrel" over the future of the play. When the curtain went down on the fiasco and Samuel Ireland had left the theatre, this exchange was pretended to have taken place:

KEMBLE. Well, Sir, you cannot doubt that the play is a forgery.
SHERIDAN. Damn the fellow, I *believe his face is a forgery.* He
is the most specious man I ever saw.

This tale was being recounted in 1851.

Mrs. Freeman, an avenging angel, was quick to write to Talbot to enlist him on their side against William Henry. Even though no one who has known William Henry has ever observed "the least trait of *literary genius*" in him, she writes, he is now telling everyone that he and he alone is the author of the Papers and the two new plays. She, for one, does not believe a word of this nonsense, and considers his conduct "unparalleled in history." She asks Talbot to reflect on the father's despair at having for an open enemy his very son, "and then think if any punishment can be devised adequate to the enormity of the crime, a crime that involves his whole family in *ruin.*"

If Mrs. Freeman was indeed William Henry's mother, as Westall, Farington, and Libbis have categorically stated, she certainly seems like the most unmotherly of women toward her son. Yet there have been women who have hated their children—popular cant to the contrary. Perhaps, too, her dubious position in Ireland's household may have worked upon her to make her thoroughly disagreeable. Ireland is said to have treated her unceremoniously before others. If so, she was not the first woman to respond to rough treatment with fierce loyalty, and her loyalty was clearly to Ireland. It is, in addition, a matter of record that she was in some quarters disliked. When the Linleys moved to Norfolk Street from Bath, they became intimates of the Irelands— and through them Ireland became friendly with the Linley son-in-law, Sheridan. Jane Linley became a lifelong friend of Jane Ireland's, and after Ireland's death (1800) Mrs. Freeman invited her to stay with her and Jane. It was from the Ireland house that Jane Linley was married, but her fiancé, Charles Ward, was opposed to the arrangement; "I find my dislike increasing with every occasion," he said of Mrs. Freeman. Sheridan held similar views. She was plainly not an agreeable woman.

When her plea to win over Talbot failed, Samuel Ireland threatened to exert political influence to have the young actor cast out of the Dublin troupe. Talbot's response was to pen a half-heartedly defiant doubt that Ireland had any such connections; and even if he could contrive the young man's dismissal, Talbot was "not dependent on the stage for a livelihood," and could in any case procure an acting position elsewhere. Besides, he had been thinking of emigrating to America.

On monday, july 4,* William Henry went to St. James's Church at Clerkenwell, there to be married (two persons named Crane acting as witnesses) to an unattractive "shortish" young woman who was apparently unknown to any member of his family, one Alice Crudge. Nothing was less to be anticipated in William Henry's harebrained career than this marriage. He never accounted for it himself.

If we accept his father's dating of William Henry's birth, he was about twenty-one in 1796; if we accept his own, he was only nineteen. He certainly appeared at the moment to be without any hope of means of supporting a wife. But he was an attractive-looking youth with, moreover, the highly approved air of melancholy which in that era was universally construed as a sign of the poetic. The very notoriety of his name must have rendered him romantic in the eyes of some maidens. The comparison with Chatterton must have occurred to many. How on earth did it happen that he could make no better marriage than that with the unhandsome Miss Crudge?

One can only theorize. It will be remembered that Samuel Ireland thought Mr. H.'s handwriting to be feminine. Did William

---

* *The Dictionary of National Biography* and Mr. Mair erroneously date this event as occurring in June, just prior to his leaving his father's house.

Henry procure the services of some young lady in penning Mr. H.'s letters (it would have been foolish to use even a disguised version of his own, when writing a modern hand, since his father must surely have been familiar with his son's script) and was that young lady Miss Crudge? Was she, too, possibly the young woman who contributed the lock of hair which had to pass as the Bard's? If William Henry had thus entangled Miss Crudge in his affairs, it might have seemed natural to the boy, in the midst of his troubles, to form a permanent alliance with one who knew the truth about him and loved him none the less for it.

Or if such was not the case, one might take a clue from the experiences of two young men infinitely more gifted than William Henry who, both of them, contracted marriages that were merely disastrous: Coleridge, whose nuptials had taken place only the year before, and Shelley, whose first marriage was to take place fifteen years later. Both these geniuses were wrapped in clouds of future glory when they were whisked into matrimony by the young women in question. Such young men are always a ready prey for girls who are willing temporarily to become disciples—if that will lead to the marriage altar. James Branch Cabell was of the opinion that it is the particular function of women to cure all men of their dreams. Possibly William Henry, absolutely dazed by the possibilities of his own talents, had an experience similar to that of Coleridge and Shelley. The to-do about his forgeries had convinced him that he had a brilliant future ahead of him as a poet and dramatist—he, who had been able to pass off his own compositions as those of the Matchless Bard!—and he was in a very vulnerable position for any girl who was willing to give him the attention and acknowledgment his father had stubbornly withheld.

For the present his way of fortifying his illusions about himself was to behave like a man of fashion. He was often to be seen on horseback about town, always with a groom following. Nightly he put in an appearance at the theatre. The funds for these extravagances were necessarily borrowed. On Sundays he walked in Kensington Gardens with his short, unhandsome wife.

Beyond this, we know almost nothing concerning Alice Crudge Ireland. The last time we hear of her is in a letter of 1798, from William Henry to his father. She must have died before 1804, for in that year William Henry married for a second time.

In the meantime, he was indulging a sense of freedom from the parental roof. It was at this period, he tells us, that he was frequently invited to the home of the Thompsons. The head of the family was a member of parliament. "On one particular occasion he introduced me at dinner to a foreign gentleman, who had frequently heard of the Shakspearian fabrication, and who was a staunch adherent to the principles of Lavater the physiognomist. Some time after the cloth was drawn, the above gentleman riveted his eyes upon my face for a considerable time, at length replenished his glass, and, after drinking my health, addressed himself to Mr. Thompson, stating that he had carefully examined the character of my physiognomy, and that, although he could not from the principles of Lavater have precisely indicated the subject on which I have been occupied, he should nevertheless have known that some circumstance of an uncommon and public nature had for a length of time overpowered every other consideration in my mind." William Henry was bound to consider himself phenomenal, and nine years after the event recounts it smugly, though disclaiming any desire to be self-complacent or to suggest his acceptance of Lavater. The incident, he tells us, "is given solely because of its singularity."

He himself was behaving with enough singularity. At Covent Garden he had so far overextended his welcome with unsolicited oratory that Harris, by midsummer, had cooled on the possibility of producing *Henry II*. Though from every point of view the play is a considerable advance over *Vortigern,* it never was to be produced.

Without notice, William Henry's threatened exile into Wales

became a fact. Out of concern for him Byng arranged with some friends, the Winders of Vaynor Park, Montgomeryshire, that William Henry be welcomed as a guest; the idea was that the young man might find it attractive enough to desire settling down on their farm. When he set out, Byng gave him at least five guineas so that he need not feel impoverished. While staying with the Winders, William Henry composed some lines on "Avarice" to prove to his hosts that he had been quite equal to the Shakespearean forgeries. As his money began to disappear, Mrs. Winder loaned him five guineas, which Byng later repaid.

It was now the end of July, 1796, and the Chancellor of the Exchequer during the Rockingham administration, Mr. Dowdeswell of Pull Court, Worcester, was visiting the Winders, and so met William Henry. Mr. Dowdeswell invited him to stay at Pull Court, giving him a letter to his agent there—for Wales had seemed less than enticing to the young vagabond—and also loaned him five guineas. William Henry accepted the gracious invitation, but left Pull Court before August 12, first, however, borrowing twelve guineas from Mr. Stone, Dowdeswell's agent. (On April 17, 1798, Mr. Dowdeswell wrote to Samuel Ireland that of these sums, £12 7s. had remained unpaid.)

William Henry continued traveling south. At Gloucester he encountered a friend of an old acquaintance of Samuel Ireland's. He introduced himself as formerly of the Eighty-first Regiment, and at present in passionate pursuit of antiquities, though his new acquaintance remarked that he did not seem to have enough funds to buy one old book. His melancholy, however, had been left behind him in London. The gentleman described him as very sprightly—even dashing—and, of course, very talkative. It was very hard to believe, he thought, that anyone so young, and particularly this young man, could possibly have sat down in one place long enough even to transcribe the Shakespeare Papers, much less compose them.

From Gloucester William Henry went on to Bristol, and made

the Ostrich Inn on Durdham Downs his headquarters. While there he called on a Mr. Cottle in Bristol, and wrote some specimens for him of the Shakespeare fabrications. He found his inn "perfectly retired as well as Romantick" in situation. When he was able to get his hands on the London papers, he was happy to see that they were concerning themselves very little with his forgeries, and at times he optimistically assumed that the whole matter was probably forgotten. He was, of course, quite incorrect.

He wrote to Byng, begging him to speak to his father in his behalf. Now he was quite ready to set himself up as a writer in his own right. He was engaged, he says, on a story, or possibly a play which was to have "songs, etc., castles, etc., wonders, etc." But he was totally without funds. As for his writing, he had already deposited in Wallis' hands the "written outlines of dramas on some few of our monarchs' reigns which had not occupied the genius of our bard. The theatrical production descriptive of the reign of queen Elizabeth I intended to have entitled The Virgin Queen. The subject of William the Conqueror had . . . greatly occupied my attention." These plays which Shakespeare had neglected to write were originally, of course, among the contemplated forgeries. Now nothing need impede his claiming them as his own. All he had to do was write them. That he never got around to doing.

His choice of Bristol was hardly accidental. Probably every day of his life for years his thoughts had dwelt on that town as the birthplace of Chatterton. He was drawn to the neighborhood of the dead poet as to the haunts of a spiritual brother. "Curiosity," he records, "naturally prompted me to visit the turret of St. Mary Redcliffe church wherein were deposited the papers to which Chatterton had access, and from which he pretended to have drawn his Rowley's poems. It contained the old chests, which were empty; being in every other respect a cheerless stone room—After inspecting this chamber, I waited upon Mrs. Newton, Chatterton's sister; who, as usual, produced the letters received from her brother, which she styled the only remaining relics of her dear Thomas. After having given them a very careful perusal . . . I proceeded to make more minute inquiries respecting Chatterton than were usually made by the few strangers that were prompted from curiosity to visit her." He asked her about Chatterton's childhood. Had he shown any personal singularities? Yes, "he was always reserved and fond of seclusion." Did he betray "any extraordinary symptoms when young?" Yes, he preferred to read from old black-letter type. That detail "very forcibly struck" William Henry. She told him about the austerity of Chatterton's character and his high moral standards. William Henry expresses his reverence for the dead poet's talents, "whose fate I commiserate with unfeigned tears of sympathy; who, had he lived, would have undoubtedly ranked with the first men of genius that have graced our isle."

Then William Henry called on "a bookseller in a bye street," and steered the conversation to Chatterton. The bookseller told how he had permitted the youth to borrow any volume he chose. Chatterton had never been "very communicative; merely bowing his head as he entered the shop, and making a similar obeisance on retiring."

William Henry was back in London sometime around the end of October or the beginning of November. He soon learned that his father was under greater harassment than ever. The newspapers had by no means dropped the affair, and the popular dramatist Frederick Reynolds had put Samuel Ireland into a play, *Fortune's Fool,* which was presented at Covent Garden on October 29.

As a matter of fact, from this perspective of time, *Fortune's Fool* seems little more than good-natured funmaking. Samuel Ireland figures in it as Sir Bamber Blackletter. In order to curry favor with him, Ap-Azard is urged to praise his library; Sir Bamber boasts that it does not contain any modern "trash"—there is not a "book publish'd within the present century, except John

Gilpin in four volumes." Surprised, Ap-Azard says that Gilpin would not fill one column of a newspaper. But Sir Bamber has extended it to four octavos by "notes, alterations, illustrations, emendations." Miss Union singles out a coat "once worn by the immortal Dryden," and Sir Bamber indicates shoes that belonged to Rochester, a waistcoat of Wycherley's, and a wig that was Hudibras'. Ap-Azard brings in a bust of Chaucer; delighted Sir Bamber is ready to make Ap-Azard his heir. Also he thinks of marrying Miss Union because she owns "Trickerinda, that ancient poem written by Dan Chaucer." However, he reflects, "though I'm fond of old books because they fetch a great price, I've no attachment for old women, for they fetch no price at all." Ap-Azard reads him an original stanza of the Matchless Bard's, "written for one of the witches in Macbeth." It has never been published:

> Hinx, spinx, the Devil winks,
> The fat begins to fry;
> Nobody at home but jumping Joan,
> Father, mother, and I.
> O, U, T,
> With a black and a brown snout
> Out! Pout! Out!

Sir Bamber is much impressed, and asks to hear it again. Miss Union owns a small trunk out of which she is about to extract the manuscript of Chaucer's *Trickarinda*. In anticipation Sir Bamber cries, "I shall die—expire in all the agonies of an expecting lover!" She opens the trunk and takes out the manuscript. Sir Bamber is in ecstasies: "Oh how the touch thrills me!" Presently he reads from it:

> On yon green bank where Trickarinda sleeps
> The wind laughs round her, and the water weeps!
> And lo! a monk all hollow'd from the cloyster
> Grey as the morn and white as any oyster.

In the end it turns out that Chaucer and Miss Union wrote the very same hand, and Sir Bamber awakes to his folly. The satire is nowhere very cutting.

But all that Ireland could make out of this or any other satire at his expense was that the whole world seemed to scorn him. His other productions, including his published books and prints, were not selling at all. The distrust attached to the Shakespeare Papers had fastened on everything connected with him. He decided, against the advice of his friends, that it was now important to write a pamphlet himself, clearing himself of all guilt and answering the charges of Malone. Such a publication could only delay the eventual death of the contention over the Papers, but Ireland was not to be dissuaded.

William Henry knew in advance that his father would surely insist that the Papers were genuine, despite his own confessions. Besides, he was in the mood to claim authorship of the forgeries with pride, as evidence of his genius. He had already threatened to publish his own pamphlet, and now determined to do just that. "I once more consulted Mr. Albany Wallis; giving it as my opinion that the only means of exculpating Mr. Samuel Ireland from any censure whatsoever, would be my publication of a pamphlet stating concisely every fact. With this opinion Mr. Wallis did not coincide; advising me rather to suffer the matter to die away than give such a testimony to the public. What was to be done in this posture of affairs? Mr. Samuel Ireland still believed the papers genuine; he demanded the remainder which had been promised; he exhorted me to confess the truth, which, though already made known, he would not believe; and lastly, he peremptorily insisted on my clearing his character to the world from every aspersion which had been thrown upon it. . . . Knowing no better mode to free him from censure . . . I determined to act in opposition to the advice of Mr. Wallis, and give to the world a concise statement of the facts."

Informed by Wallis of his son's intentions, Ireland agreed to meet the boy at Wallis' on December 12, in order to talk him out of issuing a pamphlet. It was a most unsatisfactory interview. He had not seen his son since the flight from Norfolk Street five months earlier while he himself had been in Berkshire. Possibly all would have gone well if he had greeted William Henry with some warmth and a willingness to listen. But he was chilled at once by William Henry's repetition of his claim to authorship of the Papers; angered, he asked his son whether he felt equal even to writing a pamphlet. He had not allowed Wallis to leave the room, preferring a witness instead of permitting the healing air of intimacy between himself and the young man. He remarked to Wallis that if his son persisted in writing a pamphlet, it would be so ill-written that it would only prove everything he said in it a lie. Wallis told Ireland that he had already expunged a great many poor passages from what had been shown him. Stung, William Henry vowed to issue the work in any case, for he was in great need of money.

The next day he wrote to his father that he was about to send for his armor, bookcase, press, and desk, so that he could sell them all to pay his debts. Then, as though to give vent to a long-pent-up frustration, he signed the note "W. H. Freeman."

When his *Authentic Account of the Shakspearian Manuscripts* appeared as a forty-three-page pamphlet later in December, it betrayed all the marks of hasty composition in its structure. Its punctuation and syntax, as always with William Henry, were fantastic. In it he hopes that his account "will meet with favor and forgiveness, when considered as the act of a boy." He stresses the importance of that unforgettable day at Clopton House, outside Stratford, and his father's anguish on hearing that baskets of Shakespearean documents had just been burned. In his first forgery, "I had no intention whatever of attempting anything further, my object was only to give my father pleasure, that wish accomplished, I was satisfied." There follows a brief account of the various forgeries and of the assistance rendered by Montague Talbot. Though the world condemned *Vortigern* "that did not lessen the satisfaction I felt in having at so early an age wrote a piece which was not only acted, but brought forth as the work of the greatest of men." His father has been wrongly blamed for the forgeries, but persists in thinking "*Shakspeare* the author of the papers and me totally incapable of writing them." Vanity over-powering him, William Henry takes two whole pages to quote a speech "On Contemplating Westminster Abbey," from his projected play on William the Conqueror. He leaves the "world to judge of its merits if it possesses any." He is now willing to make an affidavit to the whole truth as well as the following declarations:

> *First,*—I solemnly declare that my father was perfectly unacquainted with the whole affair, believing the papers most firmly the production of *Shakspeare.*
>
> *Secondly* [*sic*],—That I am myself both the author and writer, and have had no aid or assistance from any soul living, and that I should never have gone so far, but that the world praised the papers so much, and thereby flattered my vanity.
>
> *Thirdly,*—That any publication which may appear tending to prove the mss. genuine, or contradict what is here *stated,* is false,—this being the true account.

After this veiled warning to his father, he once more pleads for forgiveness for "the act of a boy, without any evil or bad intention," and concludes optimistically: "Should I attempt another play, or any stage performance, I shall hope the public will lay aside all prejudice my conduct may have deserved, and grant me that kind indulgence which is the certain inmate of every *Englishman's* bosom."

The *Monthly Mirror* called this "a *triumphal avowal* of the FORGERY. . . . The style of the pamphlet is contemptible and strongly insinuates the incompetency of W. H. Ireland to compose the Play of Vortigern and the Profession of Faith. . . . If anything can equal the infamy of a late literary forgery, it is the impudence with which it is avowed." The editors would not accept this as the truth; in short, the real villain had to be Ireland senior. This was the opinion, too, of the *True Briton*, which found in the pamphlet not a vestige of talent or feeling such as are manifested in the manuscripts. The *Morning Chronicle* wryly remarked: "W. H. Ireland has come forward and announced himself author of the papers attributed by him to Shakspeare; which, if *true*, proves him to be a *liar*." The *Gentleman's Magazine*, with which Steevens was associated, branded this attempt "to exonerate his father . . . ill-written"; the forgery itself was "most impudent and unparalleled," inferior to Chatterton's though exceeding it in success.

Five hundred copies to be sold at a shilling were issued and at once bought up. A few years later they were selling at a guinea.

William Henry's admissions were very rapidly followed by his father's *Mr. Ireland's Vindication of His Conduct Respecting the Publication of the Supposed Shakespeare Mss.* In an attempt to justify himself, he quotes letters and documents: William Henry's statement of November 10 and Talbot's letter of November 25, 1795, detailing the "discovery" of the manuscripts, are given as the authority for his publication of the Papers. The number and variety of them rendered the theory of forgery incredible, he was certain. Moreover, his acquaintance with Talbot "placed him [Talbot] . . . beyond even the possibility of suspicion, his fairness and honesty in the transaction appeared invariable." Besides, the papers were all given to him by his only son. "A father is not very eager to entertain surmises that affect the moral credit of one so dearly connected with him as his only son, and when the same declarations were made by him in the most solemn and awful manner, before crouds [*sic*] of the most eminent characters, who came to my house, I could not suffer myself to cherish the slightest suspicion of his veracity." Furthermore, every curious person was invited to Norfolk Street to view the documents; "of these the greater part consisting of the most celebrated literary characters this age has produced, expressed their opinions, not in the phrase of mere assent, but in the unequivocal language of a full and overflowing conviction. Some were even desirous of subscribing without solicitation, their names to a certificate, in which their belief might be formally and permanently recorded."

He tells how Boswell drew up such a certificate, and how Parr revised it to make it more energetic. He quotes Parr's statement and the names of the signatories; he describes Boswell's falling on his knees and thanking God for having allowed him to live to witness the discovery of the Papers; he provides a full catalogue of the manuscripts; he quotes the second Certificate of Belief, drawn up by Wallis in March, 1796, as a result of his comparing his own documents with the Irelands', and the names of the signatories to that; he quotes his son's statement of the same month, declaring Ireland's ignorance of the origin of the Papers; he cites the advertisement drawn up by Wallis and signed by William Henry for the *True Briton* of May, 1796, publicly exonerating Ireland senior from any acquaintance "with the source from whence they [the Papers] came"; he quotes Talbot's letter of April 15, 1796, attesting to Ireland's innocence; he describes the formation of a committee in April, 1796, and its proposals for discovering the source of the Papers; he gives at full length the schedule drawn up by William Henry and presented to the committee, in which were listed all the many manuscripts and articles still to be delivered to Ireland; he excerpts a more recent letter from Talbot exonerating him anew ("I beg leave to assure you that I shall feel the greatest pleasure in standing forward to screen you, who are an innocent sufferer. Sept. 16, 1796"); he quotes Malone's malign advertisement warning the public against the Papers; and he proceeds from that to an attack on Malone's talents as a Shakespearean scholar.

Ireland's book won no sympathy or credit for him.

On January 3, 1797, William Henry sent a remarkable letter to his father. He had thought of appearing on the stage, but his recent pamphlet has definitely put an end to that idea. Hence, "if you are *really* my father, I appeal to your feelings as a Parent, if not, I am the more indebted to you for the Care of my youthful Education etc. and though I cannot expect so much, yet I shall hope from you that degree of feeling due to every Man from a Fellow Creature—I have said *if* you are my parent, being at a loss to account for the expressions so often us'd to Mrs. Freeman, and which she has repeatedly told me of 'that you did not think me *your son*,' besides, after slight altercations with Mrs. F. you have frequently said that when of age you have a story to tell me that would astonish and (if I mistake not) much shock me. Mrs. F. after my bringing forward the Papers us'd ironically to say 'that now you was glad enough to own me for your son.' If, my dear Sir, you know anything relating to myself, I intreat you to inform me of it. But should it be merely a story appertaining to my *mother* which might give me pain, I trust you will bury it in oblivion, nay, I am sure you will, for Delicacy, I am convinced, is no stranger to your bosom. That I have been guilty of a fault in giving you the MSS I *confess* and am sorry for it, but I must also assure you it was without a bad intention or a thought of what would ensue. As you have repeatedly said, 'Truth will find its Basis,' so will your *Character* (notwithstanding all aspersions) shortly appear unblemish'd to the world. To the above Expression *I* also appeal, and though my Pamphlet, compar'd with *my* Vortigern and *my* Henry II etc. etc. may for the present convince the world that I am not the *author* of them, yet, Sir, I may sacredly appeal to my *God,* that Time which develops truth will authenticate the contents of *my Pamphlet* and thereby 'Never Erring Truth Find Its Basis.' I am exceedingly sorry that you did not (before the Publication of your Book) inspect the Papers in Mr. Wallis's possession (and which I understand you might have seen), as they contain no other than a similar account to that already publish'd by me."

Since he is in desperate financial circumstances he asks his father to see whether one of his many friends can help him to any kind of situation. The money he received for the pamphlet is almost spent, "and as to writing for the stage, I can do that at my leisure Hours but can place no *certain* dependence on it."

It is surely something to William Henry's credit that in no letter does he throw any of the burden of the forgeries on his father. Yet certainly Ireland's greed to have more and still more was a powerful spur to his son's dishonesty.

This particular letter places the Ireland household in a new perspective, and reveals the lack of security with which William Henry was asked to be part of it. That he was very probably not Ireland's son is made evident by his troubled words—as though at last the misery gnawing at his vitals had dared express itself. We gather, too, not only Mrs. Freeman's ill-usage at Ireland's hands, but also her own cold contempt for William Henry. Surely, the real answers to William Henry's activities as a forger are more revealed in this touching letter than in anything we know about the boy.

There is no evidence that Ireland answered his son's anguished query about his origins. What we do know is that he was very soon blaming Wallis for William Henry's pamphlet, and demanding a new public statement retracting all that the pamphlet declared. To protect Wallis, William Henry, on January 31, 1797, sent a formal letter to the attorney, exculpating him from the charge of having encouraged the writing of the pamphlet, and testifying, on the contrary, to Wallis' urging him to maintain silence and allow the affair to "die away."

It is natural to speculate on what could possibly have been the great revelation which, as we read in William Henry's letter to his father, old Ireland had promised to make. There are a number of mysteries here.

William Henry had heard Ireland declare that he did not believe the boy to be his own son—a remark often made to Mrs. Freeman. Later, when the Papers began to multiply, Mrs. Freeman had ironically observed that Ireland would now be glad enough to acknowledge the boy as his. All this would seem to imply that *Ireland himself had doubts about who William Henry's father was.*

Though Mrs. Freeman generally passed as Ireland's "housekeeper," this was accepted as a euphemism. Farington categorically states that she was not only Ireland's mistress but also the mother of his children. She herself was baptized Anna Maria de Burgh, and it is strong evidence that she was the mother that the elder daughter of the Ireland household was named Anna Maria. Also, William Henry, when he married a second time, named *his* elder daughter *Anna Maria de Burgh Ireland;* he was plainly naming the child not after his sister, but after the woman he felt sure was her grandmother.

We are told that for years the children bore the name of Irwin and that the girls passed as the nieces of Mrs. Freeman. That would not include William Henry. But Malone must have had some dim knowledge that the Irwin name had played a role in the Ireland home, for he insisted, by citing evidence which has never been found, that William Henry had been baptized as W. H. Irwyn. Samuel Ireland's own origins are shrouded in obscurity, and "Irwin" sounds enough like "Ireland" to make one wonder whether that had not originally been his name. (The great authority on his beloved Hogarth, by the way, was his own contemporary, John Ireland.)

It is said that Mrs. Freeman had been the mistress of the lecherous Lord Sandwich, a nobleman who for years had led a most profligate life in the company of the notorious John Wilkes and other rakes. If she had been his mistress (a likelihood fortified by her wealthy, prominent brother's disowning her), is it not possible that the Ireland children were sired upon her by Sandwich? Sandwich had several children by the Miss Ray whom the Reverend Mr. Hackman shot.

On the other hand, the great revelation promised and the

doubts of parentage seem, according to William Henry's letter, to fasten on him alone. Since there were doubts, is it not possible that the Ireland girls were the offspring of Samuel, but that William Henry was the son either of Sandwich or of some member of Sandwich's dissolute circle who came again into Mrs. Freeman's life for a brief time? A nobleman can be argued only because Ireland had promised William Henry that the revelation would be both astonishing and shocking—and nothing less than a man of rank could so affect Ireland's middle-class mind.

My own thoughts lead me to the following conclusions—though I am by no means prepared to vouch for them as fact, where there is so little fact to go on. I am convinced that Anna Maria Ireland was the daughter of Anna Maria de Burgh "Freeman." If she was, so must have been her younger sister, Jane. For the rest, I waver between two theories. First, one may suppose that Sandwich was the father of all three children. After her break with him Mrs. Freeman became Ireland's housekeeper-mistress. She is said to have had a fortune of twelve thousand pounds. Was this the gift of Sandwich? And how was Ireland, who started out in life as a "mechanick," able to devote himself to the joys of engraving and collecting (his silk-weaving business had ended in bankruptcy in 1793)—unless he had been set up in life by Sandwich as a reward for relieving him of a no-longer-desired mistress? It would explain why Ireland never married her, and was often rude to her. It might also explain her possible unwillingness to marry him! Such arrangements had been made frequently in that century. On the other hand, it is possible that the two girls were Samuel Ireland's by Mrs. Freeman after she came to live with him, but some indiscretion (either with Sandwich or someone else of rank) had been responsible for her giving birth to William Henry. If Ireland had tortured her about it, it might explain her consistent dislike for the boy. I incline toward the first of these two theories, and there I must leave the matter.

What did Ireland do about William Henry's moving request

for an answer? We shall never know. Did he refrain from replying because the facts were too shameful to reveal at this juncture, or only because he was too much annoyed with William Henry to tell him anything? Or did he actually reveal the facts to the boy in a letter which William Henry at once destroyed?

In any event, when they met once more, and for the last time of their lives, at Wallis' during the month of March, 1797, William Henry certainly behaved as though, for the first time, he had been intolerably affronted by Ireland. He neither tipped his hat nor offered his hand to the older man, and refused to utter a syllable in the way of "contrition for what had passed." Ireland, angered, reiterated his past, present, and future conviction that William Henry was not and could not have been the author of the Papers. The youth responded that he no longer cared what the world believed, and that he was well assured that Ireland would never accept the truth. Heated words ensued, and Ireland, unaccustomed to being addressed by William Henry without respect, refused to listen to any more, and stamped out of Wallis' house.

These were the circumstances of their final leave-taking.

ELEVEN

The Last Days of Samuel Ireland

THE SCANDAL was kept alive by the mere fact that the pamphlets of both father and son continued to be reviewed during 1797 and 1798.

Of William Henry's, the *British Critic* asks, is not "the young man *too* candid when he accuses himself of all the forgeries?" The *Critical Review* declares that the imposture leaves "far behind it" the lies and deceptions of Psalmanazar and Chatterton in both "ignorance and audacity"; it is indeed "the most impudent forgery that ever disgraced literary talents or abused honest credulity." The young forger "seems to glory in that which ought to cover him with shame and confusion; and while his solemn declaration tends to the acquittal of the father, the pride of Shakespearian imitation supports the son against the effusions of public censure."

As for Ireland's *Vindication* the reaction was no more gratifying. One may indeed raise one's eyebrows in astonishment at the declaration of the *British Critic* that Ireland "may safely be pronounced one of the best writers of the present day." For at its worst his prose confuses syntax almost as much as does William Henry's; and at its best it is clumsy and stuffy—and might almost have been taken as a model for that incomparable satire, *Augustus Carp, Esq. by Himself.* Nevertheless, this magazine's praise has a sting in its tail: "And we cannot but wonder that a person so completely a master of style, should have been deceived by the papers." The *Critical Review* finds his gullibility beyond pardon; and the *Analytical Review* assures him that he would do better "not to keep the public attention awake to so shameful, and to him particularly unhappy, a transaction."

But Ireland did not take this sage advice. The icy reception that met his new book, *Picturesque Views on the River Wye,* and its consequent financial failure seem to have caused him to lose whatever little common sense was native to him. Though his health was failing, and his mental distress could only have made it worse, he insisted upon stirring up new dust with a sequel to his *Vindication,* a long and dull attack on Malone's qualifications as a scholar, *An Investigation of Mr. Malone's Claim to the Character of Scholar or Critic,* which was published in August, 1797.

In the turmoil of his thoughts, he had absurdly fastened upon Malone as the source of all his woes, and now accuses him of "invading the peace of a private family." He therefore feels obliged to "expose his unworthy and disingenuous conduct as a Man." As for the Papers, he writes, "I have scrupulously abstained from the declaration of any opinion respecting the authenticity. . . . The truth may probably be ascertained at some future period when literary animosities shall have subsided." With a complete want of judgment, he feels that he must take the world into his confidence concerning his relations with his son: "Near to me as by the ties operating the author of that narrative [William Henry's pamphlet] is, it must be with sincere regret that I feel myself compelled to announce that he withdrew himself from my house and family in the beginning of June 1796, that during this period, no intercourse beyond a short communication at two different times, but neither of them under my roof, has subsisted between us. . . . Of whatever interpretation his conduct may be susceptible, cannot in the least affect me." There is much pointless argument over Malone's attempts to see the Papers elsewhere than at the Ireland home, and even to borrow them as though "every thing that belonged to Shakspeare was his own exclusive property." Most of the space is devoted to proving Malone's exceptions to the spelling and vocabulary have no basis; here Ireland is no match for Malone, though on a few heads he is able to prove Malone incorrect. The book as a whole is feeble, and was certainly not worth the energy that the ailing man spent upon it. At the end he states that he does not wish to be thought "an advocate for the authenticity of the controversial Mss." That is, he concludes, a totally different subject.

A far more qualified scholar, George Chalmers, made two attacks on Malone in the same year, in his *Apology for the Believers,* and a *Supplemental Apology.* The *Apology,* 628 pages in length, reminds Malone of his own words that Shakespearean curiosities might very well be anticipated to emerge from houses of some of the old families. Then he tries to show that Elizabeth could have written the letter to Shakespeare by demonstrating that the Queen was actually the young man of Shakespeare's sonnets! Some of Chalmers' satire is extremely heavy-handed, as when he says of Malone: "Truth strikes the shears and measure from his hand; yet does he continue to set out, with a nimble haste, but without a yard, his linsy-woolsy, in open market." The passage does, however, prove him an enamored reader of Elizabethan prose.

Though his book was widely praised for its learning, it was disposed of by Steevens in his usually venomous way: "Having dismissed the *Imposture* it was fair to presume we should have no more of the Folly of those on whom it was practiced. . . . When men confess themselves knaves, there is an end of Detection. The Imposture once admitted, as it now is in its fullest extent . . . what discredit can be imputed on a writer, who saw the most glaring internal evidence of it from its first appearance? . . . And, if the Detector's high-blown pride indulged a free contempt of such a palpable and notorious cheat, can the spirit of Englishmen be unmoved at seeing such tricks played

with their immortal Bard, and not justify every means to expose
them? Whether in view of the list of those Believers who signed
the certificate of their own confusion, with the ostentatious
Jemmy Boswell . . . at their head or [if we] attend to the first
argument in their behalf advanced by the Apologist, that the
probabilities of finding fragments of Shakspeare were encouraged
by the idea or hope that some might exist; the delusion is not les-
sened, nor the credit of these profound Scholars, Antiquaries, or
Heralds saved. . . . Neither the nineteen certifiers to the authenticity of the MSS, nor the innumerable others that might have been
obtained, can boast of having in their company one person conversant with Shakspeare lore, or experienced in the knowledge of
our records."

SAMUEL IRELAND was rather worse off than ever. Toward the
end of the year William Henry wrote once more to his father
about his desperate condition; he had been living by the sale of
his wife's "cloaths, linnen, furniture, & c. for the best part of six
months." He had tried getting a position as an actor, but his applications had been everywhere scorned. He begged his father to
destroy the letter and to refrain from telling anyone else about it;
it is bad enough to be poor "without enjoying either the world's
facetious pity, or cool contempt." Ireland, on the contrary, kept
the letter and let it be seen by many. William Henry, on his part,
was further embittered by the suspicion that Ireland was responsible for the low gossip being circulated that Alice Crudge Ireland was his mistress and not his lawfully wedded wife.

On December 1, 1797, Gillray, the brilliant caricaturist, published a sketch of Ireland as "Notorious Characters # 1," with a
malicious inscription by Steevens implying that Ireland ought to
be classified among "convicts and persons otherwise remarkable,"
and a set of verses underneath by William Mason:

> Four forgers born in one prolific age
> Much critical acumen did engage:

276

> The first was soon by doughty Douglas scar'd
> Tho' Johnson would have screened him had he dared;
> The next had all the cunning of a Scot;
> The third, invention, genius,—nay, what not?
> Fraud, now exhausted, only could dispense
> To her fourth son, their threefold impudence.

The first forger was William Lauder (d. 1771) who, in his enthusiasm to prove *Paradise Lost* largely a plagiarism, invented a great deal of his evidence; the second was Macpherson; the third, Chatterton; the fourth, Samuel Ireland.

The whole business was certainly libelous, and Ireland consulted the great Erskine on the wisdom of taking action; Erskine advised against it. Tidd, however, was willing to undertake the case, though pointing out that its success would largely hinge upon William Henry. Ireland began to institute proceedings, but receiving no backing from anyone, by degrees allowed the matter to drop. He was, moreover, becoming increasingly ill. His condition was not much improved by the appearance of two other much-talked-about engravings, John Nixon's "The Gold Mines of Ireland" and Silvester Harding's "The Spirit of Shakspere Appearing to his Detractors." (For reproductions of the engravings themselves, see the illustration section.)

"The Oaken Chest or the Gold Mines of Ireland a Farce" has under the title the motto, a perverted version from *Macbeth:* "The Earth hath Bubbles as the Water has & these are them." The verses beneath the engraving read:

> In A musty old garret some where or another,
> This Chest has been found by some person or other.
> Yet by whom is A secret that must not be told
> For your mystery puzzles the young and the Old:
> But the Chest being here the contents you shall see.
> Subscribe but four Guineas as part of my fee.
> The first thing I show you is a relick most rare,
> An astonishing Lock of the great Shakespeares hair!
> Out of which twenty rings more or less have been made;
> Nor a Single Hair miss't from this wonderful Braid.
> The next is the Manuscript play of King Lear:

It is true Master Critic so pray do not sneer:
In its own native form by no Editor drest;
And in Adam Like Nakedness simple and chaste.
An original Sonnet I now shall present,
From Sweet Willy to Anna Hatherrewaye sent,
Plainly telling in numbers so simple and new,
That Willye thye Willye to his Anna still trewe
With drawings and leases and deeds without number,
And fifteen new Plays that have lain by as lumber,
Which shall soon be brought forward to pleasure the town,
All our pocketts to fill and labour to Crown!
For genious like Ours that's so little regarded,
Ought some way or other to be well rewarded.
Hark great Vortigern comes now ye criticks be dumb!
This is Shakspeares I'll swear—if 'tis not 'tis a Hum.

"The Spirit of Shakspere Appearing to his Detractors" has a motto from *King Lear:*

Tremble, thou wretch,
That hast within thee Undivulged crimes,
Unwhipp'd of justice.

Then follow the verses:

Ah me, Ah me, O dear, O dear,
What Spectre's this, approaching here.
Surely 'tis Shakspeare's injur'd shade.
It fills my soul with so much dread
It is, it is, thus on our knees,
Let's strive his anger to appease.
O Father of the British Stage,
Whose wit has charm'd from age to age,
Pardon the base unworthy flame,
That Burnt to rob thee of thy fame.
But now this solemn mock'ry's o'er
Thy gracious mercy wee implore
We'll never more disgrace thy page.
Our Brains were gone a pilgrimage.

Despite the debilitating effects of diabetes, from which he was dying, Ireland persisted in his one-man crusade to establish the authenticity of the Papers. It seems to have been the one thing he was living for. He approached Harris anew at Covent Garden for

the once-promised production of *Henry II,* the complete rights
for which his son had given him. Harris now made the excuse
that the play needed considerable polishing. Undaunted, Ireland
asked the help of the popular dramatist Arthur Murphy, and
offered to divide the profits from a production equally with him.
Murphy responded that he could not conscientiously accept that
much, for a successful play would be worth at least £700. Since
the alterations would take about two months, Murphy suggested
an advance payment of £150 without any further claim on the
play. Ireland's own affairs were in too deplorable a condition to
justify such a risk. Nothing more was said about performing
Henry II.

In the meantime William Henry was picking up a precarious
living by extra-illustrating books for a number of collectors, and
by accepting orders for new "forgeries" in Elizabethan script
from persons interested in having such curiosities. In 1798 with
money of his wife's he partly paid for 1,200 novels with which he
opened a circulating library at 1 Princes Place, Kensington. For
the very last time he wrote to his father, telling him that the man
to whom he owed the rest of the money for the novels would consider the debt discharged in exchange for ten volumes of Samuel
Ireland's own publications; William Henry vowed to make good
their value as soon as he had the money. Ireland never answered
him.

In 1799 Ireland gave new life to a dying topic by foolishly
publishing both *Vortigern* and *Henry II.* What can have possessed him to do it? In the Preface to the first he says that he
prints it to "give it the opportunity of a more unbiassed [*sic*] and
temperate examination." The attacks in the newspapers on the
"eve of its representation, and the ludicrous manner in which the
principal character was sustained" entitle the editor to complain
of "injurious treatment. . . . Every undue stratagem, and every
mean and petty artifice, was resorted to within doors and without, to prejudice the public mind." There follows a brief attack on

Malone's book, which he calls a "mass of dulness and self-conceit," and which "established nothing." Not a word has anywhere been said to induce Ireland "to believe that great part of the mass of papers in his possession are the fabrication of any individual, or set of men of the present day." He thanks Linley for his music, and Mrs. Jordan and Mrs. Powell for their acting in *Vortigern*. Had Kemble and Phillimore done the play any justice, "it might still have received and might have promoted the interests of the Theatre . . . whoever may have been the author of the piece."

In the Preface to *Henry II* he says that some time after he had seen *Vortigern* he received "from the hands of his son, about four hundred lines of this play in his own handwriting, and with them a solemn declaration that they were faithfully copied from ancient and original papers." Of that old manuscript only the title page and two other leaves were ever shown him, and he was informed that no more would be seen because the "supposed original proprietor of the papers" had "expressed much dissatisfaction at the objections made by the public to the uncouthness of the orthography." Ireland tells us that he pressed his son for the rest of the play, but had to wait many months. When his son at last gave him the complete drama it was with the apology "that the gentleman who gave them was of a capricious disposition, and would only suffer them to be copied at certain times, when he was in the humor." William Henry assured his father that the papers were all authentic, nor does Ireland believe any of the "assertions that have since been made from the same quarter; as they stand in direct opposition to what had been before solemnly stated as a fact."

Then, to prove his title to publish both plays Ireland quotes William Henry's letter of June 14, 1796, in which he begs his father to accept full property in both works. Ireland considers it a noteworthy coincidence that several months after having been given the play, he "accidentally met with a passage in the Biographica Dramatica" listing a "Henry I and Henry II by William Shakespeare and Robert Davenport. In the books of the Stationers Company, the 9th of September, 1653, an entry is made of the above title. . . . When the fact above related was mentioned by the Editor to his son, *he expressed much surprise and satisfaction;* observing that *'he presumed the world would now no longer entertain a doubt of the validity of the papers.'* " The fact that so many of the documents were scorched, the editor adds, has made him conclude that they must have been part of the Warburton collection, most of which was destroyed by fire. He reflects: "This is probably the last time he may ever find occasion to address the public on the subject of these mysterious papers." He wishes the world to know that "he has had no intercourse or communication with the cause of all this public and domestic misfortune for nearly three years, the period at which the party alluded to quitted his house, except one meeting [there had actually been two meetings] had at the request and in the presence of Mr. Albany Wallis." At this meeting "for the first time the party above-mentioned declared himself to be the author of all the papers." The editor asks the world to have the reasonableness to believe that he has never published any papers "whatever they may be" which he does not believe to be genuine.

In spite of everything Ireland was not convinced yet!

In July, 1800, Samuel Ireland breathed his last.

Dr. Latham, whose patient he had been, has left us an interesting account. He did all he could for Ireland and had prescribed a "strict abstinence from vegetable diet." That helped "as much as I believe was possible to be done in his worn and emaciated constitution; but his spirits were gone, and his heart was broken, for notwithstanding the world did not give him credit for his assertions respecting his concurrence, or even connivance, at his son's literary fraud; yet I have the strongest testimony (and in justice to his memory I think myself called upon . . . to record it as his death-bed declaration) that he was totally ignorant of the deceit, and was equally a believer in the authenticity of the manuscripts as those which were even the most credulous."

Poor befuddled Ireland! He was not spared ignominy even in death.

The obituary in the September issue of the *Gentleman's Magazine* was pitiless: "At his house in Norfolk-street, Strand, Samuel Ireland, esq., author of a number of elegant and esteemed works, and particularly known to the world as the possessor of the forged MSS, ascribed to Shakspeare. He was originally a mechanick in Spitalfields, but, taking advantage of the prosperity of the age, commenced speculator in books, prints, and drawings. . . ." After an account of his Picturesque Tours, it continues: "The next transactions in which Mr. Samuel Ireland solicited the attention of the publick was the disgraceful forgery of the Shakspeare papers, in 1796. In that year, after an ostentatious display of the supposed treasure at his house in Norfolk-street, Mr. I. published in a four-guinea volume, 'Miscellaneous Papers. . . .' The circumstances attending the discovery and exposure of the audacious attempt on the public confidence are too public and too recent to require recapitulation. It was averred both by father and son, that the imposition originated with and was entirely conducted by, the young man, without the privity or participation of his parent, but this fact many strong circumstances lead us to doubt: the complicity appears obvious, and it even seems that some part of the forgery could not have been conducted by the son alone. The father seems also to have felt the indignation of a disappointed speculatist, which he vented in two angry pamphlets against Mr. Malone. . . ."

Ireland's good friend Byng, unwilling to allow this to pass, wrote a letter to the editor of the magazine doing him credit as a human being: "Having read in your Obituary, p. 901, a seemingly impartial account of the late Samuel Ireland esquire, I have no doubt but you will permit me to rescue the memory of an unfortunate man from the statements of some malign critics and to lay his character smoothly in the grave, however scarred by the pen of hatred, malice, and uncharitableness, attacked and massacred like the Swiss guards in Aug. 1792. Mr. I's fame has been exposed in the highway for the abuse and detraction of a wicked world." If Ireland was a "mechanick," that only redounds to his credit since he developed into "a literary man, a man possessed of many sciences." Everyone knows that Ireland purchased many books. "But why is he to be termed a speculator more than can be any other gentleman book-collector who buys, sells, and exchanges? No man has a right to heap the term disgraceful forgery upon the deceased (to whom it was deadly), unless the writer could prove his assertions." As to Ireland's display of the Papers, any eager man might be pardoned "when he gave up his time, without any remuneration, for his civil, hospitable, fatiguing display" of the documents. "Living, beloved by his family, and esteemed by many men of worth and learning, Mr. I. gained an honest liveli-hood by his engravings, and by his writings on various topics." Ireland, like few men, was draughtsman, engraver, and penman. Now these accomplishments are used to defame him. He "died a martyr to false hope, easy credulity, and despair; and but for an imposition almost forced upon him, might now have flourished an healthy and happy man. From a warmth of hope, from the advice of his friends, and from the suffrages of the learned, Mr. I too eas-ily believed a mass of forgeries handed to him by his only son. Flattered to ruin, destruction, and death, he struggled on (nei-ther a planner nor assistant in the fraud) till, deserted by many who should have shielded him, he fell a victim to a shaft shot from the nearest hand. The latter months of Mr. I's life would frame a most melancholy tale. His forgiveness to the youth who drew the fatal bow, his tender parting with his family, and his resignation to his hastened end, should have screened him from the envenomed sting even of an enemy."

Kind Byng! It is obvious that he had crossed William Henry off his books. But Ireland's forgiveness of his son was a fact. In

Ireland's will we read: "I give to my son William Henry Ireland the repeating watch I have generally worn with the seals appendant and as I wish to die in peace and good will with all mankind I hereby freely and sincerely forgive my said son for having made me the innocent agent of mischief and imposition and do give unto him 20 pounds for mourning."

TWELVE

Sputtering Candle

❊ ❊ ❊ ❊ ❊ ❊ ❊ ❊ ❊ ❊ ❊ ❊ ❊ ❊ ❊ ❊

ON THURSDAY, MAY 7, 1801, and for the following seven days (Sunday excepted), Leigh, Sotheby, & Son, at their house in York Street, Covent Garden, sold by auction the "Books, Paintings, Miniatures, Drawings, Prints, and Various Curiosities, the Property of the late Samuel Ireland."

It was well that Ireland was safely buried, for the mad enthusiast for antiquities must surely have died anew of an apoplectic fit had he been present at the bidding to hear how his prized collections, gathered so eagerly and painfully, were valued by the public after his disgrace. The auctioneer, for instance, was unable to sell numbers 2, 3, or 4 of the sales *Catalogue*—the mummy cloth, the piece of Charles I's cloak, and the piece of Wyclif's vestment—and was thus reduced to selling them as one lot for the miserable price of 1s. One can imagine the snickering as these cherished "historical" pieces were each offered up—and at the very beginning of the auction! Lady Lovelace's pinked leather shoe had also to be sold with two other items for a contemptible 3s. The garter worn by James II at his coronation brought only 6d. Shakespeare's purse fetched 2s., Ann Boleyn's 1s., and the three Roman rings 1s. 6d. Obviously any antiquity connected with Ireland was suspect. However, a thing of more contemporary interest, the ring with the hair of Louis XVI, brought £1 2s., though that may have been because of the gold of the ring. But Shake-

285

spearolatry was not dead: "a goblet made of Shakspeare mulberry tree and mounted in silver" was purchased for £6. There were twelve small pictures and miniatures, and six miniatures painted by Jane Ireland. Of the latter, one of Milton brought £1 4s., one of Jonson £1 15s., and one of Shakespeare £2 6s. There were plaster casts and models; fifteen Van Dyck portrait etchings and drawings; a great many prints, including a "Vortigern and Rowena" (which sold for 13s. 6d.), a group of "various etchings" by Miss Anna Maria Ireland, which sold for 9s. The prints and etchings by Ireland himself brought excellent prices. There were also many fine Hogarths which were purchased for adequate sums.

The books were the last objects to be sold; there were 588 separate lots. Malone's attack "filled with marginal remarks by Mr. Ireland" brought a surprising £5 5s., whereas the 1640 edition of Shakespeare's Poems only £2 6s. There were nineteen quartos of plays attributed on their title pages to Shakespeare, all of which now, with the exception of *The Two Noble Kinsmen*, are included among the Shakespearean Apocrypha. Fifty-one titles formed the "Shakespearean Library with Manuscript Notes."

The final item up for sale was the collection of the forgeries themselves, "The Complete Collection of Shakspearian Papers," including *Vortigern* and other manuscripts received too late for Ireland's published volume, all "elegantly bound in russia and green morocco cases." It went for £130.

Eventually the collection was owned by the dramatist W. T. Moncrieff, and he made a gift of it to the Shakespeare Memorial Library at Birmingham. In 1879 all the papers were destroyed by fire. *Sic transit.*

MRS. FREEMAN died the next year, in 1802. After her death, Jane Ireland destroyed all the remaining copies of the folio edition of the *Miscellaneous Papers* which her father had so proudly published hardly more than a half dozen years earlier, and also defaced the copper plates from which the facsimiles had been printed.

WILLIAM HENRY's burst of fame was over but, quantitatively at least, his literary career had hardly begun. Whatever his faults, he was not idle—his celerity and application in the forgeries exonerate him from that charge. While trying to earn his living after his break with Ireland, he certainly must also have been busy writing, for in 1799 he published under his own name a three-volume Gothic romance, *The Abbess*. He died in April, 1835; in the thirty four years between 1799 and 1833 he published not less than sixty-seven original titles (among which I do not include his translations from the French, his translations into French of some of his own works, or his Prologues and Epilogues to various plays); another novel, *Rizzio* (1849), was posthumous. In addition he left twenty three unpublished works.

His forgeries had given him a discipline in, if in nothing else, speedy writing, if that is to be considered a virtue rather than a vice. From what we know of his later life, vicious though hasty composition may be, it was lucky for his personal needs that he could manage it.

Though the theatre was his love, he saw only one of his other plays in print: a blank-verse historical drama, *Mutius Scaevola, or The Roman Patriot* (1801), as much of an advance over *Henry II* as that was over *Vortigern*. Though its setting is in the early days of the Roman republic, it has its pietistic moments; for instance, as Mutius is leaving the city to deliver it from the Etrurian enemy:

1ST PLEBEIAN. May Providence to Rome propitious prove. . . .
ALL. Heav'n preserve our hero.

It is certainly an eighteenth-century version of ancient Rome which the dramatist creates, as the stage directions for the final scene illustrate: the main characters "enter in procession . . . Senators . . . Vestal Virgins, Patricians, Soldiers, Plebeians &

c. . . . Guards . . . grand march playing while arranging round the stage." Nevertheless, the play was not inferior to the general run of theatrical pieces at the London playhouses of that day (which, of course, is not to praise it much). But it was not accepted for production despite William Henry's persistent efforts, for his name was anathema in the theatre, and he met with rebuffs when he submitted the work. Necessity dictated his employing his pen in forms more likely to bring in the shillings. He can have had little rest from ceaselessly grinding out his many books and translations. In the same year he published *Ballads in Imitation of the Antient,* the stories being mostly about historical persons. The next year he was back to his pseudo-medievalism again, with *A Ballade Wrotten on the Feastynge and Merrimentes of Easter Maunday Laste Paste,* the very title a flagrant imitation of Chatterton.

Chatterton and the gnawing question of his own origins were still very much with him in 1803 with his book of *Rhapsodies,* which no biographer of William Henry seems to have taken the trouble to look at. The title page announces that the author is he "of the Shaksperian Mss.," and the very first poem is "Elegiac Lines to the Memory of Thomas Chatterton." William Henry still identified himself with the Bristol Shakespeare, and the piece concludes sentimentally:

> Farewell, sweet youth! one bosom still can melt,
> Still gaze with anguish, and thy woes deplore;
> Still vainly soothe the suff'rings thou hast felt,
> Those agonies, which thou canst feel no more.

But even of more interest is the fact that this volume contains three poems in succession, entitled "The Bastard," "The Bastard's Complaint," and "Reply to the Bastard's Complaint." In the first of these, William Henry unconsciously reveals the motivation at the core of his notorious fabrications:

> Alone thou stand'st, a wretched Bastard born,
> Go, let thine acts thy friendless name adorn

. . . .
Whose soul unshackled soars above mankind,
And leaves the world and all its cares behind.
. . . .
May Bastards, tho' bereft of friend and name,
Feel in their breasts eternal thirst of fame!

In "The Bastard's Complaint," we read:

In vain I claim a father; none is near;
In vain I weep; no mother dries the tear.
By these denied, by parents thus forgot [italics mine],
Who shall commiserate the Bastard's lot?

It is most unusual that a bastard should have neither parent;
he is usually equipped with a forsaken mother. But, as was apparently true in William Henry's case, the mother (probably Mrs.
Freeman) had discarded him as completely as the father. These
lines would fortify the conclusions to which we have come concerning his parentage. The same extraordinary situation is repeated in "Reply to the Bastard's Complaint"; and the verses
throw further light upon what had gone on inside William Henry,
unremarked by the family that could give him no warmth:

Why should the Bastard rail his hapless fate?
The proud in suff'ring are supremely great.
. . . .
Thou know'st no father's love, no mother's sigh,
No kindred but the fost'ring Power on high,
By one neglected, and the other's shame,
Thy sole inheritance the Bastard's name.

These thus-far neglected pieces throw considerable light on William Henry's personal problem and his defiant solution of it.

In the meantime (1802), he had been employed by Princess
Elizabeth to compose a series of interludes to be performed at an
entertainment arranged for the birthday of George III. He had
been commanded to engulf the monarch in every kind of flattery.
He was so much disgusted by the fulsomely extravagant doggerel
which he composed that he was sure the piece would be rejected.

On the contrary, everyone involved was pleased and he was highly praised. Indeed, he was asked to superintend the rehearsals at Windsor. The entertainment was a vast success, and the King and the entire court greeted it "with unbounded applause." When payment was made for all this arduous and nerve-racking work, however, it turned out to be all of five pounds. Understandably offended at such a beggarly reward, he refused to accept the amount, and so received nothing.

He had become a close friend of Captain Paget Bayly, R.N., brother of the Earl of Uxbridge. Shortly after the Captain's death in 1804, William Henry married his widow. This second marriage, as it was for each of them, seems to have been a good and companionable one.

At once William Henry got busy writing the most interesting of his books, the *Confessions*. The need for funds was probably, as ever, an incentive. But I suspect that the new marriage was the real spur. This time he was well acquainted with the woman he was to marry, and may very well have anticipated happiness with her. It would be natural that he should feel, as he was turning thirty and embarking on a new life, the need to purge himself of the whole business of the forgeries by a detailed recounting of the facts (such as he had not even attempted in his brief pamphlet, written in the midst of tension and contention with his father), to afford rest to his father's perturbed spirit (he had always given Ireland more love than he had received, and was therefore probably still haunted by the wrong he had done him), and at the same time call a halt to irresponsible rumor and legend.

The more than three hundred pages of the *Confessions* are a storehouse of incident, circumstance, and document. Sometimes his memory is at fault. Sometimes there are notable omissions: few of the Papers are actually quoted; little is said about the fiction of Mr. H., and nothing of his father's correspondence with that invented gentleman (throughout the book he rarely speaks of his father except as "Mr. Ireland" or "Mr. Samuel Ireland");

nothing is said about Mrs. Freeman; nothing is said about his reasons for leaving the Ireland house; nothing is said about either of
his marriages. The book, nevertheless, contains an enormous
amount of circumstantial information.

But to the biographer the book is as much of a hindrance as a
help. The Preface promises "to give a narrative of the facts in the
order in which they occurred." Never was a promise less fulfilled.
The order of telling is so lunatic that it would be easy to make out
a case from it that its author was deranged. He was writing rapidly, as usual, and he must have put down events as he remembered them without bothering to rearrange them in proper sequence. If anyone were to attempt to get the story straight from a
reading of the *Confessions,* he could only conclude that he was
losing his own mind. Thus, while talking of his childhood education and the love he developed for matters chivalric, William
Henry suddenly inserts an acrostic he wrote years later on Chaucer; an account of the family reading of *Love and Madness*
brings up his boyhood admiration for Chatterton—but *that* leads
to an extended retelling of his visit to Bristol and the Chatterton
family, which occurred at a date later than nearly everything else
in the book; an account of Jordan, the Stratford Poet, is followed
almost immediately with the story of how William Henry hit
upon the mixture for the ink used later in the forgeries; soon
thereafter we come upon the terra cotta of Oliver Cromwell, but
that is followed by a passage that goes back years to Ireland's return from Stratford; a number of the documents are discussed—
not one in the sequence in which it was "discovered"—and *after*
that we are told about the invention of the "unknown gentleman," the donor, though in point of fact William Henry brought
word of him before ever showing any of the forgeries; pages on
the to-do over *Vortigern* are suddenly thrust in without warning,
followed by comments on publications of that play and *Henry II*
(which chronologically should have been among the last things
related in the *Confessions*); then we go back to the admission

tickets for viewing the Papers at Norfolk Street during the earlier days of the collection; it is nearly the end of the book before we are told why his father preferred to call him "Sam," etc. The story of the contention over the forgeries backtracks so many times, is so confused in sequence, and is so much interspersed with other matter that, valuable as its information is, it would be impossible to make head or tail of it without clinging grimly to one's own tabulation of the dates involved, and rearranging everything for oneself. To err in even one slight detail of the time sequence of William Henry's career is to run the risk of misconstruing the meaning of everything.

I have quoted copiously from the *Confessions* so that the reader has a good idea of that combination of pretentiousness, stuffiness, gaucherie, and confused syntax of which William Henry's prose is confected—though no doubt that prose passed in many quarters, as had his father's, as an exemplar of the elegant. What the reader can have no idea of is its amazing alternation of excess and absence of punctuation (already manifest in the forgeries), which I have felt in most places obliged to civilize to some degree.

Yet with all its defects the *Confessions* is an absorbing book, sometimes funny, sometimes touching. It is prevailingly fairly honest; its intention, I am convinced, was certainly honest. By and large it is more dependable in its facts than such a classic as Rousseau's autobiography. What is most moving is the constant desire to clear Samuel Ireland's name, the profound admiration for his father, and a complete unwillingness to blame him for anything. There is only one thing that William Henry holds against his father—for everything else he blames himself—and that is his father's absolute refusal to concede that he had the ability to compose the Shakespeare Papers.

In his conclusion there are a number of matters William Henry wishes to stress: He never intended to injure anyone. His first motive was to delight his father, and he originally had no intention of producing more than one forged paper. Even had the first been exposed, he thought "the boldness of the attempt would have gained me praise for my ingenuity rather than censure for my deceit." (The point will not seem so farfetched if one remembers Croft's pronouncements on Chatterton, and how the Ireland household worshiped the Bristol Shakespeare.) He really injured no one. Those who believed the forgeries judged them "on the mere external appearance." They should have known that the language was impossible to Shakespeare. Had not Malone averred "that the forgery was palpable to the meanest capacity"? (Here William Henry seems to have outgrown his sense that the forgeries were productions of genius.) Those who saw the Papers, delighted in them; "consequently they received no injury." (This is all very well—except for the vast injury done to Ireland.) He had no pecuniary motives. He had refused to accept anything from his father in exchange for the gift of the Papers Ireland had treasured so much. He had been content with only 90 out of the 353 pounds, the profits from the performance of *Vortigern*. He had given Ireland complete property in the manuscripts. He had done all he could to dissuade him from publishing them. (All this is the truth.) He benefited nothing from the Papers. He had had to endure all the opprobrium of his father's friends. His admission of forgery had ruined all possibilities of a career in the law. The gentlemen who viewed the Papers and praised them were somewhat responsible for the forgeries following the Mortgage Deed, for he got most of his ideas for new forgeries from their conversation. He was a mere boy at the time, and therefore might have expected treatment less savage. "I candidly submit to a generous public whether my age and the causes leading to my fabrication of the papers, should not be taken into consideration, and whether I may not be acquitted of everything except boyish folly." The reasons for his persecution are illogical. "I was a boy —consequently, they were deceived by a boy; and the imposition practised on their intellectual faculties was therefore the more galling. On the contrary, had the papers been the production of a man of known science and learning, they then would have pardoned the abuse, because he would have been more on a level with themselves: and although they would have regarded him as a dangerous forger, they would have granted that he was *a very clever man.*" (This is true only to a degree. His father was blamed far more than he, and totally without justice. On the other hand, his father did not survive the exposure by many years, while he had the rest of his life in which to live down the infamy, if he could.)

ALMOST IMMEDIATELY after his second marriage, William Henry and his wife went to France, where they mingled freely in aristocratic circles. His French was very fluent; they enjoyed themselves; she had a small income; and they spent a great deal of money. Before long they were without funds, and later in 1805 we find them back in England.

That year William Henry was close to fabrication again, for there appeared in 1805, his *Effusions of Love from Chastelar to Mary Queen of Scotland.* It was issued as a translation "from a Gallic Manuscript in the Scotch College at Paris, Interspersed with Songs, Sonnets, and Notes Explanatory by the Translator." At least one reader was not taken in by the pretense; in the copy of this rare book belonging to the New York Public Library, at Forty-second Street, the original owner has inscribed on the flyleaf: "This Book was written by My old friend W. H. Ireland of Shakespearian Notoriety." (The signature looks like *I. A.*) The Preface to the volume states that "the original Ms. and poems are written throughout in the Gallic language." Nothing could be less sixteenth-century or more early nineteenth than the inflated sentimental drivel of the contents. The hysterical style of *Love and Madness* still lingers lovingly in William Henry's recollection, the oratorical flourishes, the rhetorical repetitions, the addresses of the writer to himself, together with the multitude of dashes and exclamation points. Thus: "No, it cannot be:—Custom, hateful custom, thou art my bane, and Mary must be lost to Chastelar for ever!—For ever!—Oh horror—inexpressible!—Hold, my brain, least burning madness seize me." The end is touched with that sham religiosity so dear to William Henry: "Mary, farewel [*sic*]! . . . My queen, farewel. . . .—Till we meet above; again one last farewel, dear mistress of my heart, on this side of the grave." The "editor" has a characteristic concluding remark; he promises more "transcripts still unpublished" if this volume is well received.

Of some interest to modern readers is the title of one of William Henry's productions of 1807, *Stultifera Navis, or The Modern Ship of Fools*. Like Miss Porter, he took only the name of Alexander Barclay's volume (1508). The verses attack foolish books, fashions, old lechers, collectors of old books and prints, antiquarians. The lines for this last contain an interesting footnote (the work was published, it should be remembered, anonymously): "Among the impostors of this nature should not be omitted the Rowleian Chatterton, and the Shaksperian Ireland, whose memories will live as long as old chests and old manuscripts stand on record." Again the twinning of himself with Chatterton, and again the bid for fame.

William Henry and his wife must have dwelt for a while in Devonshire, for its countryside furnishes many a description in three successive books of narrative verse, *The Fisher Boy, The Sailor Boy*, and *The Cottage Girl* (1808–9), and years later he published a *Picturesque Beauties of Devonshire* (1833).

By November, 1810, they were living in York; more specifically, from January to July 27, 1811, William Henry was living at York Castle in debtor's prison. His old friend Mrs. Jordan sent him five pounds there. Out of the prison experience he made some poetical capital: *The Poet's Soliloquy to His Chamber in York Castle* and *One Day in York Castle, Poetically Delineated* (both 1811). They left town in August, 1812.

295

One of his books is of more than passing interest, *Chalco-graphimania* (1814) by "Satiricus Sculptor, Esq., Done in the Hudibras Manner." His Preface tells us that he wishes to be veiled "in obscurity"; that he has rewritten the work twice so that he could mingle "unsuspected" with the public. The passages on himself, his father, and Kemble are noteworthy.

On himself:

> . . . false Shaksperian lore°
> Which sprang from *Maisterre Ireland's store:*
> Whose impudence deserves the rod
> For having aped the muse's god.°°

William Henry footnotes the first of these lines with a remark that the forgeries on being resold at auction brought a very low price; the present owner "never glances at this *modern antique* without experiencing an emotion similar to that which results from the workings of a plentiful dose of ipecacuanha." The fourth of these lines is footnoted with a speculation on how amazing it is that this "literary fraud could have so long duped the world, and involved in its deception's vortex such personnages as a *Parr, Wharton,* and *Sheridan,* not omitting *Jemmy Boswell* . . . nor can I even refrain from smiling whensoever the volumes of *Malone* and *Chalmers,* together with the pamphlets of *Boaden, Waldron, Wyatt,* and *Philalethes* . . . chance to fall my way." (This is striking at foe, defector, and faithful friend alike!) There are other passages on himself:

> In autographs as ably vers'd
> As *Chatterton* the poet erst,
> Or he that later wielded fire-brand,
> The impudent and forging Ireland.
> To parent now the *son* let's add,
> Of ancient lore, the *impostor lad,*
> Who guilty was—accursed sin
> Of taking all the old ones in!

On Samuel Ireland: a footnote speaks of him as having been "no less fam'd with connoisseurs for his several volumes of Picturesque Views, than the ever memorable folio of Shakspearian relics." There is another footnote extolling his father's collection of Hogarths.

On Kemble:

> Whose AITCHES and perverted ROOM
> Shall stamp him A-s till day of doom.

(Bibliophiles will be interested in some of the sums William Henry lists elsewhere in the volume for prices paid at Evans' auction on June 17, 1812: for a 1471 *Decameron*, £2,260; for *The Recuyeil of the Histories of Troye & c.*, Caxton, 1473, £1,060 10s., bought by the Duke of Devonshire; for Gower's *Confessio Amantis*, £336.)

In April, 1814 (the year of the book just quoted), the Irelands went to France again. This time they had two daughters to accompany them. They lived near the Barracks in the Faubourg St. Germain, and stayed until 1823. They saw Napoleon's return after his escape from Elba, and the events of the Hundred Days. They were also witnesses to his abdication and to the restoration of the Bourbons. During the Hundred Days, William Henry had an interview with Napoleon, and was appointed by him to a position in the National Library. He was also nominated the Legion of Honor, but Napoleon's downfall ended that. Because of their strong Napoleonic sympathies the Irelands had to leave the country in 1823.

In the meantime a volume throwing further light on William Henry appeared in London in 1815, his *Scribbleomania, or The Printer's Devil's Polichronicon,* described on the title page as "A Sublime Poem edited by Anser-Pen-Drag-On, Esq." It is a copious series of verses, heavily footnoted, containing William Henry's judgments on his contemporaries, with passing comments on the writers of the past. Spenser is praised for his imagery; Shakespeare and Milton for their luminosity; Butler for his satire; Dryden for his sublimity; Addison, Steele, and Goldsmith for their agreeableness. Of Wordsworth he speaks highly for "the

pathos which characterises a variety of that gentleman's productions, notwithstanding his contempt for all the heretofore acknowledged rules of poetical composition." He finds Southey
sometimes pleasing, sometimes insipid, and—somewhat in anticipation of Byron's scorn (without the wit)—attacks the Laureate's
desertion of the radicals:

> Thus Southey, who once wrote for freedom—egad,
> True turn-coat, can right about face, pliant lad.

He speaks highly of Burns for his "sterling wit, vigor, pathos, and
ease." He condescends to Scott, commends the tales of Monk
Lewis, and advises Byron to apply his talents to some more "lasting topic" than Childe Harold—at present he cannot "lay claim to
real genius or originality, and with deficiencies so palpable, the
productions of his lordship could never have received those unqualified eulogiums, had not the talismanic charm of nobility in-
fused its balsam as an ingredient into the dose of criticism." William Henry approves of Coleridge for his "feeling and sensibility." And among the famous, of course, he himself must not be
omitted:

> In garb of deception boy Ireland now view,
> With *Vortigern* dauntlessly brave critic crew,
> Thus proving mere childhood can acumen blind,
> And veil youthful faults with bright flashes of mind.

(Some two decades after the event, William Henry was still
proud of his career as a forger.) These lines are footnoted: "The
fate of *Vortigern* is well known to the public; it was the effusion
of a youth of eighteen, and, if not possessed of some beauties
when read in the closet, the wisest and most able critics must
have been most egregiously deceived." The paragraph goes on to
speak of *Henry II* and *Mutius Scevola* [*sic*]: "With respect to the
merits of this writer, whose works are very numerous, it would be
unfair to have recourse to the reviewers; the stigma of having deceived the public uniformly follows his career, and, be his efforts
what they may, the lash of severest criticism at all times pursue

[*sic*] him." Ireland, he continues, is said to have issued many works anonymously and under other names, and these books have been praised. What a pity that he does not permit the world to know what he has written so that it "may be fully enabled to appreciate the extent of his literary acquirements."

After the return of the Irelands to England, William IV paid William Henry to suppress a life of the King's mistress, Mrs. Jordan. *The Great Illegitimates, the Public and Private Life of that Celebrated Actress, Mrs. Jordan* "by a Confidential Friend of the Departed" (1832) was withdrawn after a few copies had been sold. Understandably, William IV was not anxious to allow his ten illegitimate children by the generous actress to be advertised as such to the world, no matter how sympathetic the account. It is no less arresting to find William Henry, to the very end, standing up for bastards!

Of his two daughters, both of whom survived him, we know the name of only one, the girl named after Mrs. Freeman as Anna Maria de Burgh Ireland.

The burial register at St. George-the-Martyr, Southwark, records William Henry's name for April 24, 1835. (Always treading upon the heels of the Bard, he missed by only one day the anniversary of Shakespeare's birth and death, April 23!) He was fifty-nine.

IT WAS the misfortune of the Irelands, father and son, to live in an age when the understanding of Shakespeare was in no way commensurate with senseless worship of the matchless Bard. Most of the authorities were no authorities. They could not forgive either Samuel or William Henry for having unwittingly exposed their own immense lack of erudition or true appreciation of Shakespeare's qualities as a poet or a dramatist. Like hordes of modern professional scholars they felt safe only under the umbrella of external fact. They dared not trust esthetic judgment.

Yet their Matchless Bard, if he were to be appreciated at all, was not to be appreciated because of the age of paper, ink, or handwriting, but because of the qualities of the language, the verse, the drama, the human insights. Naturally, if the manuscripts were to be accepted as authentic, the paper, ink, and handwriting would have to pass the tests of age. But had they passed those tests, the manuscripts should still have won no title as Shakespeare's while their content stood so absurdly outside Shakespeare's qualities and manner as poet and dramatist.

There is little reason to doubt, I fear, that if there appeared among us today a new William Henry Ireland, more expert in procuring his materials and in imitating the Elizabethan hand, more knowledgeable in keeping within the confines of Elizabethan spelling and vocabulary, and cunning enough to have his "discoveries" emanate from acceptable archives (all of which would have to meet a more highly informed criticism today), with forgeries as poetically contemptible and dramatically ridiculous as William Henry's, his finds would be hailed by innumerable scholars as authentic. For while the Irelands' century made a great fuss about taste (exhibiting little of it in its poetry or drama), our modern professional scholars, for all practical purposes, deny the existence of taste altogether. For them esthetic judgment is too subjective to figure in literary evaluations. And for that reason their discussions of literature must be riveted to matters of dates and editions and sources (not that these are unimportant, but merely that they are quite secondary to the business of literature!)—matters which never approach the literary quintessence itself.

And since it was too humiliating to the Irelands' contemporaries to have to confess having been duped by a mere boy, they preferred to pretend, despite clear evidence to the contrary, that the older man was the culprit—and to fortify the case against him and deflect it from his son, they spread nasty little rumors about Samuel Ireland's devilish machinations.

The hour of glory for William Henry was a brief one. The chief part of our story lies within his nineteenth and twentieth years. His plea for forgiveness on the grounds of youth is fair enough. Every adolescent male is bound to be cracked to a degree—the high-minded ones rather more cracked than the run-of-the-mill. The world would be loaded with punishment and guilt if every adolescent had to pay the piper for each of his follies and "impositions." The atrophying adult, self-righteous, is but too likely to forget that.

But to me the fascination of this story is not only in its several unanswerable mysteries, its comic interludes, and its heartbreak, but most of all in the relationship of father and son.

William Henry never minded the indignation of the world half so much as the unwillingness of his father to concede him any literary talent. What he failed to perceive was that what he deemed his father's injustice to him was somewhat the product of the older man's want of critical acumen, his ludicrous overvaluation of the literary merit of the forgeries. Had Samuel Ireland seen them to be no better than they were, he might have found it possible to be less stubborn. Unless, of course, there was a larger, because unconscious, consideration which impeded his being just —something connected with William Henry's parentage, because of which he simply could not admit having been taken in by the talents of *that* youth. Possibly, just possibly, Samuel Ireland had been able to be kind—in a formal sort of way, one gathers—to that boy only so long as he could reasonably treat him as an inferior. Ireland was a bumbling man, not really mean, but he assuredly was as lacking in imagination as he was overendowed with enthusiasm. That is why he is a figure entitled to compassion. William Henry, on the other hand, tried desperately to raise himself in the regard of the man whom he loved and revered, and who could be only kind and somewhat contemptuous. That is why William Henry, despite his knavery, is entitled to compassion too.

Appendix: Bibliography

The dates are those of editions used by the author.

Angelo, H., *Reminiscences* (Philadelphia, 1904).
Anonymous, *Precious Relics, or The Tragedy of Vortigern Rehears'd* (London, 1796).
"Antenor," *A Letter to George Chalmers* (London, 1798).
Barton, M., *Garrick* (New York, 1949).
Boaden, J., *A Letter to George Steevens Esq.* (London, 1796).
——— *Memoirs of the Life of Kemble* (Philadelphia, 1825).
Bodde, D., *Shakespeare and the Ireland Forgeries* (Cambridge, Mass., 1930).
Boswell, J., *The Journals*, edited by G. Scott and F. A. Pottle (Privately printed, 1930).
——— *The Life of Samuel Johnson* (Oxford, 1922).
Boydell, J., *The Shakespeare Gallery* (London, 1803).
Chalmers, G., *An Apology for the Believers* (London, 1797).
——— *A Supplemental Apology for the Believers* (London, 1799).
Cooke, W., *Memoirs of Charles Macklin, Comedian* (London, 1806).
Croft, H., *Love and Madness* (Ipswich, 1809).
Davies, T., *The Life of David Garrick* (London, 1780).
The Dictionary of National Biography.
Dudley, H. B., *Passages by Distinguished Personages on the Great Literary Trial of Vortigern and Rowena* (London, 1796).
Genest, J., *An Account of the Stage* (Bath, 1832).
Gloag, J., *British Furniture Makers* (London, 1946).
Grebanier, B., *The Heart of Hamlet* (New York, 1960).
——— *The Truth about Shylock* (New York, 1962).
Greig, J. (ed.), *The Farington Diary* (New York, 1923).
Halliday, F. E., *The Cult of Shakespeare* (New York, 1957).

303

Hamburger, P., "Elmira, N.Y.," in *The New Yorker* (December 16, 1961).

Hardinge, G., *Chalmeriana* (London, 1800).

Hazlitt, W., *Dramatic Essays* (London, 1851).

Ingleby, C. M., *Shakespere Fabrications* (London, 1859).

—— *Shakspere, the man and the Book* (London, 1881).

Ireland, S., *Graphic Illustrations of Hogarth, from Pictures, Drawings, and Scarce Prints in the Author's Possession* (London, 1795).

—— *An Investigation of Mr. Malone's Claim to the Character of Scholar or Critic, Being an Examination of His Inquiry into the Authenticity of the Shakespeare Mss.* (London, 1797).

—— *Miscellaneous Papers and Legal Instruments under the Hand and Seal of William Shakespeare, including the Tragedy of King Lear and a Small Fragment of Hamlet, from the Original Manuscripts in the Possession of Samuel Ireland* (London, 1796).

—— *Mr. Ireland's Vindication of His Conduct Respecting the Publication of the Supposed Shakespeare Mss.* (London, 1796).

—— *A Picturesque Tour through Holland, Brabant, and Part of France Made in the Autumn of 1789* (London, 1790).

—— *Picturesque Views on the River Medway, from the Nore to the Vicinity of Its Source in Sussex* (London, 1793).

—— *Picturesque Views on the River Thames* (London, 1792).

—— *Picturesque Views on the River Wye* (London, 1797).

—— *Picturesque Views on the Upper, or Warwickshire Avon* (London, 1795).

—— *Picturesque Views, with an Historical Account of the Inns of Court in London and Westminster* (London, 1800).

Ireland, W. H., *The Abbess* (London, 1799).

—— *All the Blocks or An Antidote to All the Talents,* by "Flagellum" (London, 1807).

—— *The Angler, a Didactic Poem,* by "Charles Clifford" (London, 1804).

—— *An Authentic Account of the Shakspearian Mss.* (London, 1796).

—— *A Ballade Wrotten on the Feastynge and Merrimentes of Easter Maunday Laste Paste* (London, 1802).

—— *Ballads in Imitation of the Antient* (London, 1801).

—— *Chalcographimania, or The Portrait-Collector and Printseller's Chronicle, with Infatuations of Every Description, a Humorous Poem in Four Books with Copious Notes Explanitory,* by "Satiricus Sculptor, Esq." (London, 1814).

—— *Confessions* (New York, 1874).

—— *The Cottage Girl* (London, 1809).

APPENDIX: BIBLIOGRAPHY

——— *Effusions of Love from Chastelar to Mary Queen of Scotland* (London, 1805).
——— *The Fisher Boy* (London, 1809).
——— *Henry II*, edited by S. Ireland (London, 1799).
——— *Jack Junk, or the Sailor's Cruise on Shore*, by "the author of 'Sailor Boy'" (London, 1814).
——— *Mutius Scaevola, or the Roman Patriot* (London, 1801).
——— *Neglected Genius, a Poem Illustrating the Untimely and Unfortunate Fate of Many British Poets* (London, 1812).
——— *One Day in York Castle* (London, 1811).
——— *The Picturesque Beauties of Devonshire* (London, 1833).
——— *The Poet's Soliloquy to His Chamber in York Castle* (London, 1811).
——— *Rhapsodies*, "by the Author of the Shaksperian Mss." (London, 1803).
——— *The Sailor Boy*, by "H. C., Esq." (London, 1809).
——— *Scribbleomania, or The Printer's Devil's Polichronicon*, "edited by Anser-Pen-Drag-On, Esq." (London, 1815).
——— *Stultifera Navis, or The Modern Ship of Fools*, by "H. C., Esq." (London, 1807).
——— *Vortigern, an Historical Tragedy in Four Acts*, edited with a Preface by S. Ireland (London, 1796).
——— *Vortigern, with a Preface by the Author* (London, 1832).
Jaggard, W., *Shaksperian Frauds* (Stratford-on-Avon, 1911).
Latham, J., *Facts and Opinions concerning Diabetes* (London, 1811).
Leigh, Sotheby, & Son, *A Catalogue of the Books, Miniatures, etc., the Property of the Late Samuel Ireland, Esq., Sold by Auction on May 7, 1801* (London, 1801).
Letters in the Bodleian Library, Oxford.
Libbis, J. H., in *Notes and Queries*, March 21, 1931; April 2, 1932; April 16, 1932; May 14, 1932.
Mair, J., *The Fourth Forger* (New York, 1939).
Malone, E., *Inquiry into the Authenticity of Certain Miscellaneous Papers* (London, 1796).
Manuscript Letters in the British Museum in the *Additional Manuscripts* 30349–30353.
Marsh, C., *The Clubs of London* (London, 1828).
Nichol, J., *Literary Anecdotes of the Eighteenth Century* (London, 1812–15).
O'Keefe, J., *Lie of a Day*, in Mrs. Inchbald's *Modern Theatre*, Vol. X (London, 1811)
Oman, C., *David Garrick* (London, 1958).
Oulton, W. C., *Vortigern under Consideration, with General Remarks*

305

on Mr. James Boaden's Letter to George Steevens, Esq. (London, 1796).

Owen, G., Chalmeriana (London, 1800).

Payn, J., The Talk of the Town (London, 1885).

Prior, J., The Life of Malone (London, 1860).

Reynolds, F., Fortune's Fool (London, 1796).

Shakespeare, W., His True Chronicle History of the Life and Death of King Lear and His Three Daughters. With the Unfortunate Life of Edgar, Sonne and Heire to the Earle of Glocester, and His Sullen and Assumed Humor of Tom of Bedlam (London, 1608).

Smith, R. M., Shakespeare's Folios and Forgeries of Shakespeare's Handwriting (Bethlehem, Pa., 1927).

Spenser, H., Shakespeare Improved (Cambridge, Mass., 1927).

Sprague, A. C., Shakespeare and the Actors (Cambridge, Mass., 1944).

Stow, J., A Survey of London (London, 1598).

Taylor, J., Personal Reminiscences (Bric-a-Brac Series, New York, 1876).

Theobald, L., The Double Falsehood (London, 1728).

Waldron, F. G., Free Reflections on Miscellaneous Papers (London, 1796).

Webb, F., Shakspeare's Manuscripts in the Possession of Mr. Ireland, by "Philalethes" (London, 1796).

Wheeler, R. B., The History and Antiquities of Stratford-upon-Avon (Stratford-upon-Avon, n.d.).

Woodward, G. M., Familiar Verses from the Ghost of Willy Shakespeare to Sammy Ireland (London, 1796).

Wright, T., An Historical and Descriptive Account of the Caricatures of James Gillray (London, 1851).

Wyatt, J., A Comparative Review of the Opinions of Mr. James Boaden (London, 1796).

PERIODICALS OF THE PERIOD CITED

The Analytical Review.
The Annual Register.
The Anti-Jacobin.
Argus.
The British Critic.
The Brittanic Magazine.
The Cambridge Intelligencer.
The Critical Review.
The English Review.
The European Magazine.
Frazer's Magazine.

APPENDIX: BIBLIOGRAPHY

The Gentleman's Magazine.
The London Monthly Review.
The London Review.
The London Times.
The Morning Chronicle.
The Morning Herald.
The Monthly Mirror.
The New Annual Register.
The Oracle.
The Picture of the Times.
The Pocket Magazine.
The Telegraph.
The Theatrical Review.
The Tomahawk.
The True Briton.
An unidentified magazine of which several pages for the month of April, 1796, are in the Stead Collection of the Theatre Wing of the New York Public Library.

THE WORKS OF WILLIAM HENRY IRELAND
A sampling of the not less than sixty-seven original titles by Ireland published between 1799 and 1833, exclusive of his translations.

NOVELS
The Abbess (1799)
Rimualdo (1800)
The Woman of Feeling, 4 vols. (1803)
Gondez the Monk, 4 vols. (1805)
The Catholic (1807)
Les Brigands de l'Estramadure, 2 vols., published in Paris as a translation from the English of W. H. Ireland (1823).

VERSE
Ballads in Imitation of the Antient (1801)
A Ballade Wrotten on the Feastynge . . . (1802)
Rhapsodies (1803)
The Angler (1804)
Flagellum Flagellated (1807)
All the Blocks (1807)
The Fisher Boy (1808)
The Sailor Boy (1808)
The Cottage Girl (1809)
The Cyprian of St. Stephens (1809)
Elegiac Lines (1810)

307

The Poet's Soliloquy to His Chamber in York Castle (1811)
One Day in York Castle (1811)
The State Doctors (1812)
Neglected Genius (1812)
Chalcographimania (1814)
Jack Junk (1814)
Scribbleomania (1815)

BIOGRAPHY AND ANECDOTE
The Confessions of William Henry Ireland (1805)
The Napoleon Anecdotes (1822)
Memoir of the Duke of Rovigo (1823)
The Life of Napoleon Bonaparte (1823)
Memoirs of a Young Greek Lady (1823)
Memoirs of Henry the Great (1824)
The Hundred Days of Napoleon Bonaparte (1827)
Life of Napoleon Bonaparte, 4 vols. (1828)
Authentic Documents Relative to the Duke of Reichstadt (1832)
The Great Illegitimates (1832)

DRAMA
Mutius Scaevola (1801)

MISCELLANEOUS
Stultifera Navis, or The Modern Ship of Fools (1807)
The Pleasures of Temperance (1810)
France for the Last Seven Years (1822)
Shaksperiana (1827)
History of Kent, 4 vols. (1828–34)
The Political Devil (1830)
The Picturesque Beauties of Devonshire (1833)
Shakspeare Ireland's Seven Ages (n.d.)

Besides the posthumously published *Rizzio* (1849), William Henry left at the time of his death at least twenty-three other unpublished works. These include several plays (e.g., *Bretville*), several novels (e.g., *Fantasies of Love*), many poems (e.g., *Chatterton*), and a poetical satire called *Johannes Taurus, the Don Juan of England by Byronus Secundus*.

In publishing William Henry frequently used his own name. Eight times he published anonymously; four times under the pseudonym of W. H. C. I.; four times as H. C., Esq.; thrice as Ben Block; twice each as Cervantes, Paul Persius, and Henry Boyle; and at other times as Charles Clifford, Flagellator, Flagellum, AEre Perennius, Sam Satiricus, Amicus, Satiricus Sculptor, Esq., Anser-Pen-Drag-On, Esq., and Thomas Fielding, Esq.